# The Framers
# and Fundamental Rights

## THE RIGHTS EXPLOSION

*Robert A. Licht, series editor*

THE FRAMERS AND FUNDAMENTAL RIGHTS

IS THE SUPREME COURT THE GUARDIAN OF THE CONSTITUTION?

OLD RIGHTS AND NEW

# The Framers and Fundamental Rights

Edited by Robert A. Licht

The AEI Press

*Publisher for the American Enterprise Institute*
WASHINGTON, D.C.

1991

This book was funded in part by a grant from the National Endowment for the Humanities.

Distributed by arrangement with

National Book Network
4720 Boston Way
Lanham, MD 20706

3 Henrietta Street
London WC2E 8LU England

**Library of Congress Cataloging-in-Publication Data**

The Framers and fundamental rights / edited by Robert A. Licht.
     p.   cm.—(AEI studies ; 541)
    ISBN 0-8447-3788-7
    1. Civil rights—United States.   2. United States—Constitutional
history.   I. Licht, Robert A.   II. Series.
KF4749.F67   1991
342.73'085—dc20
[347.30285]                                   91-19602
1  3  5  7  9  10  8  6  4  2                CIP

AEI Studies 541

The AEI Press
Publisher for the American Enterprise Institute
1150 17th Street, N.W., Washington, D.C. 20036

*Printed in the United States of America*

# Contents

EDITOR AND AUTHORS     vii

**1** INTRODUCTION   *Robert A. Licht*     1

**2** CONSTITUTIONAL RIGHTS—
DEMOCRATIC INSTRUMENT OR DEMOCRATIC
OBSTACLE?   *Benjamin R. Barber*     23
    The Tradition of Rights   24
    Rights Claims and Equality Claims   28
    "Parchment Barriers"   30
    Rights Absolutism   33

**3** FUNDAMENTAL RIGHTS AND THE STRUCTURE OF THE
GOVERNMENT   *Judith A. Best*     37
    Republican Government   39
    The Large Republic   41
    The Independent, Energetic Executive   51

**4** CONGRESSMAN MADISON PROPOSES AMENDMENTS TO THE
CONSTITUTION   *Robert A. Goldwin*     57
    Why Congress Ought to Consider Amendments Now   58
    The Amendments   61
    Madison's Arguments in Favor of His Amendments   70
    Appendix: Madison's Speech to the House of
       Representatives, June 8, 1789   75

5 THE CONSTITUTION AND "FUNDAMENTAL RIGHTS" *Lino A. Graglia*    86
   Individual Rights in the Constitution  88
   The Supreme Court's Improvements on the
      Constitution  93
   "Fundamental Rights"—A Euphemism for Judicial Defeat
      of Majority Rule  97

6 REPUBLICANISM AND RIGHTS  *Thomas L. Pangle*    102
   Republicanism in the Constitution  104
   The Classical Conception of Republicanism  107
   Liberal Government Centered on Rights  111
   The American Synthesis  116

7 THE FEDERALIST AND THE INSTITUTIONS OF FUNDAMENTAL
   RIGHTS  *Mark Tushnet*    121
   Institutional Design  122
   Extending the Republic  124
   On Judicial Review  132
   The Enumeration of Rights  134
   Failure of the Deferral Strategy  136

8 THOMAS JEFFERSON ON NATURE AND NATURAL RIGHTS
   *Michael P. Zuckert*    137
   Nature  139
   Human Nature  147
   Natural Rights  152
   The Right to Life  157
   The Right to Property  158
   The Right to Liberty  160
   The Right to the Pursuit of Happiness  161
   Civil Rights and Political Imperatives—Some
      Implications of Natural Rights  163
   Appendix I: On Reading Jefferson  167
   Appendix II: Natural Rights and the Moral Sense  168

NOTES    171

INDEX    189

# Editor and Authors

ROBERT A. LICHT is resident scholar and director of constitutional studies at the American Enterprise Institute. Mr. Licht taught philosophy at Bucknell University and liberal arts at St. John's College in Annapolis. He has been a visiting scholar at the Kennedy Institute for Ethics and a National Endowment for the Humanities fellow at AEI. He is the author of "On the Three Parties in America" and "Reflections on Martin Diamond's 'Ethics and Politics: The American Way'" and the coeditor of *Foreign Policy and the Constitution* and *The Spirit of the Constitution*.

BENJAMIN R. BARBER holds the Walt Whitman Chair of Political Science at Rutgers University, where he is director of the Whitman Center for the Culture and Politics of Democracy. He is the author of eight books, most recently *The Conquest of Politics: Liberal Philosophy in Democratic Times*. He was for ten years the editor of the international quarterly *Political Theory* and has been a Guggenheim fellow, Fulbright research scholar, visiting fellow at the New York Institute of Humanities, and senior fellow at the American Council of Learned Societies.

JUDITH A. BEST is Distinguished Teaching Professor of Political Science at the State University of New York at Cortland. Professor Best is the author of various books, including *The Case Against Direct Election of the President*, and has written several articles on the executive power and the political theory of the American founders.

ROBERT A. GOLDWIN is resident scholar at the American Enterprise Institute and former director of constitutional studies. He has served in the White House as special consultant to the president and, concurrently, as adviser to the secretary of defense. He has taught at the University of Chicago and at Kenyon College and was dean of St.

John's College in Annapolis. He is the editor of a score of books on American politics, coeditor of the AEI series of volumes on the Constitution, and author of numerous articles, many of which appear in the collection *Why Blacks, Women, and Jews Are Not Mentioned in the Consitution, and Other Unorthodox Views.*

LINO A. GRAGLIA is A. Dalton Cross Professor of Law at the University of Texas. He was an attorney with the U.S. Department of Justice and practiced law in Washington, D.C., and New York City before joining the Texas law faculty in 1966. He is the author of *Disaster By Decree: The Supreme Court Decisions on Race and the Schools.* He has written widely on current constitutional issues and the role of the Supreme Court in the American system of government. Professor Graglia has been awarded the Distinguished Faculty Award of the Delta Theta Phi Law Fraternity.

THOMAS L. PANGLE is a professor of political science at the University of Toronto. He is the translator of *Plato's Laws* and of *The Roots of Political Philosophy: Ten Forgotten Socratic Dialogues.* He is the author of *Montesquieu's Philosophy of Liberalism: A Commentary on "The Spirit of the Laws"* and *The Spirit of Modern Republicanism: The Moral Vision of the American Founders and the Philosophy of Locke.* Mr. Pangle's latest work (forthcoming from Johns Hopkins University Press) is *Ennobling Democracy: The Challenge of the Post-Modern Era.*

MARK TUSHNET, professor of law at Georgetown University Law Center, has written extensively on constitutional law and legal history. His book *Red, White, and Blue: A Critical Analysis of Constitutional Law* was published in 1988. He is the coauthor of casebooks on constitutional law and federal jurisdiction. His book *The NAACP's Legal Strategy Against Segregated Education, 1925–50,* published in 1987, won the Littleton-Griswold Prize of the American Historical Association. He is the author of a forthcoming biography of retired Justice Thurgood Marshall.

MICHAEL P. ZUCKERT is Congdon Professor of Political Science at Carleton College. He is the author of many articles on the American political tradition and early modern political philosophy. He has recently completed a book titled *Natural Rights and the New Republicanism: Studies in the Anglo-American Whig Tradition.*

# 1

## Introduction

*Robert A. Licht*

The American Constitution is not an artifact of a departed civilization, and the study of its central ideas—liberty and self-government, individual rights—is not merely a chapter in the history of ideas. The scholars who have contributed to this volume are well aware that their inquiries are animated by developments that have both political and intellectual urgency. The "rights explosion," a crude but sufficiently precise characterization of these developments, signifies a proliferation of grievances, individual and social, whose central focus is the word "rights."

This issue is momentous and, at the same time, hard to grasp. It is momentous because the political conflicts arising from it are more than a matter of clashing interests; otherwise, the usual constitutional mechanisms would have found a way to mediate among them. But because the most notorious of the present-day rights conflicts address questions of the moral definition of persons and of groups, they are resistant to political compromise. The national courts have become the constitutional instrument for political closure because we seem to believe that constitutional jurisprudence is, in some way, intellectually and politically privileged. The courts are thus seen as the appropriate venue for solving the politically intractable intellectual questions of fundamental rights. The constitutional role of the courts has, however, itself become the focus of considerable controversy.

The rights explosion, then, is momentous because it brings into the political commons matters that are intractable, which in turn stress and distort the central institution of polity, the Constitution.

That the rights explosion is hard to grasp is only to be expected. The eminent historian James H. Hutson characterized the era of the founding as "a period (not, perhaps, unlike our own) in which the public's penchant for asserting its rights outran its ability to analyze them and to reach a consensus about their scope and meaning."[1] Surrounding and contributing to the complexities of the issue at present is the intense academic revival of political and moral theory and of theoretical jurisprudence. But be not deceived. For all the intellectual sophistication displayed, another Thomas Hobbes, or John Locke, or Jean-Jacques Rousseau, has not arisen. Rather, we have the much permuted traditions of their thought.

Nor, unhappily, do we have deeply thoughtful statesmen of the order of Madison, Jefferson, and the other founding luminaries—men capable of clarity, conviction, foreknowledge, and persuasion, men equal to the task of founding a democratic republic. We have instead the tradition of self-government built on that foundation, a very great thing indeed, but not the same as the founding in its intellectual demands.

Our intellectual traditions, which for better or worse must now nurture our political traditions, are best described as favoring a way of inquiry that continually reappropriates, redefines, or attempts to overturn the past. Such a tradition is perhaps not the best support for stability in politics. Paradoxically, the American polity has nevertheless been remarkably stable. In any event, we would not dare to purchase political stability with the coin of stifled inquiry.

So we have entered a phase, the significance of which is not yet evident, of acute intellectual and political ferment over the oldest theme of the American founding: rights. Our intellectual tradition does not allow us simply to depart from the past in the name of what is "right." We are compelled to reexamine the past if we are to understand and to achieve our purposes in the present. It is in this context that this volume, and the series of which it is a part, should be understood.

The question I posed to the authors in this volume—What are the fundamental rights and where are they in the Constitution?— elicited responses that fall clearly in the intellectual and political tradition alluded to above. Although diverse in their approaches to this question, sometimes radically so, the essays can nevertheless be dialectically linked according to the questions they pose. I shall do so in what follows, but my reading should be taken neither as an interpretation of their thought—they speak quite eloquently for themselves—nor as the correct intellectual sequence and relation of the essays. I am interested in where their thought joins—or butts—and I hope to provide the reader a map to the territory in which they have each staked a claim. The attentive reader will see that while each essay stands on its own, it also may be brought into dialogue with the others, in various, often unexpected ways. All of them address the American situation, but the question remains: Is there a *decisive* standpoint from which to view the relationship of rights and constitutional government? I invite the reader to enter the dialogue.

## The Constitution and Fundamental Rights

It is fitting for me to begin with Lino A. Graglia's essay, "The Constitution and Fundamental Rights," because Graglia takes issue with the question itself. The only truly fundamental rights provided by the Constitution, he argues, are the rights "to be governed by electorally accountable officials, and to be governed primarily by local officials." Indeed, talk of fundamental rights is itself a questionable enterprise, particularly in constitutional law. "Talk about 'fundamental rights' in constitutional scholarship perpetuates [a] misunderstanding," "the mistaken belief of the American people that judicial declarations of unconstitutionality are in some sense based on the Constitution."

This distortion of the Constitution has its own history, which began with the Bill of Rights itself and continued through the so-called Civil War Amendments. But the critical difference came with the Fourteenth Amendment, which gave "the federal government a role in the relationship between the individual state citizen and his state that was quite different from anything contemplated before." Although the purpose of the amendment was itself limited, the use made of it has been such as to alter profoundly the very notion of constitutionality—in particular, to allow for "judicial policy making." If the Bill of Rights was originally meant to protect the states against possible encroachments of the federal government, then successive judicial interpretations of the Fourteenth Amendment have reversed that role; the Bill of Rights has come to be used by the Court against the states, by virtue of "incorporation" into the Fourteenth Amendment.

> The justices became keenly aware that the reduced status of the states meant that the Court, as an arm of the federal government, had the de facto power, even if not the legitimate authority, to substitute the policy views of a majority of the

justices for the views of elected state and local representatives.

The justices found a "constitutional basis for frustrating the political process," for the sake of one version or another of enlightened social policy. This basis was found in the famous due process clause, which in time became the doctrine of "substantive due process," whereby the Court gave "itself the veto power over state law that Madison in the Constitutional Convention had unsuccessfully sought to give to Congress."

The subsequent history of the Court's activism has given rise to serious questions as to the source of its constitutional interpretations.

> It is obvious . . . that the vast bulk of constitutional decision making involves state, not federal, law and is almost entirely based on a single constitutional provision, the Fourteenth Amendment, and indeed, on four words, "due process" and "equal protection."

The Court's rulings of unconstitutionality "almost always represent the transference of decision-making power on issues of social policy from electorally accountable officials . . . to a majority of nine lifetime appointees." But these rulings "are not based on interpreting the Constitution in any ordinary sense." Rather, they are said to be based on "moral and political principle. Where these supposed principles are to be found is unclear."

Apart from the very few personal rights found in the Constitution, the substantive rights added in the Bill of Rights, and the small number of rights expressed in subsequent amendments, such as the grant of basic civil rights to blacks and the extension of the right to vote, "All other alleged fundamental constitutional rights are the product of judicial policy making." These rights represent the value choices of an intellectual elite and of judges.

> Value choices must be made, and the meaning of representative government is that they should be made by officials subject to electoral control. To have them made by judges through the supposed discovery of fundamental rights on the basis of moral and political philosophy is simply to have them made in accordance with the judges' rather than the electorate's value judgements.

The notion of fundamental rights is a fraud perpetrated by America's intellectual elite, who view the idea of government with the consent of the governed to be "undesirable in America."

## *The Federalist* and Fundamental Rights

Graglia maintains that the right to self-government through elected officials has been undermined by judicial policy making, which is itself the outcome of a process of amendments and even more of judicial interpretation. This thesis is radicalized in Mark Tushnet's "*The Federalist* and the Institutions of Fundamental Rights." Tushnet argues that judicial policy making is in a sense the inevitable outcome of a flawed constitution. He offers an analysis of the theory of the Constitution, as defended by Publius in *The Federalist*, in which the structure of the theory of the Constitution may be seen to undermine itself.

In Tushnet's view, the system of government the authors of *The Federalist* defended was based on certain fundamental assumptions about human nature. According to these assumptions, however, it was difficult to explain how the Constitution would resolve the inherent tension between energetic government and the protection of liberty. The *Federalist* authors therefore relaxed their views of human nature.

> Because they understood that they could not adequately defend these relaxed assumptions, the authors created a rhetorical structure in which the confrontation between energy and the protection of liberty was repeatedly deferred.

This strategy of deferral may be traced

> from the citizenry to Congress, then from Congress to the courts, then from the courts under the original Constitution, then to the courts under a Constitution amended to include a bill of specified rights, and finally to the courts under a Constitution with a relatively undefined protection of rights.

*Federalist* 10 is designated by Tushnet as the decisive statement of the assumptions about human nature: "The fallibility of human reason gives rise to different opinions, the connection between reason and self-love amplifies the importance of those differences, and 'the latent causes of faction are thus sown in the nature of man.' " It is the celebrated *cure* of the disease of faction, the institutional design of the Constitution, that Tushnet questions. The "representative republic [that] extended over a large territory," the proffered solution to the problem of majority faction, is where "the first strains in the scheme of *The Federalist* appear."

Representation, according to Madison, will bring to the fore "the most diffusive and established characters," and the people, through the mechanisms of representation, will choose representatives "bet-

5

ter than the citizens themselves." Tushnet adduces several reasons why representation per se offers no assurances of superior character in elected officials.

The defects of the extended republic have also become apparent over time. The creation of national political parties and the improvement of communications have increased the ease of forming majorities. Moreover, although majorities change over time, their legislation remains in place. Incumbency and ambition also work toward the creation of dominating majorities.

> If the extended republic is not sufficient to solve a problem, then the solution can be deferred to the operation of the institutions . . .[:] the bicameral legislature, the presidency and the courts.

An analysis of the legislative system comes to a similar conclusion. Although the legislative function was intended to limit the power of majorities, here too the inherent tendency of legislatures themselves—to defend their own rights and thereby to maximize their own power—moves them away from their purpose.

The fear of legislative dominance, according to Tushnet, led the opponents of the Constitution to demand the addition of a bill of rights. Although Publius objected that no language would be adequate to provide the guarantees sought because of an "unavoidable inaccuracy" of terminology, he also conceded that over time the terminology might become fixed by usage. Indeed, the courts did develop and apply this view, but its influence was eventually eroded. So Publius' view that the language might become fixed "needs careful qualification." Therefore, in the end, "as Publius understood, one might design another institution" to enforce the "mere parchment barriers." The institution is that of judicial review, which is a further step in the strategy of deferral.

But the constitutional guarantees of judicial independence themselves act against the desired results of judicial review. "These protections provide judges with the opportunity to operate as their own faction," which is "worse than a minority faction controlling the legislature." Publius tries to allay this fear by asserting that judges "have neither *force* nor *will* but merely judgment." Moreover, they are more likely to be "fit characters." Tushnet finds this unpersuasive. Their very professionalism factionalizes judges, and the process of selection is no guarantee of better character. Moreover, judges are skilled in the rhetorical arts: "By exercising their rhetorical skills the judges may cloak their own will in the guise of judgment." Finally, the "independent will" of the judges might lead them to make common

6

cause with a majority, "thereby defeating the possibility that the judiciary would defend fundamental rights against the will of a majority."

Regardless of the efficacy or inefficacy of judicial review, Publius

> cautioned that the inclusion of a bill of rights might cause people, including judges, to believe that the national government could do anything it wished so long as it did not invade the specified rights. This conclusion was inconsistent with a careful enumeration of powers conferred on the national government.

The advantage of a bill of rights lay in its specificity: "The existence of specified rights . . . would provide a benchmark. . . . Rights would allow people to criticize legislators . . . and thus provide a political check against oppression." But "where the Constitution is less clear, the political check cannot operate effectively"—particularly in the area of deciding whether one branch of government has overstepped its constitutional bounds.

Under judicial review, the courts themselves might violate fundamental rights, "in the guise of enforcing limitations on the political branches." Publius nevertheless embraced the institution of judicial review, and in so doing he was forced to depend on the professionalism of judges. But if, as Tushnet argues, that faith in professionalism is itself "theoretically ungrounded," then "the dangers to the constitutional system are substantial."

The "strategy of deferring difficulties in the theory of the Constitution" reaches its end point in the Ninth Amendment. "It is an end point that demonstrates the failure of that strategy." The amendment specifies that "the enumeration in the Constitution, of certain rights, shall not be construed to deny or disparage others retained by the people." There is a tendency "not precluded by the terms of the amendment and its intellectual setting" to use a natural-law interpretation. The effects of such an interpretation are to license "the courts to develop constitutional limitations on the authority of legislatures by references to notions of natural law." But in the absence of any belief in or agreement about natural law, "the prospects for a stable constitutional law are rather slim." Thus "an enormous gap" opens between energetic government and the preservation of liberty. The temptation of the judges, following a natural-law interpretation of the Ninth Amendment, will be to create a "constitutional law of unenumerated rights." If the strategy of deferral was an attempt to limit the power of legislators and of judges to overreach—that is, to protect the liberties of the people against the power of energetic government—then here, in the Ninth Amendment, that strategy finally fails.

## Fundamental Rights and the Structure of the Government

Tushnet's view, that the theory of the Constitution undermines itself, deserves to be contrasted with the framers' own view of how the theory was supposed to work. Judith Best's account of that theory as it appears in *The Federalist*, in "Fundamental Rights and the Structure of the Government," points out that the essentially *republican* character of the Constitution and of its mechanisms is the key to securing fundamental rights. Securing rights requires strong government. The difficulty with strong government, however, is its potential threat to rights. The task of the founders, therefore, "was to propose a government that would be powerful and balanced, both energetic and safe, both stable and free." Precisely how the mechanisms of the Constitution solve this conundrum is her thesis.

American republican government is founded upon consent, both original—"no rational man may consent to the destruction of his unalienable natural rights"—and ongoing—"the people's role of judging is to be incorporated into the governing process by free and frequent elections." According to the historical evidence, however, republican government is also weak and unstable.

To address the historical weaknesses of republican government, the founders made "two innovations that appeared to be antithetical to republicanism . . .[:] the large republic and the independent energetic executive." The large republic "is necessary for political liberty as Locke and Montesquieu defined it—safety and security of person and property." Against foreign threats, union or strong national government provides the physical strength that derives from "plenary authority to command and direct the enormous resources of the large republic."

Against domestic insurrection, Article IV of the Constitution, which guarantees a republican form of government to every state, means that "the rest of the union can come to the aid of a part." This means that a minority cannot hold the majority hostage. A large republic allows the rule of law to have force.

Minorities must be protected, however, against a majority faction. It is necessary for the majority to rule with the consent of the minority. Here, too, the large republic is a prevention of the disease of majority faction—a disease that can be acute in a small, homogeneous society. The remedy, therefore, is to "extend the sphere" and allow a multiplicity of factions and interests to flourish. In particular, the promotion of commerce will both advance the cause of protecting "the diverse talents of men" and foster a desirable heterogeneity of interests. "A large commercial society develops many different *kinds* of property, many different kinds of economic interests . . . around which minority factions will form." Minority factions will join together to form "concurrent majorities, majorities created by the temporary and changeable" coalitions, formed through "compromise and accommodation." Minorities will consent to majority rule when they see that they too will have a role in forming majorities.

But the large commercial society cannot, by itself, protect against majority faction. It is the political function of the federal system of government so to divide constituencies into districts that it becomes "difficult for a majority faction to unite and use national elections as an opportunity to act." Moreover, the separation of powers divides "the national government into three distinct branches having shared powers." This division and the various modes of representation and election "act like a brake" and "slow down the transformation of the will of the majority into law."

Other features of separation of powers also act to protect individuals and minorities against government by limiting its power. These features are the famous "checks and balances," including bicameralism, the veto power, and judicial review. Although it is not clear whether the founders understood the consequences of an independent judiciary, judicial review is "an almost incredible innovation in democratic government," and it necessarily gives the judiciary a policy-making role.

> The written Constitution itself creates a special task for an independent judiciary . . . of measuring the correspondence of governmental action against declared rule. . . . Judicial review is at least latent in a written constitution that decrees an independent judiciary.

There are dangers to the Constitution in an independent judiciary, however, and judges thus "must recognize that they themselves are bound by the Constitution."

The other innovation of the founders was the independent energetic executive, perceived as a major departure from republicanism at the time of the founding. The energetic executive is the "specifically designated champion of the Constitution. . . . The executive office is the efficient cause of government, and government, if properly constituted, is the essential cause of human liberty." Indeed, it is the energy of the executive that makes the separation of powers effective: "Without energy in the executive the separation of powers would produce either deadlock or legislative tyranny."

The republic of the founders is then the means by which government is the guardian of liberty, and the Constitution is the means by

9

which the guardians themselves are watched. The solution to guarding the guardians is to "divide *all* the guardians into distinct and separate parts and set them all to watch each other." But in the end, the people are sovereign: "The supreme and final guardians, the people themselves, must be divided into multiple and diverse parts each to counterpoise, each to help offset the factional interests of the others."

## Congressman Madison Proposes Amendments

If the unamended Constitution, in its structures of government, contains the key to securing liberty and individual rights, then why was there such great agitation for a bill of rights, and what effect did the adoption of it have on the framers' design of the Constitution? Robert A. Goldwin, in "Congressman Madison Proposes Amendments to the Constitution," examines closely the thoughts of Madison on these questions in his speech to the House of Representatives on June 8, 1789. Goldwin regards this speech as "one of the most consequential political orations in American history."

Goldwin asks how Madison, who "did not start out as a supporter of the idea of a bill of rights," eventually came to deliver a speech that made him "the father of the Bill of Rights"? Goldwin follows the sequence of Madison's speech, which explained, first, why he thought it was "timely and prudent" to consider amendments; second, Madison's proposed amendments; and finally, the arguments in support of the amendments.

Madison's reasons for considering a bill of rights were two: "to reassure those uneasy Americans who needed reassurance; and . . . to avoid changing anything in the Constitution." Madison's strategy, according to Goldwin, was to divide those who needed reassurance from those who truly opposed the Constitution—the Anti-Federalists. A "great mass of the people" were ready to support the Constitution if they could be reassured on the point of rights. The opponents of the Constitution, however, desired fundamental changes in its very structure; this structure, they believed, and not the absence of a bill of rights, was the greatest threat to liberty. Hence they desired a second constitutional convention—to make "profound structural changes" to the Constitution. And Madison sought to divide the opponents of the Constitution from its potential supporters:

> Madison was acutely aware that there was a genuine constitutional problem to be addressed, but the problem was not in the document; it was in the public mistrust of the document and of the powers of the new government it established. For a constitution establishing popular government,

based on consent of the people and majority rule, with powers limited so as to secure the rights of the minority—for
such a constitution it is not enough to have majority support. . . . Such a constitution must have the allegiance of
"the great mass of the people."

Madison's speech to the House was addressed not to the opponents of the Constitution, but to his allies—to "those who supported
the Constitution as he did." He proposed to them the adoption of
amendments that would satisfy "the great mass of people" on the
score of rights but would not affect the structure of the Constitution.
To this end he made two proposals that were not adopted but are
revealing of his strategy.

First, he proposed to *insert* into the body of the Constitution "all
of what are now the First, Second, Third, Fourth, Eighth, and Ninth
Amendments." They were to be placed in Article I, Section 9, between
clauses 3 and 4. This section already has "the character of provisions
of a bill of rights." That is, they are limitations on government, and
they take the form of negative imperatives: By inserting into the body
of the Constitution the limitations on the power of government,

it would have been difficult to think of them collectively as a
body to be called the Bill of Rights. . . . They would have
more likely been seen as integrally part of the Constitution
. . . and thus less likely to be considered as some sort of "corrective" of a defective original.

The second proposal would have added what Goldwin calls a
"pre-Preamble" to the Constitution, the main purpose of which was
to assert that "all power is originally vested in, and consequently derived from, the people"; that the purpose of government is for the
sake of the benefit of the people, particularly their "enjoyment of life
and liberty, with the right of acquiring and using property . . ."; and
finally, that the people have the "right to reform or change their government." The proposal, even after it was revised, was "denounced,
reviled, ridiculed, and rejected." Nevertheless, Madison's purpose
may be detected in his reference to this proposal as what "may be
called a bill of rights." In this sense it was like the Massachusetts State
Constitution of 1780, which was prefaced with a similar bill of rights.

If this was what, in the public mind "may be called a bill of
rights," then it can be said that the pre-Preamble, as a constitutional provision, would have been at once useful and innocuous.

Thus the two proposals of Madison that were not accepted are
nonetheless instructive:

11

The combination of the pre-Preamble and interweaving would have served well Madison's dual purposes, first, to reassure . . . second, to protect the Constitution against significant change.

If we look at the substance of Madison's proposed amendments to the Constitution, the result is similar:

What Madison did was to separate the proposals having to do with civil rights from those that altered the distribution of powers between the states and the government of the United States.

The right of the Congress to impose direct taxes was challenged by a proposal, perhaps the most important to the Anti-Federalists, "that was close to a return to the indirect system of apportionment of taxes by states under the Articles of Confederation." Their great concern was that the powers of the national Government threatened "the annihilation of the state governments." As Goldwin observes,

What they meant was that the threat of the new government to religion, press, speech . . . was not a specific danger, or if a danger, it could not be resolved by these new words in the Constitution. What was a danger . . . to all liberty, was an all-powerful central government able to tax from a great distance . . . and thus render state and local governments relatively powerless.

Although Madison did not prevail in several of his proposals, he nonetheless succeeded in his main goals:

[H]e reassured the part of the public that had been uneasy about the new Constitution and thus brought to an abrupt halt the popular movement for a second constitutional convention; he saved the Constitution from every contemplated radical amendment; and he gave an instructive display of a new kind of statesmanship—democratic statesmanship on the national scene—political wisdom artfully joined to popular consent.

### Democratic Instrument or Democratic Obstacle?

Judith Best shows that the Constitution is a structure designed to secure rights; Robert Goldwin shows that the Bill of Rights, whatever it may have accomplished in securing rights, nevertheless did not tamper with that structure of government. Benjamin Barber's thoughts in "Constitutional Rights: Democratic Instrument or Democratic Obstacle?" carry us further down the path pursued by Mark Tushnet. Barber points out a flaw in the Constitution even more radical than the one Tushnet indicates, a flaw that is to be found in the very perfection that Best and Goldwin extol: the Constitution is antidemocratic precisely because of its republicanism. In this sense, far from securing rights, it thwarts them.

Rights, in Barber's view, cannot be understood apart from equality, for which *democracy* is the only adequate regime.

It is ironic and troubling to find today that the language of rights is often deployed in a fashion adversarial to democracy, rights have become privatized and are being construed as possessions of individuals.

Rights, properly understood, certainly have their roots in the individual and in his natural necessities: "The hungry man *wants* to eat; the ravenous man *needs* to eat; the starving man *has a right* to eat." Nevertheless, to understand rights as only individual is to misunderstand them: "The naked self is perforce a social self whose claims on others implies equality and reciprocity." Rights then imply or require democracy as their proper political form of realization. When we look at the framers of the Constitution, however, we see "a primarily antidemocratic bias." Both Federalists and Anti-Federalists agreed in this: "Neither had much trust in the people from whom popular government took its legitimacy." Moreover, "The word equality fails to make an appearance in the Constitution's language, and almost every device of government contemplated was aimed not at embodying but at checking popular power." At the Constitutional Convention, "radical democratic models calling for a unicameral legislature and universal white male suffrage . . . were given short shrift." The mechanisms of the Constitution—federalism, the separation of powers, indirect election of president and senators, judicial review—combined to bury "any incipient tendencies to popular government." The very meager number of amendments—sixteen in the 200 years since the original ten—"does not suggest a very democratic instrument."

But the spirit of the Constitution, quite apart from the mechanisms, is "the spirit of democracy" and is as old as the republic. So the question for Barber is, What is the relation of rights to this democratic *spirit*, rather than to the antidemocratic *letter*? "There is a simple but powerful relationship between rights and democracy: rights entail the equality of those who claim them; and democracy is the politics of equality." Thus the "right to suffrage turns out to be the keystone of all other rights." The history of America since the nineteenth century—especially the Thirteenth, Fourteenth, and Fifteenth Amendments—is a history of the growth of the spirit of democracy into the letter of the Constitution: "The actual history of rights talk in America unfolds as an increasingly progressive and democratic story." There is then a tension between the democratic substance and the republican forms of constitutional government. Democracy is "defined by universal suffrage and collective self-legislation," while republicanism "elicits the consent and accountability but not the participation and judgment of the people."

Historically, the successful attempts at redress "by those who felt left out of the American way" have entailed the framing of a cause "in the name of the American founding." But in this century, "the powerful alliance between rights and political emancipation, between the claim to be a person and the right to be a citizen, has come unstuck." The reason for this separation is the growing "rights absolutism,"— the privatization of rights, which "cease to be a civic identity to be posited and won; they become a natural identity to be discovered, worn, and enjoyed." Their function as a "mediator of political discourse" has been "transmogrified into a discourse that denies politics." Here Barber and Graglia agree: the consequence of "rights talk" has been to distort the role of the judiciary. But Barber sees this as a consequence of the "'filtration' of the public mind favored by the founders"; that is, "judicial government" is a consequence of the antidemocratic letter of the Constitution. What America needs now is "not lessons in the rights of private persons but lessons in the responsibilities of public citizens; not a new view of the Bill of Rights but a new view of the Constitution as the democratic source of all rights."

## Republicanism and Rights

From the perspective of Barber, the framers were simply antidemocratic. From the perspective of Best and Goldwin, they held this attitude because republican government was the best way to secure the right to liberty. But if the framers' antipathy to purely democratic forms of regime is undeniable, the reasons for their attachment to republicanism is by no means self-evident—particularly in view of their attachment to the idea of rights. According to Thomas Pangle in "Republicanism and Rights," the American republic, precisely because of its attachment to rights, is also a unique and novel event in the history of republican thought and institutions.

Pangle asks, "What is the relationship between republicanism and rights?" Although in America this relationship seems very close, when viewed through the history of ideas, it is "more ambiguous than it appears." "Republicanism" is a theme that reaches back to antiquity, while the tradition of rights derives from seventeenth century Northern Europe, primarily England. The tradition of rights by itself does not entail republicanism.

The originator of the modern theory of rights, Thomas Hobbes, "precisely because he believed that individual rights are fundamental . . . was no friend of republicanism." Hobbes stood equally against the "moralistic ancient theorists" and the "radically amoral republican principles of Machiavelli and his followers."

Closer to modern times, thinkers like Hume and Montesquieu also had "serious doubts as to whether republics were likely to secure rights, or to curb their own tendencies to violate rights." This doubt was also to be found in the Anti-Federalist tradition in America as well as in the thought of Alexander Hamilton.

From this perspective, it would appear that republicanism is "a genus," of which "the American republic [is] the first example in history of one relatively new species . . . that puts individual rights at the center of attention." Questions then arise from both sides—the republican tradition and the rights tradition. What is "republicanism per se," and what "new qualification" or "supplement" to the tradition was necessary to bring it together with the rights tradition? As to rights, "What change in the original theoretical understanding" of that theory was required to bring it into close relationship with republicanism?

Pangle begins by looking at the republicanism of the framers of the American Constitution. They defined it as "popular sovereignty, or majority rule, expressed and channeled through elected . . . institutions and checked and balanced by the separation of powers, including an independent judiciary." What is new in Madison's definition of a republic is its *representative* character, which is to be distinguished from democracy, the form of government where "the people meet and exercise the government in person." Rather, Madison insists, the new form of democratic republic excludes "the people, *in their collective capacity*, from any share in government." But this definition is truly innovative, departing even from the definition of Montesquieu of a republic as that in which "the body of the people, or only a part . . . has the sovereign power. . . . When the sovereign power is in the hands of a part of the people, this gives itself the name *aristocracy*." Montesquieu's definition, in turn, harks back to the classical understanding of a republic—that is, to a "tradition, as the American founders were to varying degrees aware, [that] was fundamentally *aristocratic*." The notion now appears mistaken that republicanism is a genus of which the American form, which marries republicanism to rights, is a species. Rather

> The difference between . . . the American founding and clas-
> sical republicanism is a difference not of the species but of
> the nature of the genus. The two types . . . dispute the basic
> principles of republicanism.

In the classical view, according to Pangle, "freedom and rule" are
inseparable, and access to rule is a prerequisite of republicanism. But
"freedom seems incompatible with being ruled by others." Nevertheless, "in the light of self-critical scrutiny," this relationship undergoes
a significant change: there must be rotation of rule, so that "to be free
is . . . to belong to a society in which one rules and is ruled in turn."
In other words, "one must *deserve* to rule."

*Virtue* is thus the central consideration of ancient republicanism.
But "the rule of the wise and the virtuous must be qualified by the
principle of popular consent, that is, by the principle of majority
rule." So aristocracy must be "mixed" with democracy. But the legitimacy of majority rule stems from the superior strength of the many.
Thus, consent in the classical republic "is a distinctly . . . second-
ranked principle of legitimacy." And popular sovereignty, strictly
speaking, is "an abridgment of civic justice, that is, of the sovereignty
of the just."

Virtue is the "heart or core of happiness" and is the chief end of
the life of the republic. But the contention that virtue is the core of
happiness is itself disputed. Troubling facts threaten to undermine it:
to wit, that "the security, prosperity, glory . . . of the republic as a
whole sometimes seem . . . to depend upon actions and men who are
not virtuous." Moreover, virtue "requires the . . . coercive, awe-
inspiring, and frightening authority of the law." If virtue then requires
such external supports, "the question arises whether such virtue can
be the true response to humanity's deepest natural needs."

> The fundamental problem is in a sense solved, but at the
> same time deepened, by the introduction of the divine law,
> or the natural law, conceived as the reasonable edict emanat-
> ing from a divinely ordered cosmos.

This "solution," which gives an awesome support to the law, also
raises the question, "Who or what are the true gods, and how do we
know?" These questions "open the door to philosophy in the classical
republican (Socratic) sense." The philosophers radically address the
question, What is virtue? They find an answer "in thinking or in the
genuine self-knowledge that comes from thinking." This is the discovery of a virtue "which is truly and radically nonutilitarian." But the
activity of the philosopher "poses the danger of undermining the traditions, bonds, and healthy limits on public speech" on which repub-

lican communities and leadership depend. Philosophers must "communicate and publicize" their philosophic speculation with a caution that acknowledges "the threat" to republican institutions. Their "most appropriate role" is as teachers of "decent, politically ambitious, and talented men."

> Republican life is compelled in almost all actual situations to substitute some kind of approximation to wisdom or virtue. . . . The complex task of constitution-making and ruling, . . . is . . . the weaving together of the necessarily impure simulacra of the twin roots of political authority— wisdom and consent.

By contrast, "the new liberal thinking rejects" the preoccupation with virtue and its problems, proposing in its place "an alliance between reason and passion." In this alliance, reason is "not the end or purpose of human existence," but the servant of the passions. The passions are harnessed for "the common benefit of each," in Machiavelli's phrase. A "moral primacy" is bestowed on those passions "which are by nature irresistible and therefore blameless." They are the "natural rights" of security, liberty, and property. Duties are subordinate to these rights, and the preeminent duty is to join in constructing government, a "rationally constructed artifice by which individuals contract with one another" to create mutual security or the limitation of everyone's pursuit of the passions. Just how to construct this artifice is the question that animates "the whole history of modern liberal political philosophy." Hobbes' successors, notably Locke and Montesquieu, "propose a series of . . . institutional schemes . . . by which even imperfectly enlightened, selfish pursuits of power can be made to issue in constructive competition."

In Pangle's view, the central concern of modern liberal thought is a "need for education—of an intellectual or scientific, rather than a moral and habitual sort." The need only grows greater in the innovations of Locke and Montesquieu, which increase the numbers who share in political power. Also, free enterprise increases prosperity, but at the same time it increases inequalities.

> Given the principled universal equality as well as liberty at the foundation of the modern liberal political teaching about rights, what is to ensure that the mass of men will not grow restive under the very unequal distribution that follows from the protection of the equal liberties embodied in the natural rights?

There is then a need for moral education as well as mass technical education for the restraint of selfish passions, particularly in the light

17

of the Lockean right of rebellion. Locke proposes two approaches to this problem. The first is "a Christianity reinterpreted" and "radically liberalized." The second is the "new stress on moral education," which now becomes a private, not public matter. Of necessity such education is restricted to the few, since mass moral education would require governmental involvement in the formation of character, which "trenches on the sacred private sphere of basic individual rights to liberty and the pursuit of happiness."

But Locke's successors, notably Hume and Montesquieu, are "less sanguine . . . as to the degree to which liberal political systems and principles are likely to spread and take root throughout the world."

In this context, Pangle addresses the "American synthesis," or "the American attempt to join republicanism and rights." The great departure of American liberalism is its "continuing dedication to popular self-government."

> The American notion of republicanism introduces the egalitarian and libertarian . . . principles of the underlying social contract directly into the constitutional organization and administration of the government.

From this perspective it can be seen that on the one hand, "the most prominent American founders" were prepared to "jettison the cautions and qualifications that had been the greatest theme of Hume, Montesquieu, Blackstone," and others. The Americans, in their insistence upon individual and private rights, are "at most only the distant heirs of the English republican tradition." On the other hand, there is "a sense of kinship with the classical republican tradition" of men of virtue and the spirit of the people as "a bulwark against tyranny." Unhappily, the American founders made little provision for the education that would foster the excellences of character that the classical outlook requires.

> The question looming from the beginning bulking ever larger . . . especially in the last forty or fifty years, is whether and how the system provides for the moral and civic education of a people that becomes more fragmented in every sense, even as it is given more power and responsibility.

The framers approached the problem by looking back toward the classical political virtues. But this approach suffered from an inner contradiction. They celebrated the civic virtues of sacrifice of life, martial manliness, and brotherhood in arms, "while creating a society in which commerce was to reign supreme, explicitly displacing . . . heroic republicanism." Even these "slender threads" of connection to classical republicanism, however, have become "weaker and weaker." The author wonders "whether the country might not be entering upon an irreversible trajectory."

## Thomas Jefferson on Natural Rights

If Pangle's account answers the question of why the framers chose a synthesis between republicanism and rights, Michael Zuckert's analysis may be said to address why they found a doctrine of natural rights to be compelling. In "Thomas Jefferson on Nature and Natural Rights," Zuckert examines Jefferson's only book, *Notes on the State of Virginia*, and reveals its carefully thought-out reflection on nature, human nature, and the natural rights of mankind.

Jefferson's most famous work certainly is the Declaration of Independence.Though that work speaks easily of "Nature and Nature's God," it is difficult to see the careful thought that lies behind its "air of quiet confidence." *Notes*, on the other hand, while seemingly a "glorified guidebook," is also, in the words of Merrill Peterson, "touched with philosophy."

Particularly revealing of the philosophic character of the *Notes* is the reflection on nature based on the existence of sea shells "found far from the seashore." These shells could not have resulted from a "universal deluge," as described in the Bible. The outcome of this discussion, in Zuckert's analysis, is that "the 'laws of nature' are . . . identical to the 'laws of nature's God.'" "The 'ultimate reality' to which the Declaration appealed is thus nature."

*Notes* is organized around the difficult distinction between the natural and nonnatural, or nature and human artifice:

Virginia as a physical entity is . . . a complex intermixture of nature and artifice: nature cannot so readily be extricated from nonnature.

The "intermingling of nature and human artifice" as a theme leads to a discussion of whether nature can be seen in itself. "When all use is stripped away, nature stands revealed as an awesome array of forces." But if nature is seen this way, "how can nature be the source of guidance for human life?" The "natural bridge" of Virginia provides a way to discuss this question, since it both is natural and "resembles a product made by human beings for human use."

The natural bridge is remarkable because it "combines two very different views." There is the experience of the bridge from above, looking down, which is fearful, and the experience of viewing it from below, which is "delightful" and "sublime." The natural bridge is a "parable" that reveals the limits of human domination and use of nature. From the perspective of human insecurity, the bridge shows the terrors of nature.

But seen from below, "man, nature, and heaven are all joined in a beneficent harmony."

The twofold human perspective of security and insecurity "is itself natural":

> There exist two irreducible perspectives and a thoughtful person stands undecided before them. A yet more thoughtful person, perhaps, affirms the deeper truth beneath the two: the point of reference for both is the human drive for security.

*Human* nature thus becomes intelligible from this reference, and the discussion in the *Notes* provides another link to the Declaration and two of its themes—natural equality and rights. It is human intelligence that allows humans to be flexible and variable in their adaptation to natural conditions. The life of the Indians, who "were as close to nature or natural man as Jefferson thought he could get," provides an example of this resourcefulness in what to Jefferson was a Lockean "state of nature." In the absence of law and government, according to Jefferson, the Indians live by "their manners, and that moral sense of right and wrong, which . . . in every man makes a part of his nature." There is then no "pure" state of nature, since human beings "add something to their strictly natural endowment." But nature is also inadequate; although it "may provide the moral sense, . . . that is insufficient to produce just or moral social relations." Where men live by moral sense alone, the ultimate rule is by force, since the moral sense of itself cannot overcome the selfish passions. Force destroys the natural condition of equality. Hence civilization is necessary to *restore* the natural condition.

It is the discovery of rights that makes it possible to tame the selfish passions and to advance beyond the moral sense to more just social relations. Rights are superior to the moral sense in both respects:

> With their intimate ties to the passions, rights are more effective than the moral sense; but rights also supply the specific standards of political action.

Jefferson's treatment of natural rights in the *Notes* is concise but "very carefully thought through." Rights are divided into three entities: "selfish passions, the initial rights, and the later rights." These stages Zuckert divides in two, referring to the first as "proto-rights" and to the second as "rights-in-the-proper-sense."

From the natural drive for security arise the proto-rights. They derive from a law of nature that is amoral. Rights-in-the-proper-sense, however, arise from the recognition of the necessity for the mutual recognition of rights. The origin of mutual recognition is the obvious fact that proto-rights are defective, because the weak cannot preserve their claims against the strong, and the strong cannot be secure from one another. Thus, the needs for mutual recognition and such rights "acquire a genuine moral quality."

But are rights-in-the-proper-sense "natural?" In one sense they are not:

> What derives from nature are the selfish passions, which in themselves produce only selfish claims. . . . What transforms the claims of the passions into rights is the 'civilized' figuring out of the system of mutual respect for rights.

In another sense, though, in the Declaration these rights as they derive from the Creator are indeed natural. Zuckert reconciles the two accounts by showing that "the core of nature is the human drive for security; the core of rights is the same. . . . In this quite meaningful sense, the rights thus arrived at are indeed natural rights."

Zuckert goes on to show that the enumeration of natural rights in the Declaration is incomplete, but that a complete list may be derived from the *Notes* and from an 1816 letter of Jefferson's to Pierre Samuel du Pont. They include the right to life; the right to property; the right to liberty; and the right to the pursuit of happiness. All of these rights, however, may be seen in the right to liberty:

> As a right, it is constituted by its service as a means to the preservation of life. But it also betokens the human quest [for] the human transcendence of mere survival as an end. Liberty is thus a most comprehensive right. As it often did for writers of the founding generation, it can stand as a shorthand expression for all the rights.

Zuckert concludes his analysis with a discussion of civil rights. They must be distinguished from natural rights, "which individuals hold in the first instance vis-à-vis other individuals." Civil rights are a "whole new class of rights" whose origin is the institution of government, "against which rights hold." Individuals must now be protected against the coercive force of government. "The individuals, or now citizens, have a new right—the civil right to protection in their natural rights."

Although the primary civil rights are embedded in constitutional law, Zuckert observes that "the founders' constitutional science is far

21

more a form of political science than a form of constitutional law." The doctrine of rights "shaped the very task of political construction."

With Zuckert's essay we return to the beginning. The thought of the framers looks in two directions: toward the natural and human foundations of a just political order, and toward the edifice to be constructed by political art and science on those foundations. The discussion of rights at the present time must share the same twofold outlook, but apparently not with the same conviction about the foundations or about the edifice built upon them.

# 2

# Constitutional Rights—
# Democratic Instrument or
# Democratic Obstacle?

*Benjamin R. Barber*

If there is a single theme upon which Americans agree and have always agreed it is that ours is a regime rooted in rights. Rights are how we enter our political conversation; they are the chips with which we bargain, collateral in the social contract. They are the ground of both rebellion and legitimacy, of our inclinations to anarchism and our proclivities toward community.

Any American, without coaching, will cry out: "I know my rights!" or "You got no right!" or "What about my rights?" or "Read him his rights!" Corporations mimic the individual; they are zealous devotees of rights as barriers against the public pursuit of goods inimical to private profits. The Philip Morris Company recently paid the National Archives $600,000 to associate itself with the Bill of Rights, presumably to promote its view of advertising as a First Amendment right essential to selling tobacco in a democratic age of public health advocacy. Rights are how Americans have always advanced their interests, whether as individual or corporate persons. Some might say, as I do below, that there is an element of obsession in the American devotion to rights, that we sometimes risk a rights absolutism as unbalanced in its political effects as the fabled "tyranny of the majority" against which rights are often deployed as the primary defense. Yet there are good reasons for the focus on rights.

The naked self comes to the bargaining table weak and puny: the language of rights clothes it. The naked self extends hardly beyond that bundle of desires and aversions that constitute its raw, prelegitimate wants: rights carve out a space for it to operate in—call it autonomy or dignity or, in its material incarnation, property. Wants become needs, and needs acquire a moral mantle that, as rights claims, cannot be ignored. The hungry man *wants* to eat; the ravenous man *needs* to eat; the starving man *has a right* to eat. Rights turn the facts of want into powerful claims—powerful, at least, in civil societies that recognize and legitimate rights rhetoric. For, as we shall see, even the naked self is perforce a social self whose claims on others imply equality and reciprocity. If, as this suggests, democracy may be the regime form especially suited to the language of rights, it is ironic and troubling to find that today the language of rights is often deployed in a fashion adversarial to democracy; rights have become privatized and are being construed as possessions of individuals. But this is to get ahead of our story.

### The Tradition of Rights

Borrowing its early norms from the English dissent traditions of Puritanism and from republicanism (Machiavelli, James Harrington, and Montesquieu), America has always been a civil society hospitable to rights. Its institutions, even in colonial times, had a contractarian flavor; they treated government as an artificial body instrumental to the religious and secular interests of individuals. The Mayflower Compact, for example, though scarcely a document concerned with natural rights, saw the Pilgrims "covenant and combine" themselves "together into a civil body politick, for [their] better order and preservation." The question of how democratic this society, which is so hospitable to rights, was, or became in time, offers one way of determining whether rights and democracy can cohabit and perhaps even reenforce one another.

On the face of things and in keeping with the eighteenth century view, the answer would seem to be no. Both Federalists and Anti-Federalists understood the Constitution as a tool of rights; the former saw in the Constitution's governmental powers their own explicit political expression; the latter saw the Constitution's provisions as a set of rights-regarding limits on governmental power. Historically, these standpoints were both complementary and in tension in the same

24

way that the contractarian perspectives of Thomas Hobbes and John Locke were both complementary and in tension. In the Federalist case, there is a Hobbesian faith in strong contract-based government as a guarantor of rights; in the Anti-Federalist case there is a Lockean distrust of strong government that issues in a strong version of rights understood as constraints on government. Both positions share a conviction that government is an artificial means of preserving rights that are anterior to politics—that exist in a "natural" or "higher" pre-political form.

Returning to our question then, the terms of the Federalist–Anti-Federalist debate suggest that the American rights tradition in both its Federalist and its Anti-Federalist forms had a primarily antidemocratic bias. For in the case of the Federalists, the problem appeared as how to insulate the power in which rights were expressed and by which liberty and property were to be safeguarded from popular majorities and private opinion. James Madison warned against "an infinity of little jealous clashing commonwealths, the wretched nurseries of unceasing discord." He essayed to design a constitution that would supply republican remedies to treat with republican vices (among which democracy was paramount!)—for example, indirect election of representatives and an expanded compass for civil society. By multiplying the number of factions and groups, their capacity for divisiveness might be attenuated.

In the case of the Anti-Federalists, the aim was to limit government *tout court*. Despite the democratic mood of the devolution of power strategy favored by Thomas Jefferson, the object remained to check and limit central power and thus to curtail the exercise of a unitary popular sovereignty. Here the Bill of Rights figured as a studied obstacle to centrally organized popular power. Locke had worried about how "polecats and foxes" (ordinary men, quarrelsome and contentious) might protect themselves from the sovereign lion brought in to police their disputes. The Federalists wanted to keep the "people" from riding the lion; they believed that only the best men could subdue its power and divert it to their virtuous ends. The Anti-Federalists were less concerned with the rider, hoping rather to imprison the lion itself in a cage of rights. Neither had much trust in the people from whom popular government took its legitimacy. Alexander Hamilton is said to have expressly calumnized the people as a great beast, "howling masses" not fit to govern.

It is hardly a suprise then that the founders created a form of government in many ways antipathetic to the popular sovereignty that was its paper premise. Moreover, they wrote a constitution whose letter was self-consciously distrustful of democracy. Popular sovereignty could not for them mean popular rule. The abstract status of sovereign permitted "we the people" to establish a government, but did not license us to participate in the government it brought forth. The word equality fails to make an appearance in the Constitution's language, and almost every device of government contemplated was aimed not at embodying but at checking popular power. The real democrats (such as Sam Adams, Patrick Henry, Tom Paine, and Jefferson himself) were not present at the Philadelphia creation, and radical democratic models calling for a unicameral legislature and universal white male suffrage of the kind represented by the Pennsylvania Constitution were given short shrift.

Jefferson had written of the Virginia Constitution: "Try by this as a tally every provision of our constitution and see if it hangs directly on the will of the people."[1] By this measure, the federal Constitution, which he did not much like, perhaps because he subjected it to just such a tally, failed; thus, for the suspicious founders, it succeeded. As Patrick Henry dryly remarked, as far as he could see, the people had given the founders no power to use their names. Any incipient tendencies to popular government that might have been insinuated into the constitution by "democrats, mobocrats and all the other rats" (as the slogan had it) were warded off by the provisions of the separation of powers, with its immobilizing checks and balances; by federalism as a forced vertical separation of powers enhanced by the Tenth Amendment; by the indirect election of senators and the president, which interposed a filter between the people and their servants; by judicial review as a check on popular legislation (and in time a warrant for judicial legislation); and by the division of popular will into two parts equal and opposed—one represented by the House of Representatives, the other by the presidency.

The two expressly democratic instruments—the House of Representatives and the amendment process—were hedged in with restrictions. Limitations on suffrage, which the states could decide at their own whim, left the Constitution, in Henry Lee's scathing indictment, "a mere shred or rag of representation." The powers to amend the Constitution detailed in Article Five, popular sovereignty's most potent constitutional instrument, were made sufficiently complicated and unwieldy to turn it into a last and improbable recourse of what would have had to be a wildly dissatisfied and endlessly energetic people, if they were really to have used it. Sixteen amendments in 200 years (I count the Bill of Rights as part of the original Constitution) does not suggest a very democratic instrument or a very engaged popular sovereign.

The letter of the Constitution and the intentions of the framers are, however, only part of the story. The spirit of democracy is as old as the republic—equality had its ardent advocates then as now—and found its way into the spirit and the logic of the Constitution, even where it was contradicted by the letter of the Constitution itself. This democratic spirit arises not in opposition to rights but from the political context which gives rights meaning and force. There is a simple but powerful relationship between rights and democracy: rights entail the equality of those who claim them; and democracy is the politics of equality. Without democracy, rights are empty words that depend for their realization on the good will of despots. Rights in their own turn promote and promise emancipation, suffrage, and empowerment. Even Madison recognized that rights without supporting political institutions were so many "parchment barriers" to tyranny; this was one reason for his early opposition to a separate Bill of Rights. Late in his life, in 1821, like so many Americans who had once feared the people as a rabble, he had come to take a less harsh view of democracy. He would not, perhaps, have agreed with Louis Hartz that "the majority in America has forever been a puppy dog tethered to a lion's leash," but on the question of the enfranchising of those without property, he came to acknowledge that

> Under every view of the subject, it seems indispensable that the Mass of Citizens should not be without a voice, in making the laws which they are to obey, in choosing the Magistrates, who are to administer them, and if the only alternative be between an equal and universal right of suffrage for each branch of the government and a containment of the entire right to a part of the citizens, it is better that those having the greater interest at stake namely that of property and persons both, should be deprived of half their share in government; than that those having the lesser interest, that of personal rights only, should be deprived of the whole.[2]

Madison's use of the language of "an equal and universal right of suffrage" just thirty years after a founding consecrated to limiting both popular suffrage and popular access to government seems startling, but rights language permitted no other evolution. If popular government and laws understood as self-prescribed limitations on private behavior are the real guarantors of liberty, if natural rights are secure only when political rights are guaranteed by popular government, then the right to suffrage turns out to be the keystone of all other rights. This principle was increasingly recognized in the real democratic politics of the early nineteenth century and was eventually written explicitly into the Constitution with the Thirteenth, Fourteenth, and Fifteenth Amendments.

## Rights Claims and Equality Claims

I mean here to advance both a logical claim and a historical claim. I want to say rights can be shown theoretically to entail equality and democracy. At the same time, I want to argue that the history of rights talk in America unfolds as an increasingly progressive and democratic story. From a philosophical viewpoint, rights claims are always and necessarily equality claims as well. To say "I have a right" is to posit that I am the equal of others and at the same time to recognize the equality of the persons to whom, on whom, or against whom the claim is made. No master ever said to a slave: "Give me my rights!" for rights can be acknowledged only by equals. Likewise, the slave who proclaims "I have the right to be free" says in the same breath, "I am your equal," and hence, "You are my equal." In a certain sense in speaking of equal rights one speaks redundantly: rights are equalizers. Equality is expressed in the idea of rights. Individuals may use rights to insulate themselves from others, to wall in their privacy, but their rights claims depend entirely on the proposition that as claimants they are the equal of all others, that no persons living in a free and democratic society are privileged by virtue of race, gender, religion, or other conditions.

More than anything else, this is why a constitution rooted in rights cannot systematically exclude whole classes of persons from citizenship without becoming inherently unstable. Even where it is antidemocratic in its institutional provisions, it will incline to democratization, tend over time toward greater inclusiveness. This is exactly what happened to the American polity in the course of the nineteenth century. That the Constitution included provisions implicitly recognizing slavery, such as the three-fifths compromise, was a shameful comment on the founders and perhaps on their motives; nonetheless, such provisions sat like undigested gruel on the Constitution's rights-lined stomach, and they were in time regurgitated not simply from pressures brought to bear from the outside, but because rights talk is inherently universalizing and pushed against artificial boundaries of every kind, making inequalities increasingly indigestible.

If rights imply citizenship and citizenship appears as a right—like the right to liberty, the right to self-legislation, and the right to be included in a civic polity founded on "popular" (that-means-me!) sovereignty—the idea of the citizen will always have an aggressive, liberating, even imperial character with respect to the category of "persons," which pushes to extend its compass to the very periphery of the universal. In Rome, in early modern Europe, and in America, the idea of the citizen has been expansive in its logic and liberating in its politics. Today, as rights continue to press outward, reaching the very edge of our species boundary, we can even speak of animal rights or fetal rights and still seem to be extending rather than perverting what it means for beings to have rights.

Rights are also linked logically to democracy and equality as a consequence of their essentially social character. Rousseau had already observed in the *Social Contract* that, although all justice comes from God, "if we knew how to receive it from on high, we would need neither government nor laws. There is without a doubt a universal justice emanating from reason alone; but to be acknowledged among us, this justice must be reciprocal. . . . There must be conventions and laws to combine rights with duties and to bring justice back to its object."[3] In a classical nineteenth century idealist argument, the English political philosopher T. H. Green elaborates Rousseau's argument by insisting that "there can be no right without a consciousness of common interest on the part of members of a society. Without this there might be certain powers on the part of individuals, but no recognition of these powers . . . and without this recognition or claim to recognition there can be no right." Recognition entails the mutuality of a common language, common conventions, and common consciousness: in other words, civility. Citizens alone possess rights, for as Green says rights "attach to the individual . . . only as a member of a society." When Green suggests that a right "held against society is a contradiction in terms" he seems to echo Edmund Pendleton, who repeatedly insisted that there is no quarrel between government and liberty. This is to say that Green underwrites the necessary linkage between democracy and rights.

Rights attach and pertain to citizens, whose evolving perceptions and needs generate evolving claims that become effective, practical rights only insofar as they succeed in eliciting the mutual recognition of citizens. The Constitution could be regarded by a number of Federalists as, in and of itself, a Bill of Rights because, by breathing air into the American polity, the Constitution gave life to the substance of rights. The "We" in "We the People" constituted the nexus of mutual recognitions upon which rights depended. Rights may have preceded the formal structures of the Constitution, and may therefore be thought to constrain and limit these structures; but rights become real (that is, realized) only in the setting of mutuality and common recognition, which in turn conditions the Constitution.

Now if rights entail equality and require a civic context of mutual recognition to be effective, the form of regime most compatible with rights is neither a decentralized, limited government based on the model of the Anti-Federalists nor a screened and filtered representative government based on the republican model of the Federalists, but quite simply democracy—defined by universal suffrage and collective self-legislation. For democracy is the rule of equality. Limited government is indifferent to who rules so long as the rulers are constrained. Republican government elicits the consent and accountability but not the participation and judgment of the people; this is why Jefferson sometimes called representative government elective aristocracy. Rights do best, however, where the claimants and those on whom their claims fall are the same—where sovereign and subject are united in one person: a person to whom we commonly give the name citizen. Without citizenship and participation, rights are a charade. Without responsibility, rights cannot be enforced. Without empowerment, rights are decorative fictions. A constitution is, after all, a piece of paper, and "parchment barriers" are never much use against lead and steel and chains and guns.

## "Parchment Barriers"

In what may be the world's most effusively rights-oriented constitution, a famous document not only guarantees citizens "freedom of speech," "freedom of the press," "freedom of assembly," and "freedom of street processions and demonstrations," but also offers judges who will be constitutionally "independent and subject only to the law" and "separation of church from state," as well as the "right to education," "the right to work," "the right to rest and leisure," and "the right to maintenance in old age and also in case of sickness or disability." And, if these were not enough, it provides equal rights to women "in all spheres of economic, government, cultural, political, and other public activity." Finally, it guarantees universal elections in which all citizens have the right to vote, "irrespective of race or nationality, sex, religion, education, domicile, social origin, property status or past activities." This unprecedented fortress of human liberty was bequeathed to its people by the Constitution (Fundamental Law) of the Soviet Union, a nation in which, however, as everyone including the Soviets themselves have finally been persuaded, rights have been paper parapets from which no defense of liberties can possibly be undertaken.

Madison understood the weaknesses of parchment barriers well enough, for it was he who used the term in questioning the value of a Bill of Rights detached from the Constitution. "Repeated violations of . . . parchment barriers," he observed, "have been committed by overbearing majorities in every state. . . . Whenever there is an interest and power to do wrong, wrong will generally be done and not less readily by a powerful and interested party than by a powerful and interested prince."[4]

Philosophical argument finds persuasive historical expression in the American setting. Successful popular movements aimed at the emancipation of slaves, the enfranchisement of women, and the re-mediation of the condition of the native American Indian tribes, as well as at the empowerment of the poor, the working class, and others cast aside by the American market, have all had in common a devotion to the language of rights. Indeed, the single most important strategic decision faced by those who have felt left out of the American way of life has been whether to mobilize against or in the name of the American founding, understood as the Declaration of Independence, the Constitution, and the Bill of Rights. Movements that have made war on the Constitution, holding that its rights promise no salvation to the powerless, have on the whole failed. Movements that have insisted that the founding can and must make good on the promise implicit in its universalizing rights rhetoric have succeeded.

The explicit mimicry of the founders' language and the citation by progressives of great rights jurists like Blackstone provide a clear example of holding rights language up to the test of its own entailments.[5] The bold women at Seneca Falls in 1846, for example, captured the essence of their own militant rights claims—"we hold these truths to be self-evident," they asserted, "that all men and women are created equal." And although the radical abolitionists at times seemed to declare war on America itself, one of their most fiery leaders understood the entailments of the American tradition well enough. William Lloyd Garrison burned a copy of the Constitution in Framingham on July 4, 1854. Nevertheless he declared in *The Liberator,* in his "To the Public," and in impassioned speeches throughout the North, that he "assented to the 'self-evident truth' maintained in the American Declaration of Independence, 'that all men are created equal, and endowed by their Creator with certain inalienable rights—among which are life, liberty and the pursuit of happiness.' On this foundation," he concluded, he would "strenuously contend for the immediate enfranchisement of our slave population."[6]

Some might say these radicals were trying to drive a wedge between the Declaration and the Constitution in the fashion of the later progressive historians. But when John Brown went looking for legitimacy he found it in the preamble to the Constitution as well as in the Declaration. When he offered the people of the United States a "Provisional Constitution," its preamble read:

31

> Whereas slavery, throughout its entire existence in the
> United States, is none other than a most barbarous, unpro-
> voked, and unjustifiable war of one portion of its citizens
> upon another portion . . . in utter disregard and violation of
> those eternal and self-evident truths set forth in our Decla-
> ration of Independence, therefore we, citizens of the United
> States, and the oppressed people (deprived of Rights by Jus-
> tice Taney) . . . do ordain and establish for ourselves the fol-
> lowing Provisional Constitution and ordinances, the better
> to protect our person, property, lives and liberties, and to
> govern our action.[7]

From this perspective, the Civil War amendments ending slavery and
involuntary servitude and guaranteeing universal suffrage for men,
due process, and the equal protection of the laws to all U.S. citizens
were not a reversal of America's constitutional history but the culminating event in the history of the Constitution's rights commitments
as manifested in the practical politics and the civic life of the nation.
Justice Taney's decision in *Dred Scott* was by the same token the last
gasp of those trying to stem the flood tide on which rights were
sweeping through history. Taney's problem was how to construct
rights that had an ineluctably universalizing thrust in narrow, self-
limiting terms. He had to show that "we the people," which is syn-
onymous with "citizens," was intended to exclude the Negro race.
His decision turns on the historical fact that Negroes "were at that
time considered as a subordinate and inferior class of beings," but
studiously and prudently avoids a careful examination of what such
crucial terms as person, citizen, and right might entail. For he is
trying to construct an argument precisely against those entailments.[8]

Even at the time of the founding there had been powerful opposition to slavery as an embarrassment to the language of the Declaration and the Constitution's preamble. John Adams and John Jay were
vigorously eloquent in their opposition to it (although not at the convention), and a number of statesmen would sympathize with George
Mason's refusal to sign the Constitution because its twenty-year extension of the slave trade was "disgraceful to mankind."

James Madison had acknowledged the "moral equality of blacks"
and in *Federalist* 54 allowed that Negroes did "partake" of qualities
belonging to persons as well as to property and were thus protected
in "life and limb, against the violence of all others." The slave, Madison said, "is no less evidently regarded by the law as a member of the
society, not as part of irrational creation; as a moral person, not as a
mere article of property."[9] Now to be sure, Madison also had supported the thesis that slaves were property, and when Missouri ap-

plied for admission to the Union, he had argued that its Negroes should be removed. But rights were seeping into American history, which helped Madison to change his tune; in 1825 he wrote "the magnitude of this evil among us is so deeply felt, and so universally acknowledged, that no merit could be greater than that of devising a satisfactory remedy for it." [10] It was not so much the moral argument but the logic of what it meant to be a person that is captured by Madison; it was this logic that created the problems for the hapless Taney.

## Rights Absolutism

In our century, the powerful alliance between rights and political emancipation, between the claim to be a person and the right to be a citizen, has come unstuck. Rights have retreated into the private space won for them by their civic entailments allowing us to forget that they have meaning only for citizens. The communities that rights once created are now pictured as the enemies of rights, and the political institutions by which we secure rights are made over into external, alien adversaries—as if they had nothing to do with us. The sense of rights as a claim for political participation—and of participation and civic responsibility as the foundation of rights—has yielded to peculiarly privatized notions of rights; they are considered the indisputable possessions of individuals who acquire them at birth and who need do nothing to enforce them, and they exist and are efficacious only so long as they are noisily promulgated. Rights cease to be a civic identity to be posited and won; they become a natural identity to be discovered, worn, and enjoyed.

As a consequence, young people today are as likely to use rights to deny government as to affirm it; to deny the civic community the power to conscript or interfere with them, as if it were not *their* community, as if there could be a democratic government in the absence of a willingness and responsibility to serve it—to constitute it—by its citizens. Similarly, many Americans seem to think of voting as a right to be exercised or not at will, rather than as a responsibility on which the preservation of all rights inevitably depends. Towns and municipalities find themselves unable to govern because inhabitants who have forgotten that they are citizens and that *the* town is actually *their* town—nothing other than the citizenry represented and embodied in a civic whole—express their rights by bringing lawsuits against their elected officials.

Rights are expressed not in citizenship but in litigiousness. But a litigious citizen is a contradiction in terms: the lawsuit is a denial of connection, a denial of responsibility; when the defendant is the civic

33

community, it is a denial of civic membership, in other words, a denial of citizenship. Once the bond between the citizens and the civic community is severed, citizens willingly become the clients of government. This is but a new form of servitude disguised by bureaucratic benevolence and judicial paternalism. Recently, volunteer fire departments have been vanishing for want of volunteers; fire protection is viewed as a service provided by the government to citizens who are understood as its clients. Therefore when the service is unsatisfactory, litigation appears an appropriate response.

The precarious balance between individual and community, which rights properly understood can mediate, is upset, and rights are introduced on only one side of the scales, leaving the community without a justificatory base for advancing the public good. As Amitai Etzioni has wisely observed, and as the new American Alliance for Rights and Responsibilities is showing on a case-by-case basis, the obsession with private rights has induced a kind of rights absolutism in Americans.[11] Rights become trumps, trumps become trumpets, then drums, hammers, sledge hammers, cannons, and finally heavy weapons of judicial overkill. From their role as a crucial mediator of political discourse, rights are transmogrified into a discourse that denies politics.

The American Civil Liberties Union only follows this mood when it assumes a stance of rights absolutism in which the political context of rights is made to disappear. In recent years, in addition to its traditional and healthy concerns with the sanctity of political speech and the right of assembly, the ACLU has dug itself into a foxhole from which it can engage in a firefight with democracy, the commonwealth, and the public good. It opposes airport security examinations, decries sobriety checkpoints (which were recently declared constitutional by the Supreme Court in a six to three decision), argues against the voluntary fingerprinting of children in areas with a history of kidnapping, and generally makes privacy into a super trump card in a deck of individual rights that, with respect to all other goods, is already trump to start with. In the case of the *Michigan Department of State Police v. Sitz*, a leading argument held that sobriety checkpoints abridged the constitutional rights of Michigan motorists by causing them "fright and surprise" during a ninety-second inspection that was tantamount to "subjective intrusion upon liberty interests." Consider the liberty interests of other drivers who are potential victims of drunken driving accidents. These interests, usually thought of as the rights of the community, or the responsibility of the body politic, are not weighed and found wanting; they are ignored. The language of rights simply is not permitted to extend to them.

Rights absolutism feeds into the historical mistrust that some Americans still feel toward popular government in a way that disenfranchises the very citizenry that rights were once deployed to empower. The new strategy links a Federalist distrust of popular rule with a form of judicial activism that permits courts not merely to enforce rights but to legislate in their name whenever the "people" are deemed sufficiently deluded or insufficiently energetic. It is not at all clear that rights, enforced within an obstinate citizen body rendered passive-aggressive (that is, quiescent but angry) by an encroaching court, are really made more secure over the long haul. But it is certainly clear that a "democratic" government that will not permit its citizens to govern themselves when it comes to rights will soon be without either rights or democracy. Perhaps the development of such a government can be seen as an extension of the original federal strategy against democracy, which produced judicial review as a limit on popular legislation. Since *Brown v. Board of Education* in 1954, rights activists, properly impatient with the slowness of the democratic process, have allied with courts that are willing to act as surrogate legislators where they find the people have failed to act. The "filtration" of the public mind favored by the founders takes the modern form of judicial government.

In the recent Supreme Court case that upheld a lower court's decision concerning Kansas City, Missouri, school desegregation, the majority ruled in favor of a judicial intervention whose outcome was the raising of taxes. In a complicated case, the Missouri court did not itself directly levy taxes, but Justice Anthony Kennedy issued a sobering caution about the insidious logic of a judiciary that acts as a legislative surrogate. He wrote in dissent: "It is not surprising that imposition of taxes by a [judicial] authority so insulated from public communication or control can lead to deep feelings of frustration, powerlessness and anger on the part of taxpaying citizens." [12] Frustration, powerlessness, and anger have been precisely the currency in which Americans have reacted to the usurping of their political authority in the name of their political rights.

Democracies do not always do justice. They frequently do injustice. But the remedy for this, as Jefferson noted a long time ago, is not to disempower citizens who have been indiscreet, but to inform their discretion. Publics can become more discreet and competent over time. The ravages done by Proposition 13, which initiated the tax revolt in 1978 and thus limited state expenditures, have over time educated the people of California and brought them to an appreciation of their civic responsibilities. In the spring of 1990, quite on their own, without the mandate of a court, Californians approved a referendum raising taxes.[13] What America needs most now are not more interventionist courts but more interventionist schools; not lessons in the rights of private persons but lessons in the responsibilities of public citizens; not a new view of the Bill of Rights but a new view of the Constitution as the democratic source of all rights.

If the rights obsessions of our times prove anything, it is that Madison might have had a better understanding of rights than the advocates of a separate bill of amendments when he argued for including rights in the substantive text of the Constitution. For by placing them there, where they would be read in context, rather than isolating them in a document that might make them seem a natural possession of passive private persons, their civic and social nature as part and parcel of the fabric of democratic republicanism would have been crystal clear.

On this 200th birthday of the Bill of Rights, we need to learn for ourselves what the first seventy-five years of American history, culminating in the Civil War, taught our ancestors in a still young America; rights stand with, not against, democracy, and if the two do not progress together, they do not progress at all.

# 3

# Fundamental Rights and the Structure of the Government

*Judith A. Best*

*History proves that dictatorships do not grow out of strong and suc-
cessful governments, but out of weak and helpless ones. If by democratic methods people get a government strong enough to protect
them from fear and starvation, their democracy succeeds; but if they
do not, they grow impatient. Therefore, the only sure bulwark of
continuing liberty is a government strong enough to protect the interests of the people, and a people strong enough and well enough
informed to maintain its sovereign control over the government.*

FRANKLIN DELANO ROOSEVELT
Fireside Chat, April 14, 1938

By its very form, our government not only reveals that its end is human liberty; it also institutes and mandates a process that produces
that end. The rule of law emerging from the form of our government—the democratic federal republic, with its separation of powers—is the ongoing guarantee of our fundamental rights. These fundamental rights are expressed in and secured by a competent and
balanced governing process, not by mere "parchment barriers."

It is possible to make a list of fundamental rights, especially in
the form of prohibitions on government, and then to emboss them on
parchment. One of the dangers of this kind of enterprise, however, is

37

omission—either through lack of foresight or through failure to recognize the potential breadth and complexity of liberty. Awareness of this problem produces disclaimers like that in the Ninth Amendment: "The enumeration in the Constitution, of certain rights, shall not be construed to deny or disparage others retained by the people." This disclaimer is at once a notice of the incompleteness of the list and a confession of the inadequacy of the effort. As the Ninth Amendment makes clear, it is ultimately the people who must continuously define and refine their rights in time and place. For this they need a process.

The major and overriding problem with relying on parchment prohibitions is revealed by the questions: Where does the danger to fundamental rights arise? Against whom must they be protected? Who or what is to secure them? The answers to these questions are: Dangers to liberty arise in all times and places, and under unpredictable and changing circumstances. Rights must be protected against all comers—against threats from individuals and organizations of all kinds, both inside and outside of our own society. They can only be secured by the people employing a properly structured governing process. Government, not parchment prohibitions, is the solution to the problem of securing rights. And as the Declaration of Independence proclaims, men have a right to institute government—a right to form a fully competent government as the agent and tool of their safety.

Madison pointed out that liberty must be secured against private persons and outside enemies and also against the government itself. So he said, "You must *first* enable the government to control the governed; and in the next place oblige it to control itself."[1] The point is that liberty exists through government and not just against government. This point cannot be overemphasized, as we are far too prone to think exclusively of liberty as freedom from governmental oppression, and to neglect the idea that government is absolutely essential to liberty. In the absence of competent government a man's freedom depends on his personal ability to protect himself, and he cannot be free unless he is strong, smart, and above all lucky. Our founders did not neglect the point, for they believed that weak government is a greater danger to liberty than strong government.

Yes, liberty must be secured against government; but mere prohibition on anyone, including government, will be ineffectual unless there is an agent with the "means and motives" to enforce the prohibition. Thus our founders put their faith in a governing *process* and not in a set of parchment prohibitions.

Their task was to propose a government that would be both powerful and balanced, both energetic and safe, both stable and free. In a word—moderate. It is the combination that made the task difficult and necessitated a new science of government. It is relatively easy to institute either a stable or a free government, but each would lack the excellence of the other. The stable might not be free, and the free might not be stable. To establish a governing process that would be both was the real challenge of statesmanship. The challenge was met by the republican form of government, modified by two innovations that were republicanized into a governing process regulated by the two great structural principles of the Constitution—the separation of powers and the federal system.

## Republican Government

The founders were committed republicans, which is to say first that they agreed government must stand on the original and *ongoing* consent of the governed. This understanding is not only modern, it is Lockean—although Locke was not necessarily a republican. The Lockean principle requiring not only original but also ongoing consent reflects the motive for consent—to preserve and enlarge freedom. A rational man will consent to be governed to his benefit, and no rational man may consent to the destruction of his unalienable natural rights—his fundamental rights.

From the Lockean perspective, political liberty exists through and because of government. Thus we give our original consent; we *manu*facture government to guard our rights. But then, who is to guard the guardians? The Lockean answer is that the people shall guard the guardians. The people shall judge the government. This is the ongoing consent that may be withdrawn at any time by a deliberate and solemn act of a majority of the incorporated people, of society itself—although according to Locke, the people will not act precipitously but only after suffering a "long train of abuses."

The *fully* republican version of ongoing consent takes that consent one step beyond where Locke left it in what is often called the right of revolution—the right of the people to dissolve the government and to replace it with an entirely new one. That republican step is to require ongoing consent in the administration of the government, to require that all "the persons administering it be appointed either directly or indirectly by the people," and those appointed hold their offices "during pleasure for a limited period, or during good behavior."[2]

Those who administer the government are to be kept dependent upon the people themselves and not on some specially favored class. It is this step that makes a government of and by the people as well as for them. The people's role of judging is to be incorporated into the governing process by free and frequent elections rather than to stand outside and above the governing process.

Because the republican principle of free and frequent elections formalizes ongoing consent, making consent tangible and not tacit, making popular oversight continual and not rare, this principle serves both stability and freedom. The justification for giving the people the task of judging the government arises not only from the principle of natural rights, but also from political prudence. Those who wear the shoes know best where they pinch. The republican, elected-representative principle is prudent because it injects information about the pinch into the governing process on a timely basis, while it is still a pinch and not yet the bleeding sore that leads us to throw out the shoes. The governing process can be corrected or adjusted continually by replacing those who administer it, thus avoiding the long train of abuses that leads to the extreme remedy of abolishing the government and replacing it with a new one.

The republicans had indeed improved upon the principle of ongoing consent by incorporating it into the governing process. Republics, however, like all pure or simple forms of government, suffer from the vices that attend their virtues. Republics were relatively small, compared with monarchies, and in democratic republics the people are the final sovereigns. Thus the diseases of republican governments are weakness and factionalism. Factionalism, that union of individuals into groups "adverse to the rights of other citizens or to the permanent and aggregate interests of the community,"[3] is in the nature of man. Dogs will bark, geese will migrate, and men will form factions as long as they are free to do so.

To protect our fundamental rights governments must be powerful custodians, and powerful custodians must be constantly watched. But by whom? The democratic republican answer—Watched by the people, in free and frequent elections—is not sufficient, because of the factionalism rampant in a republican people, a free people.

The founders were not only dedicated republicans, they were a new breed of republicans. Committed to the success of the form, they turned their attention to its all too numerous failures in history and in their own experience, under colonial and state governments and under the Articles of Confederation. They openly discussed and analyzed the diseases of republics that they might find "a republican remedy for the diseases most incident to republican government."[4] And they believed they had.

Their cure, however, consisted in two innovations that appeared to be antithetical to republicanism; at least this was the conclusion of the traditional republicans. Their two innovations were the large republic and the independent, energetic executive. The founders maintained that although a large nation and an energetic executive frequently are characteristics of monarchy, these characteristics would solve the problems of weakness and factionalism if they could be republicanized and regulated through a federal system and the separation of powers. They concluded that it was essential to adopt these innovations for the preservation of liberty.

## The Large Republic

The arguments for the large republic, for union, and for the supreme national government boil down to one thing: they are necessary for political liberty, understood as Locke and Montesquieu defined it—as safety, as security of person and property. "The Great end of men's entering into society," said Locke, is "the enjoyment of their properties in peace and safety."[5] In *Federalist* 3 John Jay concurred, asserting the *first* object of a wise people is their safety. The contributions of the large republic to safety are three: protection from foreign enemies, security against domestic insurrection, and prevention of majority faction.

**Foreign Enemies.** The large republic will be stronger and richer, in a word *powerful,* and thus more able to defend itself against enemies abroad. Human nature being what it is, weakness invites attack; voluntary weakness is, therefore, culpable. Small republics and confederations, which are easily divided, have been conquered or controlled by large united nations whose protection the small ones must seek. As Tocqueville pointed out, "Small nations are often miserable, not because they are small, but because they are weak. . . . Physical strength is therefore one of the first conditions of the happiness and even the existence of nations."[6] Physical strength means union, means a truly national government that has plenary authority to command and direct the enormous resources of the large republic.

If the large republic is to be prosperous, the national legislature must have the power to regulate commerce to preclude the internal economic wars that one factional part would otherwise make on the others. It must be able to tap these resources with a power to tax and spend for the common defense and general welfare. It must be able to raise armies. And it must have the power to choose the most appropriate means and methods of employing its assigned powers.

The government is created as the instrument of our safety, but there is no way to define in advance of specific circumstances what is

41

requisite for defense. No nation can unilaterally define what is requisite for defense. The current enemy does that because safety from external danger depends upon having a defensive power that at the very least matches and better still surpasses that of the current enemy. Only union, only a powerful supreme national government can do the job. Or as Hamilton said, it is an axiom of political science that "the means ought to be proportioned to the end, that every power ought to be commensurate with its object; that there ought to be no limitation of a power destined to effect a purpose which is itself incapable of limitation." Our purpose is safety, and "the circumstances that endanger the safety of nations are infinite."[7]

The large republic, because united and powerful, is the sine qua non of all rights. If the republic is conquered we have no rights other than those the conqueror will allow. If the nation is vanquished the Bill of Rights is not even a "parchment barrier," for its prohibitions fall on a nonexistent government.

**Domestic Insurrection.** With its Article IV guarantee of a republican form of government to each state, the large republic is also a barrier to domestic insurrection and violence. The rest of the union can come to the aid of a part which, on its own, might not be capable of handling the problem. Liberty requires that minority rights be protected, but minority rights do not mean minority rule. In a Lockean society the majority may fire the government and hire a new one, but the minority does not have this right. Having one's say is not the same as having one's way. In a Lockean society, a society with a functioning legal process, action is to be taken through the rule of law, not the rule of force without right. Indeed, the rule of law is to be a substitute for the rule of force, but to maintain the rule of law the government must have the power as well as the authority to use force against those who would use it without right, against intransigent minorities who take to the streets with violence.

In civil society none of our fundamental rights are absolute. All of our rights are conditional upon our coexistence with others and their rights. All of our fundamental civil rights, including life, liberty, and estate, may be abridged for abuse upon conviction by due process of law. We may be fined, imprisoned, or even executed for lawbreaking. The creation and enforcement of law is the true birth of liberty. Men, Locke said, had absolute rights in the state of nature—that theoretical model of asocial men. Their absolute rights were substantively worthless, however, because there was no fully known, enforced, and effectual law, no real law to secure them. It is the creation of real law—government—that converts the worthless rights of asocial men into the actual rights of men in a civil society.

**Majority Faction.** The small republic has a tendency to weakness, but this tendency is only one of the two foremost diseases of republics. The other is majority faction. The rule of law is the condition of liberty, but the simple rule of the majority is not at all the same as the rule of law. Unstructured, it is merely the rule of the greater force. Liberty is the right to obey laws one has a voice in making. It is the right to live under a governing process that is balanced for safety, open to peaceable change, and above all controlled by the majority *with the consent of the minority.* The disease of republics is majority rule without minority consent.

The large republic, especially the large commercial republic, is the remedy of choice. For men to be factious is to do what comes naturally. Madison observed that "so strong is this propensity of mankind to fall into mutual animosities that where no substantial occasion presents itself the most frivolous and fanciful distinctions have been sufficient to kindle their unfriendly passions and excite their violent conflicts."[8] As long as men are free they will form factions; in republics, in governments dedicated to liberty, factions will flourish.

But it is not faction per se that destroys republics; it is majority faction, a faction inflamed by a common interest in oppressing a minority. It is the liberty of all, not simply the liberty of the majority, that is the aspiration of republics. The danger is particularly acute in a small republic, as the smaller it is the more homogeneous it is likely to be. The smaller the society and fewer the varieties of faction, the more likely is the formation of a majority faction. So, said Madison, "Extend the sphere and you take in a greater variety of parties and interests; you make it less probable that a majority of the whole will have a common motive to invade the rights of other citizens."[9] The disease is faction and the cure is more faction, as we fight fire with fire.

Extend the sphere and the society will be heterogeneous, will be composed of many small factions rather than dominated and oppressed by one large faction. And further, since according to Madison the first object of republican government is to protect the diverse talents of men, and since property rights originate in our freedom to use our talents, the large republic will promote commerce. Promotion of commerce will also foster heterogeneity. This axiom is implicit in Madison's recognition that this protection results in "different degrees and *kinds* of property."[10]

Conflict over different degrees and different amounts of property

43

destroyed many of the old republics. The conflict of the rich and the poor is a form of factionalism to be avoided if republics are to be preserved. A large commercial society develops many different *kinds* of property, many different kinds of economic interests, based on specialized occupations and particular industries around which minority factions will form. They will compete with each other, but no one will be a majority faction. In the large commercial republic the class struggle is avoided and replaced by the struggle of competing interests. This makes it less likely that the majorities that form will have a natural common interest. Instead the majorities formed will be concurrent majorities, majorities created by the temporary and changeable coalition of minority factions—factions actually in competition with each other in some ways, on some issues. Such factions can only form coalitions through compromise and accommodation—by tempering their factionalism. The cure is to promote the formation of the kinds of minority factions that are flexible and can compromise—as Martin Diamond argued, those based on interest as opposed to those arising from opinion or passion—and then to regulate and direct their rivalry.[11]

If the society is sufficiently heterogeneous, majorities will have to be built, will have to be constructed often on an issue-by-issue basis. This construction not only means that the threat of majority faction is reduced; it also provides the incentive for the consent of the minority. Liberty requires not only a form of majority rule but also minority consent to that rule. Why and when would a minority consent to majority rule? The answer is, only if a minority can see that on some issues important to it and on some occasions, it can be part of the majority. It would be irrational to consent to a game in which you can never win, never win anything at all. The rule of the concurrent majority, with its shifting alliances, provides a minority with the opportunity to be part of the majority some of the time and thus functions to secure minority consent.

To make this rule work, however, the *governing process* must be set up to structure and use these coalitions. The federal system and the separation of powers do both, for they are the instruments of the new science of faction that converts this human weakness into a political strength. They institutionalize rivalry: they sift and screen the contestants, schedule competition, arrange and supervise the contests.

**Structuring the Rivalry.** Madison saw "a proper federal system" as a barrier to majority tyranny, for it means "the society itself will be broken into so many parts, interests and classes of citizens, that the rights of individuals, or of the minority, will be in little danger from interested combinations of the majority."[12] Among the parts are the districted constituencies mandated by the federal system in the process of choosing our national representatives. All of our elective national offices are shaped and defined by federalism. State boundaries serve as the electoral districts for the Senate. Smaller parts of states, in most cases, are the electoral districts for the House. The number of electoral votes for president allotted to each state is tied to the number of representatives a state has in Congress, and to win the presidency a candidate must win states. Our votes are aggregated only within states, and they cannot be combined across state or district lines. We never vote as members of one all-national constituency; we never vote "in a society under the forms of which the stronger faction can *readily unite* and oppress the weaker."[13]

The result is a more moderate, less ideological politics, one that is extremely sensitive to local needs, one that recognizes that those who share the same schools and roads, the same climate and natural resources and local economy, have common interests. But it is a process that not only recognizes the needs of those who live in close proximity; it also reflects the views and interests of broad cross sections of the country, because the districted division is not simply geographic. As James Burnham pointed out, ethnic, religious, and occupational clustering means that many and various groups that are minorities from a national perspective may actually be majorities or at least powerful minorities within given electoral districts.[14] Therefore, the federal rider on our ongoing consent, our process of choosing national representatives, will give them a voice on the national level.

The federal representative principle orders and directs the multiple factions produced by the extended sphere and the commercial society. Instead of expressing their views on national policy directly, the people express their views indirectly in a framework designed "to refine and enlarge" those views. Representatives can "refine and enlarge" the public view precisely because their interest as representatives is to be elected in the first place and reelected in the second. To accomplish this in the larger heterogeneous districts required by the federal system, each representative must try to satisfy a substantial number of people whose interests are conflicting. To be elected he must synthesize and harmonize; he must transcend the selfish interest of a single voter and a single-interest group; he must build a majority, and in so doing he comes closer to expressing the common interest.

The federal system structures the representative principle to foster the formation of concurrent majorities rather than majority factions. Negotiation, compromise, and consultation with the various interests will be the means of building majorities first within the districted constituencies and second among the elected representatives themselves, when they take their places in the national government. Thus, "a coalition of a majority of the whole society could seldom take place on any other principles than those of justice and the general good."[15]

The large commercial republic goes a long way toward preventing the formation of a majority with a common tyrannical impulse, but it is not a guarantee. Both impulse and opportunity to act have to be addressed, since even in this commercial republic of over 240 million people it is relatively easy to name at least two majority factions which could form—whites and Christians. If a majority faction were to form, it must not have the opportunity to act.

The districted constituencies of the federal system make it difficult for a majority faction to unite and use national elections as an opportunity to act. The separation of powers compounds the difficulty. One of the several purposes of the separation of powers is to prevent the majority from tyrannizing a minority. It does so by dividing the national government into three distinct branches having shared powers. The members of these branches are chosen in different ways, by different coalitions of people, for different terms of office. These different modes of selection and different terms of office act like a brake. They slow down the transformation of the will of a majority into law. They serve as a cooling-off period, so that the government is not subject to temporary passions among the people. This is the appeal from the people drunk with passion and power, to the people sober.

Two-year terms for the members of the House, six-year terms and staggered elections for the Senate, a four-year term for the president, life tenure and indirect selection by the president with the consent of the Senate for the judiciary—a majority faction will find it difficult to gain control of the entire national government in a single election year.

A determined and sustained majority can gain this control over time, of course. A sincere republican would never deny the will of the people, but as Jefferson said, "That will to be rightful must be reasonable." The separation of powers is one of the devices designed to secure reasonable majorities among the people.

Martin Diamond was quite right about the founders: they were not Hobbesian pessimists; they believed men can govern themselves when they are calm and sober.[16] If the governing process is complex and balanced, if it is not immediately responsive to their temporary passions, they can reconsider and their better natures will prevail. If this is not so then self-government is a utopian dream, an imaginary republic, and no parchment barriers can withstand the force of an irrational, cowardly, unjust, or immoderate people.

**Protection against Government.**   To achieve safety, it is not enough that the republic be large and powerful in order to protect individuals against foreign enemies, intransigent minorities, and majority faction. Government itself, especially in the large republic, may be a formidable threat to safety. This is not only obvious; it was the basis of a major argument against a powerful union made by the Anti-Federalists. In recognizing the danger from government itself, however, the Anti-Federalists drew the wrong conclusion—that republican governments must be extensively limited, limited to the point of weakness. It was fear of the governing power that shaped the Articles and caused their failure. The founders judged this conclusion to be absurd and irrational. A government whose power is so limited that it can do no harm can do little good. If you refuse to give a surgeon a knife because he may harm you with it, you preclude the possibility that he can help. Government must be powerful to perform its assigned, formidable tasks.

Power can be abused, and this must be guarded against; but this means governmental power must be balanced, checked, and *vigilantly watched*, not disabled, not diminished. Both external and internal controls must be placed on government. Here the separation of powers and the federal system serve as "auxiliary precautions," auxiliary to the traditional republican control of popular elections.

**Internal Control.**   The separation of powers, with its checks and balances, is the internal control on the national government. Without a separation of powers all governmental power would fall into the hands of the legislature in a republic. Then a common ambition to aggrandize the position of legislator, to increase its privileges and power, and to secure all incumbents dissolves the motive for mutual surveillance. If there are to be internal controls on government, there must be a separation of powers to create the "opposite and rival interests" that will have the personal motives to watch each other. These rival interests must also have the power to act and not just to sound the public alarm when trespass is perceived, and so the checks and balances are inherent in a true separation of powers. Internal controls create a governing process that is continually self-correcting because of the checks and balances.

The separation of powers places each of the three branches of

47

government on guard duty, each to be sentry over the other two, each to sound the alarm if either or both of the other two abuse power, each armed with the means to check the others. And since of the three the legislature is the most dangerous branch in a republic, one of the most essential checks and balances is bicameralism. The division of the legislature into two chambers, each having an absolute veto over the bills passed by the other, makes each chamber a watchman over the other.

Abuse of power is to be forestalled by a balance of power rather than by extensive restrictions on power. "The constant aim," Madison said, "is to divide and arrange the several offices in such a manner as that each may be a check on the other—that the private interest of every individual may be a sentinel over the public rights." [17]

Each branch and chamber of the government participates in some way in the activities of the others. Of the shared functions one of the most important is the presidential veto, because in a republic an executive without a veto is much weaker than the legislature and the government would be unbalanced. "The legislative department," warned Madison, "is everywhere extending the sphere of its activity and drawing all power into its impetuous vortex." And so, he advised, "it is against the enterprising ambition of this department that the people ought to indulge all their jealousy and exhaust all their precautions." [18]

The veto is a legislative power; it provides the president with one-sixth of the legislative power, for that is the difference between the ordinary majority of one-half needed to pass a bill and the two-thirds majority needed to override a veto. As I have argued elsewhere, the veto was qualified not only to republicanize it—not only to transform its odious monarchical appearance—but especially so that it could be used freely and frequently.[19] Madison feared an absolute veto might not be firmly exercised on ordinary occasions. And Hamilton based his argument for the qualified over the absolute veto on facility of exercise. The veto is one of the clearest examples of the balancing process because of its intended usableness. A process is a series of *continuous* actions that bring about a particular result—in this case moderate government, government that is neither too restricted to do its job nor too unbalanced to be safe.

The veto has two functions. "It not only serves as a shield to the executive, but it furnishes an additional security against the enaction of improper laws." [20] To accomplish both it must be part of the ordinary, the continuous process of governing, either by actual exercise or by unceasing anticipation of its exercise. Understanding the animus of republican legislatures to executive office, the founders predicted repeated legislative encroachment on the independence and the powers of that office. Recognizing the human capacity for error, they anticipated the need for reconsideration and provided for it institutionally. A veto power that could only be used on rare occasions rather than continually and regularly would not be effective.

Another great check and balance is judicial review, the power of the judiciary to declare national laws and other official acts of the national government to be unconstitutional. This check and balance is an almost incredible innovation in democratic republican government, but it cannot be characterized as one of the founders' innovations. The innovations that can be attributed to them are the ones they fully and consciously defended and clearly and indisputably provided for in the Constitution.

Although judicial review may have been anticipated by at least some of the founders, including Hamilton, the Constitution is silent on the power—neither confirming nor forbidding. In exercising judicial review, nonelected, life-tenured judges make policy: surely an anomaly in a republic. A number of members of the Convention, such as Pinkney, Mercer, and Dickinson, expressly disapproved of a power in the judiciary to set aside national laws, though their arguments were made in the context of proposals to give the judiciary a role shared with the president in the *formation* of a law—presentation of a bill, signature of approval, or return to the legislature with objections for reconsideration or possible override.[21] Allowing the judiciary to have a role in the formation of a law involved it directly and immediately in the policy-making process. Under judicial review the time and circumstances for judicial intervention are different (subsequent and not self-initiating); the result, nonetheless, is that in exercising the power, judges make policy.

Whether or not the founders understood it, it was probably inevitable that judicial review would emerge under a written Constitution that separates the powers of government and creates an independent judiciary. The written Constitution is an actual, formally promulgated law that enables and restricts the several departments of government, and not simply an announcement of purposes and aspirations. As such it is binding and obligatory. Further, it is the law of laws, a law not created by or altered by ordinary legislative process. Thus the written Constitution itself creates a special task for an independent judiciary—the task of measuring the correspondence of governmental action against declared rule, against the highest law: the law of the Constitution. Judicial review is at least latent in a written constitution that decrees an independent judiciary.

Judicial review, however, has transformed the judiciary into a far more dangerous branch of government, because it makes it possible for judges who would rather be legislators to exercise will rather than judgment by ignoring the text—the actual words—of the Constitution, and replacing them with a personal concept of justice or of the "felt needs of the time." If judicial review is to maintain any republican legitimacy the judges must recognize that they themselves are bound by the Constitution. To paraphrase Jefferson: a constitution which may be changed by a decision of the Supreme Court amounts to having no constitution at all. The people, not the Supreme Court, must define and refine their rights in time and place. The Constitution provides two processes for this: through statutory law made by their elected representatives, Congress and the president; through constitutional law involving Congress and the state legislatures.

Unelected, life-tenured judges have a role as the guardians of our constitutional law; however, in a republic this means that they are the guardians of the constitutional *process*, not revisers or amenders of the Constitution. All guardians must be guarded against, but an unelected, life-tenured judiciary exercising the power of judicial review must be subject to extraordinary vigilance. The advent of judicial review may have converted the judiciary into the *most* dangerous branch of government.

**External Control.** The other "auxiliary precaution," the federal system, is an external control on the national government. Madison said that the federal system, which makes every citizen subject to two governments, provides "a double security . . . to the rights of the people."[22] The division of power is vertical, between the two governments, and horizontal, because both governments operate under the separation-of-powers principle. Therefore, "the different governments will control each other, at the same time that each will be controlled by itself."[23] The direct external control by the people—free and frequent elections—is supplemented by an indirect external control of the people acting through their two governments. The state governments stand on guard to prevent abuse by the national government and vice versa.

Though the two governments are not true rivals because of the essential principle of national supremacy, the state governments, constitutionally recognized as legitimate, permanent, and to some degree autonomous, serve as a platform for criticism of the national government and as intermediary institutions to act and speak for organized parts of the people. Tocqueville recognized the value of the state and local governments as intermediary institutions that support liberty when he argued that although the United States has a centralized government, it does not have a centralized administration. The national policy is administered most often by state and local officials who can to some extent adjust it to local and regional needs.

Moreover, the state governments acting in concert have one formidable power—that relating to amendments to the Constitution. They have a power of initiative on amendments. If two-thirds of them agree a convention must be called to offer amendments, including amendments to alter the power or even the form of the national government, and this even if the national government speaking through Congress is opposed. Acting on a three-fourths rule, they have the power to approve or reject all amendments, including those proposed by Congress unless Congress chooses to go directly to the people in convention. Thus both governments in the federal system can appeal to the people, who in republics must be the final judges not only of all their governments but also of disputes between their two constitutionally established governments.

## The Independent, Energetic Executive

The argument for the independent, energetic executive is competence. Incompetent government is not worthy of the name. A competent government must have an agent to vigorously enforce the laws and also to supply the defect of law itself. "We have neither troops, nor treasury, nor *government*,"[24] Hamilton cried out in his plea for union over confederation. A republic, large or small, is a form of government. Whatever the advantages of small republics, the advantages of large ones, including strength and wealth, "troops and treasury," tempt political amateurs to confederation on the premise they can have the advantages without the government. This combination is not in the nature of things. Confederation, it turns out, is no form of government at all.

**Law Enforcement.** "The great and radical vice" of the Confederation was that it was not a government. It was not a government because it could not legislate for individuals—it could not enforce its own "laws" but rather had to rely on the true governments, the states, to make individuals comply. The Confederation was an incomplete and defective government because it did not have an effectual executive power.

"Government," said Hamilton, "implies the power of making laws. It is essential to the idea of a law that it be attended with a sanction."[25] National "laws" that only the states could enforce would not be laws at all but only advice or recommendations. Gouverneur Morris had made the same point in the Convention, describing a confederation as "a mere compact resting on the good faith of the parties," and a national government as "having a compleat and *compulsive* operation."[26] Both were following Locke's definition of government as "a right of making laws with penalties of death, and consequently, all less penalties for the regulating and preserving of property, and of employing the force of the community in the execution of such laws and in the defense of the commonwealth from foreign injury; and all this only for the public good."[27]

Government and law: the terms are coessential. The advantages of government are never more conspicuous than in its absence. The logical model of anarchy, the Lockean state of nature, arises in the real world when law disappears—when there is no competent government. But it is government that is "the great instrument and means" of men's "enjoyment of their properties in peace and safety."[28] If real government means lawmaking and real laws mean sanctions, it is not enough that the national government be supreme and the national legislature be given broad powers such as to tax and to regulate interstate commerce. The executive must be energetic—laws are not self-executing.

National supremacy met with less resistance than one would have anticipated. In their first substantive decision, on May 30 the Convention voted six to one, with New York divided, that a supreme national government be established. And when with ten states present Luther Martin moved the inclusion of the supremacy clause, on July 17th, the resolution was agreed to without a dissenting voice.

Major objections arose regarding the energetic executive "as inconsistent with the genius of republican government."[29] It took the tireless efforts of some of the most influential members of the Convention to produce an executive office that Clinton Rossiter was to call "one of the few truly successful institutions created by men in their endless quest for the blessings of free government."[30]

As Morris argued, "the efficacy and utility of the Union," of the large republic, depended on the energetic executive[31]—and not only because laws are not self-executing. It is the executive office that unites the nation, for the president is the one and only officer for whom all the people may vote. (The vice president is merely a standby officer.) The president has his own power source in the people and so he is more than the chief of state; he is the voice of the people. His is the only office that can never go empty. Important though his symbolic role as the visible center in a federally fragmented nation may be, the imperativeness of the filled office, the efficacy of the union, lies in the fact that the president alone is the activating agent of the government. His is the office with the inherent power to produce results that go beyond directing and compelling obedience to law, results that extend, according to his oath, to preserving the Constitution.

The separation of powers makes the independent executive possible, but to produce an energetic executive independence is not enough. The executive power, unlike the independent judicial and legislative powers, must be unified. A plural though independent executive brings with it all the problems indigenous to collectives: unclear responsibility, vacillation, slowness, inefficiency. But unity is only the first condition for energy in an independent executive; initiative and discretion must be added, and were. Initiative is granted in treaty-making, appointments, and recommending legislation; discretion is granted in pardoning, receiving ambassadors, serving as commander in chief, and being vested with the executive power of the United States. Initiative and discretion are necessary to the energetic executive, for an executive who is a mere minion of the legislature, who is nothing more than the faithful enforcer of the laws made by the legislature, cannot supply a defect of republican governments—the weakness that arises from the rigidity and blindness, from the failure of foresight in ordinary law itself.

**Prerogative.**    True law, it is often said, is frozen wisdom. That it contains wisdom is its glory; that it is frozen is its defect. It is in supplying this defect of law with the energetic republican executive that the founders made a tremendous breakthrough. Locke had stated that in all "well-framed governments" the executive and legislative powers are separated. This separation, as he went on to explain, requires that the prerogative be placed in the hands of the executive. Prerogative, Locke said, is "this power to act according to discretion for the public good, without the prescription of the law and sometimes even against it."[32]

Why is the prerogative necessary? Locke answers: the legislature is not always in session; collectives usually are too slow to act; legislators do not have perfect foresight and cannot anticipate and provide for all necessities; in particular circumstances, strict adherence to and enforcement of law can do great harm. The will of the legislature is not the highest law. *Salus populi suprema lex.*

The president's constitutionally assigned duties give him powers of initiative and discretion so that he can act quickly and firmly in emergencies foreign or domestic, and so that he can take contingencies into account. Above all, the president has the executive power of the United States—that amorphous power undefined in the Constitution because it is undefinable. The undefined executive power makes the government flexible in the face of unforeseen circumstances. The executive power can be understood as Locke's prerogative. At least some of our presidents (and our most successful ones at that) have so understood it. Think of Jefferson's purchase of Louisiana, of Lincoln's resoluteness in preserving the Union (which included suspending the writ of habeas corpus). Clearly they believed the executive power included "the power of doing public good without a rule," Locke's description of prerogative.

As long as the executive office is filled the nation has a democratically authorized, unified agent to act for the common good. This was actually anticipated. Speaking in the Convention, Madison drew a distinction between the executive and the judiciary, declaring that "the collective interest and security were more in the power belonging to the Executive," and therefore "much greater latitude is left to the opinion and discretion" of the executive.[33] In perhaps his longest and most eloquent speech in the Convention, Morris repeatedly called the executive the "Guardian of the People."[34] This is a bold statement in a republic, but it is nonetheless true.

The energetic executive does more than provide direction and discipline in the governing process. He is bound by oath not merely to enforce the ordinary laws but instead to preserve the Constitution, that higher law created by a solemn act of the whole people, that law which forms and regulates the governing process. Just as the fact of a written Constitution creates a special task for the judiciary under the separation of powers, so it also creates a special role for the executive. He is the specifically designated champion of the Constitution. The president is the sword of the nation, its defender against all comers. The executive office is the efficient cause of government, and government, if properly constituted, is the essential cause of human liberty.

The energetic executive as opposed to the merely independent executive is the pivot of the separation of powers. Without energy in the executive, the separation of powers would produce either deadlock or legislative tyranny. Deadlock is forestalled because the president has his own powers under the Constitution and is not limited to those delegated by the legislature. He has the executive power of the nation, and that power can be vigorously and effectively wielded because of the unity of the single officeholder. Legislative tyranny is to be prevented by the independent selection of the president, the veto power, his fixed term of office, and his fixed salary, among other things. It is the energy of the executive that makes separation possible and practicable. To paraphrase Hamilton: a feeble executive implies a dependent executive. A dependent executive is but another name for a tyrannical legislature; and a tyrannical legislature whatever it may be in theory, must produce, in practice, a weak, incompetent government.

**A Republican Executive.**    The energetic executive in a republic is a truly astonishing innovation, as it goes against the deepest prejudices of republicans. Nowhere is the founders' statesmanship more evident than in the creation of this office. To accomplish this, however, they had to republicanize the office. They had to make it safe. The energetic executive, so essential to good government, like all forms of power can be dangerous. They therefore subjected the executive to frequent election—to an election process that allowed for and soon evolved into the popular elections advocated by some of the leading proponents of the office, men like Wilson. They qualified the veto. They made the executive impeachable. Add to these, of course, all the counterbalancing powers assigned to the other two branches of government and found in the federal system.

According to Locke, the control on prerogative is the acquiescence, the tacit consent of the people. If the executive misuses the power, the Lockean remedy is the right of revolution, the right of the people to dissolve the government and hire a new one. Here the republican form of government, with its institutionalized, ongoing consent in the form of free and frequent elections for the executive, with its separation of powers designating an existing body, Congress, to indict and try a usurping executive, makes the remedy less drastic and more usable. The remedy does not have to be generated; the organizations and instruments do not have to be formed after the fact. The remedy is already in place—is institutionalized. It is automatically triggered every four years, and should the abuse be too flagrant, the situation too urgent, the people acting through their agents in the Congress can intervene at any time. The entire government need not be dissolved nor the Constitution changed to remove an offending executive. The remedy provides more stability than the purely Lockean one. Once republicanized, the energetic executive is the wellhead of vigorous, competent, yet moderate government.

Powerful, energetic, and stable government is the only competent guardian of liberty. And who is to guard the guardians? Our founders answered that the only way to guard the guardians is through a constitutional process called the balance of power, a process of dividing and distributing power, a process that includes and employs both society and government. Divide *all* the guardians into distinct and separate parts and set them all to watch each other.

The official guardians, the government, must be divided vertically through the federal system and horizontally through the separation of powers. Each of the several governing parts is placed on alert, ready to raise the hue and cry and, through the various checks and balances, armed to control another—to keep it at its proper post, performing its proper functions. The supreme and final guardians, the people themselves, must be divided into multiple and diverse parts, each to counterpoise, each to help offset the factional interests of the others. With every segment of society and every subdivision of government keeping vigil, powerful government can be moderate government.

Our founders agreed with John Philpot Curran that "the condition upon which God hath given liberty to man is eternal vigilance; which condition if he break, servitude is at once the consequence of his crime and the punishment of his guilt."[35] Vigilance means more than watchfulness; it includes action—a process of acting. According to our founders, the proper process is directed by the Lockean concept that men have a natural right to rule themselves under law in order to secure their faculties and produce conditions where those faculties can properly function.

It is a process formed on the belief and assertion that there is "sufficient virtue among men for self-government," for there are "qualities in human nature which justify a certain portion of esteem and confidence."[36] The nature of man is complex, not simple. Men are rational as well as passionate, can be social as well as selfish. Yes, human passions are powerful and can blind and bind the reason; but if founders perform their task well, a process can be created that employs the power of these passions to promote the civic virtue of moderation.

It is a process informed by the policy of "opposite and rival interests," a policy that uses passion to check passion, for when the passions are curbed the reason breaks loose and bestirs man's social disposition and sympathy. From the release of reason comes the recognition that there is a common good, that the condition of men is improved by the rule of law, that we benefit *individually* when we consent to society and moderate government, when we adhere to the law of our Constitution.

Security for the fundamental rights of men depends upon a properly structured, competent governing process. Thus the Constitution itself, as Hamilton said, is "in every rational sense and to every useful purpose" the guarantee of our rights, for it established a form of government, a self-governing process that is powerful, energetic, and stable, as well as balanced, safe, and free. The Constitution, with its complex arrangements, its intricate internal and external controls, its multiple procedures, is our true bill of rights.

# 4

# Congressman Madison Proposes Amendments to the Constitution

*Robert A. Goldwin*

The speech James Madison delivered on the floor of the House of Representatives in the first session of the First Congress, on June 8, 1789, proposing the first amendments to the new Constitution of the United States, was one of the most consequential political orations in American history (see the appendix to this chapter). It may not be remarkable for eloquence or rhetorical flourishes, but it stands as an extraordinary example of democratic statesmanship in action. It would merit our careful study for its abundance of political sagacity, even had it not produced the profound and far-reaching results from which we and the rest of the freedom-loving world have benefited ever since.

How did James Madison get to the point of delivering the speech that made him the father of the Bill of Rights? He did not start out as a supporter of a bill of rights in the Constitution, and even after he became an advocate of amendments to the Constitution he did not express enthusiasm for them. Madison made no secret of his reservations about the efficacy of a bill of rights as an instrument to secure the rights of the people. He expressed these reservations on numerous occasions both public and private, in political speeches he made in Virginia[1] and in his letters to Thomas Jefferson[2] and others. He was, therefore, an unlikely candidate for the role of initiator of the amendments to the Constitution that are now known as the Bill of Rights; yet that is the role he undertook. The explanation of how and why it happened is of much more than historical interest. And much of the explanation can be found in his speech to the House of Representatives in the First Congress.

The speech is divided into three major parts: an explanation of why it was timely and prudent for Congress to consider amendments, the presentation of the amendments themselves, and his arguments in support of them. Let us follow Madison in his own sequence.

### Why Congress Ought to Consider Amendments Now

Madison begins his exposition by giving several reasons why the Congress, in their first session, despite other, urgent legislative business of major importance, ought to take the time to propose constitutional amendments to send to the state legislatures for ratification.[3] The first reason is to offer evidence to those Americans who do not yet support the Constitution, that its supporters are as devoted to liberty as the nonsupporters, by showing that they "do not disregard their wishes." Prudence dictates that they take steps now to make the Constitution "as acceptable to the whole people of the United States, as it has been found acceptable to a majority of them." The fact is, Madison says, there is still "a great number" of the American people who are dissatisfied and insecure under the new Constitution. So, "if there are amendments desired of such a nature as will not injure the constitution, and they can be ingrafted so as to give satisfaction to the doubting part of our fellow-citizens," why not, in a spirit of "deference and concession," adopt such amendments? For it is also a fact that "a great body of the people" are inclined to support the Constitution, if only they can be "satisfied on this one point" of rights.

Madison concludes this part of the argument by urging on the House members a direct and simple remedy for the widespread dissatisfaction. "We ought not to disregard their inclination, but, on principles of amity and moderation, conform to their wishes and expressly declare the great rights of mankind secured under this constitution." Madison, this last sentence shows, seems to be urging his colleagues to add to the Constitution in express terms a declaration of the rights that were already secured in the Constitution, not so much for some intrinsic reason, but rather for the sake of dispelling dissatisfaction.[4]

Two purposes are consistently linked and given equal weight in Madison's argument: first, to reassure those uneasy Americans who need reassurance; and second, to avoid changing anything in the Constitution. And the terms in which he casts the argument— "caution," "deference," "concession," "amity," "moderation," "prudence"—are clearly chosen to promote conciliation, mutual respect, and national unity.

After touching briefly on another "motive" for prompt consideration of amendments, that of bringing into the Union the two states, North Carolina and Rhode Island, that had not yet ratified the Constitution, Madison moves on to a second substantive point he says he ranks "over and above all these considerations." Keeping in mind that all power can be abused, he says,

> it is possible the abuse of the powers of the General Government may be guarded against in a more secure manner than is now done, while no one advantage arising from the exercise of that power shall be damaged or endangered by it. We have in this way something to gain, and, if we proceed with caution, nothing to lose.

Thus Madison begins a line of argument by reassuring the old friends of the Constitution that they can introduce amendments that do not "open a door" for reconsideration of the constitutional structure, while at the same time gaining new friends by opening a different door, one for "provisions for the security of rights"—amendments of such a moderate nature that they are likely to get the approval of the necessary constitutional two-thirds majority of the Congress and three-fourths of the state legislatures. As an additional substantive bonus, they might even do some good.

Madison's strategy begins to become clear at this point, as he turns to consideration of the "objections of various kinds made against the constitution," which reveal his analysis of the opposing forces. On the one hand, he seeks to persuade the supporters of the Constitution that the adversaries are formidable and that action is therefore urgently required. On the other hand, he seeks to show that the adversaries, though formidable, are not invincible. In fact, he argues, the adversaries can not only be thwarted, "the great mass" of them can be recruited as new friends of the Constitution by efforts that will cost little, if anything.

Leading opponents of the Constitution—"respectable characters," Madison calls them—were critical of it because of the structure it established and the broad powers it delegated. These opponents were the Anti-Federalist leaders in the states and in the Congress. But Madison believed that other opponents, in fact most of those still dissatisfied with the Constitution, were not disturbed for these reasons; he perceived that "the great mass of the people who opposed it, disliked it because it did not contain effectual provisions against encroachments on particular rights." Madison's analysis of those opposed to the Constitution and of their efforts to convene a second constitutional convention was that while the opposition's political leaders and spokesmen—the "respectable characters"—might want profound structural changes, their followers were indifferent to such matters, and deeply engaged only on the issue of provisions relating to their rights. Madison thus perceived that the whole movement for making radical changes in the Constitution could be undercut by making moderate, cautious, less-than-consequential additions to the Constitution.

> It is a fortunate thing that the objection to the Government has been made on the ground I have stated, because it will be practicable, on that ground, to obviate the objection, so far as to satisfy the public mind that their liberties will be perpetual, and this without endangering any part of the constitution which is considered as essential to the existence of the Government by those who promoted its adoption.

In this speech, to whom were Madison's arguments addressed as he pursued this dual line of reasoning? He did not speak to those one would consider his opponents, to convert them to becoming friends of the Constitution; he addressed, instead, those one would consider his allies, that is, those who supported the Constitution as he did. He sought to explain to them that their opponents, those who wanted to make changes in and additions to the Constitution, could be divided. A few of them would be frustrated in their desires to make fundamental changes, but the rest—"the great mass of the people"—could be won over as supporters. His analysis was that the popular support could be stripped away from the Anti-Federalists by offering not what their spokesmen sought—radical alterations in the Constitution— but rather, only explicit assurances on "the great rights of mankind"; and that that could be accomplished without altering in any way the powers of the new government. In this speech, Madison did not address the Anti-Federalists, the minority in the House, probably because he was in the act of taking away their popular support by acceding, in part, to their demands for a bill of rights in the Constitution. To succeed in this effort he needed to persuade not his opponents but his adherents: supporters of the Constitution who were opposed to amending it in any way.

## The Amendments

The whole substance of the Bill of Rights as we have it now in the Constitution was included in Madison's initial list of proposed amendments. Some of them are verbatim as first proposed; others were modified, many only slightly.[5] Everything in the ten amendments was included in some form first in Madison's speech.

But rather than review what was adopted, has long been part of the Constitution, and is therefore familiar, I propose to focus attention on two of Madison's proposals that were not adopted: primarily, on his plan to interweave the amendments into the body of the Constitution instead of placing them at the beginning, as in the state constitutions, or appending them at the end of the document, as we have them now; and on his proposal to insert several sentences before the Preamble, which I call the pre-Preamble.[6] In addition, I will consider the importance of some of what Madison did not propose, giving due heed to Herbert Storing's contention that what Madison left out was more important than what he included in his proposals.[7]

Madison proposed to insert in Article I, section 9, between clauses 3 and 4, all of what are now the First, Second, Third, Fourth, Eighth, and Ninth Amendments, and parts of the Fifth and Sixth Amendments. Placed thus, they would have followed two clauses already in the original text that have the character of provisions of a bill of rights, so that the sequence of clauses in Article I, section 9, would have read this way:

> 2. The privilege of the writ of habeas corpus shall not be suspended, unless when in cases of rebellion or invasion the public safety may require it.
> 3. No bill of attainder or ex post facto law shall be passed.

And then Madison's new articles, in the form he proposed them originally, would have followed:

> 4. The civil rights of none shall be abridged on account of religious belief or worship, nor shall any national religion be established, nor shall the full and equal rights of conscience be in any manner, or on any pretext, infringed.
> 5. The people shall not be deprived or abridged of their right to speak, to write, or to publish their sentiments; and the freedom of the press, as one of the great bulwarks of liberty, shall be inviolable.

And so most of the new articles would have continued in that place in Article I, section 9. What is now the Seventh Amendment, providing for jury trials, would have been added to Article III, along with most of what are now the Fifth and Sixth Amendments. And finally, what is now the Tenth Amendment would have been part of a new Article VII.

Interwoven in this fashion, these provisions, although substantially the same as we now have them appended to the Constitution, would have been much less obtrusive, though not necessarily less important or effective. If the House of Representatives had gone along with Madison's proposal to insert the new articles in the body of the Constitution, it would have been difficult to think of them collectively as a body to be called the Bill of Rights, or any other collective name. They would more likely have been seen as integrally part of the Constitution, in no way unlike the rest of the text, and thus less likely to be considered as some sort of "corrective" of a defective original, or of a different character, or as pointing in a different direction. With no substantive difference from what we have now, they nevertheless would have blended in and become part and parcel of the original text, instead of seeming to stand separate and apart.

It would also then have been clearer that these new articles were not, in one strict sense of the word, amendments. That is, it would have been clearer that they added to but altered nothing in the text of the Constitution. These were not the only new articles Madison proposed, of course; among the others, he also proposed an article to change the size of congressional districts, which would have amended Article I, section 2, clause 3. That proposal was passed by the Congress but not ratified by the requisite number of states. Of the ten proposed articles that were ratified, none changed anything at all in the original text.

When Congress decided not to interweave the new articles but instead to place them at the end of the original text, as an appendage after the signatures, a heading for the twelve proposed articles was composed, commencing as follows:

> Articles in addition to, and amendment of, the Constitution of the United States of America. . . .

This heading seems to distinguish two kinds of articles—one kind adding to the original text, the other amending it. Of the twelve proposed articles, one was an article "in . . . amendment of" the Constitution, and the rest were articles "in addition to" it. But the one article in amendment, changing the size of congressional districts, was not ratified. All of the ratified articles were additions, not amendments.

Thus, if the distinction is valid, the heading was not an appropriate one until the ratification of subsequent articles that did amend the Constitution.[8]

Two important consequences followed from the scheme to interweave the new articles into the original text: all of the formulations are imperative, and almost all are negative. One might contend that they would have had that form in any case, but the intention of placing them in Article I, section 9, required that they be negative and imperative or else stand out as badly misplaced, clumsily patched rather than interwoven. As we have seen, the new articles would have been placed after Article I, section 9, clause 3, and before the nine remaining clauses of the Article. Madison chose the perfect spot to insert his new provisions: every one of those ten clauses begins with the word "no" and includes the word "shall."

This essay is not the appropriate place to dwell at length on the significance of the negative and imperative character of the Bill of Rights.[9] Perhaps it will suffice here to point out that the amendments, especially as revised by Congress, make no grants of power to the government to protect or guarantee rights. Instead they consistently set forth negations, denials of power to the government, beginning with those five sovereign words of negative command: "Congress shall make no law. . . ." As for the imperative "shall" in every one of the first nine amendments, one need only compare it to the pervasive "ought" in the bills of rights of the state constitutions to appreciate that a major change was being made. In the state constitutions, bills of rights usually came at the head; it seems likely that the new form of the proposed articles was influenced by the initial expectation of placement in the body of the text, and that reciprocally the intention of designing negative and imperative articles dictated the choice of placement.

It is common usage for many who are otherwise knowledgeable about the Constitution, including Supreme Court justices, to speak of "our First Amendment guarantees" of freedom of religion, speech, and press; but of course there are no guarantees in the First Amendment and can be none where there is no grant of power, but only a denial of power. The one time the word "guarantee" occurs in the Constitution is in the aptly named "guarantee clause" (Article IV, section 4), in which the United States guarantees to every state a republican form of government. That is a clear, affirmative guarantee. The First Amendment would have a very different meaning and mode of enforcement if it were affirmative and provided that "Congress shall make laws" to guarantee the freedom of speech and press. The affirmative form would result in an accretion, not a denial, of governmen-

tal power. Awareness of the difference that the negative and imperative character of the Bill of Rights makes, in large part a consequence
of the interweaving intention, is an essential step in perceiving how
the authors of the Bill of Rights thought rights are made truly secure.

**The Pre-Preamble.** The very first addition proposed by Madison
was "that there be prefixed to the constitution a declaration,"

> That all power is originally rested in, and consequently de-
> rived from, the people.
> That government is instituted and ought to be exercised for
> the benefit of the people; which consists in the enjoyment of
> life and liberty, with the right of acquiring and using prop-
> erty, and generally of pursuing and obtaining happiness and
> safety.
> That the people have an indubitable, unalienable, and inde-
> feasible right to reform or change their Government, when-
> ever it be found adverse or inadequate to the purposes of its
> institution.

The fate of this proposed addition should not surprise us. It was
subsequently revised and condensed by the Select Committee into
less than one sentence, and in the process made even less fitting and
more awkward. It further had the misfortune of being designed to
precede the Preamble, a one-of-a-kind pre-Preamble, which would
have had the effect of stripping the Preamble of its marvelous rhetorical forcefulness. As it came from the Select Committee, the amended
Preamble would have read as follows:

> Government being intended for the benefit of the people,
> and the rightful establishment thereof being derived from
> their authority alone, we the people of the United States, in
> order to form a more perfect union . . . do ordain and estab-
> lish this Constitution for the United States of America.

In subsequent debate the proposal was denounced, reviled, ridiculed, and rejected. We can concur with the decision of the members
of the First Congress to preserve the Preamble unaltered, and yet be
instructed by what Madison was attempting to do. What could he
have had in mind?

The most obvious feature of the statement is its seeming resem-
blance to the Declaration of Independence, but there are interesting
differences. Although Madison's passage and the Declaration both
speak of "the people," Madison's formulation does not speak of individual persons, as does the Declaration, either as the source of political power or as the possessors of rights. The source of all power and

the possessor of rights is "the people." This is doctrine for a society already formed, already "one people," now in the act of constituting government. One might argue that the power of "the people" had its origin in the natural powers of each individual person, but individual powers are surrendered up to the society when it is formed. Forming individuals into a people, that is, forming a society that can be considered one body, is an antecedent step on the way to establishing a constitution; individuals do not form a constitution; we, "the people," do.

One other point of difference is worth noticing: "the . . . right to reform or change their Government" is a much modified version of the Declaration's "right of the people to alter or abolish it." The Constitution, it seems, is no place for a permanent and emphatic reminder of the ultimate consequence of the natural right to resist tyranny, however much it might be an underlying principle of the Constitution.

Rather than the Declaration of Independence, perhaps a more appropriate comparison would be to the bill of rights of the Massachusetts State Constitution of 1780.[10] It includes these passages, all close to the formulations in Madison's proposed pre-Preamble:

> All power residing originally in the people, and being derived from them. . . .
> Government is instituted for the common good; for the protection, safety, prosperity and happiness of the people. . . .
> Therefore, the people alone have an incontestable, unalienable, and indefeasible right to institute government; and to reform, alter, or totally change the same, when their protection, safety, prosperity and happiness require it.

Madison was willing to have the new bill of rights say, as did the Massachusetts bill of rights, that the people are the original source of political power; but he was unwilling to include an explicit assertion, as part of the Constitution, that the people have the right to "alter or totally change" the government, which was the language of the Massachusetts bill of rights. He was willing to propose the words "reform or change," but even this milder formulation was deleted by the Select Committee, of which Madison was a member, when they condensed the pre-Preamble. The Massachusetts bill of rights had other features that illustrate one reason why Madison was leery of state bills of rights. Its religion provisions, for example, authorized use of public funds to promote religion and limited such support not only to Christians, but to Protestants.[11]

Why then would Madison propose this pre-Preamble for addition to the Constitution? Madison, speaking of it in the speech, said "the first of these amendments relates to what may be called a bill of rights." We are now accustomed to thinking automatically of the first ten amendments, as ratified, as not only *a* bill of rights, but as *the* Bill of Rights. But that was not the state of things at the moment of this speech. In fact, as we shall see, a good part of Madison's commentary was devoted to what may be called an inquiry into the question of just what Americans meant when they spoke of a bill of rights. Since one of his chief motives was to ease the mind of those who wanted a bill of rights, if this was what in the public mind "may be called a bill of rights," then it can be said that the pre-Preamble, as a constitutional provision, would have been at once useful and innocuous.

Interweaving the additional articles in the body of the text would have made them little visible; what would have been visible, even prominent, would have been this pre-Preamble, "what may be called a bill of rights." The combination of the pre-Preamble and interweaving would have served well Madison's dual purposes: first, to reassure those who were uneasy because of the absence of a bill of rights; second, to protect the Constitution against significant change.

The ratifying conventions of seven states had urged the addition of a bill of rights and had required their representatives in Congress to do all that was reasonable and legal to achieve passage of the amendments they drew up. The scores of proposed amendments of these seven state-ratifying conventions were abundant enough to supply Madison and his colleagues in the Congress with all of the material for a bill of rights. There is nothing in the final Bill of Rights as we have it that was not already present in the amendments proposed by the state-ratifying conventions. But that is a bit like saying, as one looks at a fine sculpture, that all of it was there in the block of marble before the sculptor began chiseling away at it. Madison's legislative artistry consisted in what he succeeded in stripping away.

What Madison did was to separate the proposals having to do with civil rights from those that altered the distribution of powers between the states and the government of the United States. He included protection for "the great rights," and he excluded every provision that would diminish the powers of the new government, despite the repeated complaints of fellow representatives that he was omitting those they cherished most.

For example, several states had proposed in slightly differing versions that since a militia was an important safeguard of the liberty of the people and a standing army a threat to that liberty, the right of the people to bear arms must be ensured and there must be no standing army.[12] This proposal would have put all land military forces under state control, none under control of the United States. Madison proposed the first half and dropped the second.

The Constitution provides that the state legislatures shall prescribe the "times, places and manner of holding elections" for Congress, but that Congress may change those regulations (Article I, section 4). At least seven states proposed an amendment to the effect that

> The Congress shall not alter, modify, or interfere in the times, places, or manner of holding elections for Senators and Representatives, or either of them, except when the Legislature of any State shall neglect, refuse, or be disabled by invasion or rebellion to prescribe the same.[13]

Madison did not include such an amendment among his own proposed amendments.

Again, the Constitution provided that "The Congress shall have power to lay and collect taxes. . . ." Seven states proposed an amendment designed to prevent Congress from collecting taxes; it sought to return instead to the indirect system of apportionment of taxes by states under the Articles of Confederation, so that only the states and not the government of the United States would tax citizens directly:

> When the Congress shall lay direct taxes or excises, they shall immediately inform the Executive power of each State, of the quota of such State according to the census herein directed, which is proposed to be thereby raised; and if the Legislature of any State shall pass a law at the time required by Congress, the taxes and excises laid by Congress shall not be collected in such State.[14]

When the two Virginia senators, both Anti-Federalists, transmitted the amendments as passed by Congress, our present Bill of Rights, to the governor of Virginia, they expressed their "grief that we now send forward propositions inadequate to the purpose of real and substantial Amendments."[15] In their letter to the speaker of the House of Representatives in Virginia, the senators reported that they had omitted no effort "to procure the success of those radical amendments proposed by the [Virginia] Convention."[16] At the heart of their distress was their conviction that only "radical amendments" "may secure against the annihilation of the state governments." And as one supporter of the Constitution and the new amendments wrote to Madison about the Virginia legislators, led by Patrick Henry, "the opposition to the Federal Constitution is in my opinion reduced to a single point, the power of direct taxation."[17]

What they meant was that the threat of the new government to religion, press, speech, and other great rights was not a specific danger, or if a danger, it could not be resolved by these new words in the Constitution. What was a danger—to religion, speech, press, and to all liberty—was an all-powerful central government able to tax from a great distance, exert a power over the lives of the citizenry, and thus render state and local governments relatively powerless.

The Anti-Federalists looked less at what was in the text of the amendments and much more at what was omitted. What was omitted was what they thought to be the heart of the matter. As Representative Aedanus Burke of South Carolina said to Madison when the debates were well advanced and he and the rest of the Anti-Federalist minority were feeling forcefully the extent of their defeat, a comparison of the new amendments being approved by the House and the amendments proposed by the states would show to "any man of sense and candor" "that all the important amendments were omitted."[18]

Patrick Henry and many others were much more concerned about the amendments relating to a standing army, the power of Congress to levy direct taxes, and congressional control over elections than about those relating to added security for the rights of religion, speech, and press—not because they did not care about those rights, but because they either did not consider that the new Constitution placed them in increased jeopardy or because they did not think that such amendments could provide security against a majority intent on violating those rights. Both sides, opponents and proponents of the Constitution, caring deeply about rights, thought rights were best secured by preventing a concentration of political power. That concentration was what Henry and his colleagues feared in the new government, and that is why they sought a return to old, familiar, constitutional arrangements, as in the Articles of Confederation.

Other amendments, too, were important to them, all tending in the same direction. A strenuous effort was made to add to "the right of the people to assemble" the words "to instruct their representatives."[19] The question arose at once whether this meant that such "instructions" were to be binding on the representatives; if so, that would change the character of the government from a representative one, in which elected officials deliberated and voted in accord with their judgment, to one more like direct democracy, in which representatives acted only according to instructions from their constituents. Congress would have been not a deliberative body, but more like an international assembly of delegates, in which diplomats speak for the nation they represent always according to their instructions. Instructed representatives and senators would have been completely the instruments or mouthpieces of their districts and states.

The struggle over that one word—"instruct"—was fought as if the fate of the nation depended on it; and perhaps it did. The measure was raised and defeated more than once in the Congress.[20] The argument was, if the instructions were binding on elected officials, it was destructive of representative government, and if they were not binding, there was no reason to put "instruct" in the Constitution, because if everyone was ensured a right to freedom of speech, press, assembly, and petition, public officials would inevitably receive an abundance of advice and guidance from their constituents whenever they assembled.

The same kind of effort was made to insert the word "expressly" in the provision that "The powers not delegated to the United States . . . are reserved to the States. . . ."[21] That word "expressly" was in the same provision in the Articles of Confederation, and its omission by Madison was glaring. He successfully opposed the motion to insert "expressly" by arguing that the addition of the word would severely limit the discretionary powers of the new government—which was, of course, the intention. The motion was defeated, but it was moved again three days later by Elbridge Gerry, who argued that it was "an amendment of great importance." He was right, of course. The amendment as it is, without the word "expressly," directs us (as Walter Berns has explained)[22] to look elsewhere in the Constitution to see what powers have been delegated; but it does not tell us what powers—including implied or inherent powers—might have been delegated to the United States.

Thus if we try to look at the Bill of Rights with the eye of an Anti-Federalist, we see the importance of what is left out. What was included, Madison told his colleagues repeatedly, was only what everyone would accept, only what was uncontroversial. Whatever the differences between the Federalists and the Anti-Federalists, they did not differ in their devotion to "the great rights of mankind." The rights in the Bill of Rights were not a matter of contention between them. The Virginia Senate did not refuse in 1789 to ratify the Tenth Amendment because of what it said; they refused because it did not say "expressly"—that is, because of what it did not say. They did not refuse to ratify the First Amendment because they thought it wrong to protect the freedom of the press; they refused to ratify because they thought the protections provided were too weak and because it said nothing about the right "to instruct their representatives."

In sum, the same strategy guided Madison's formulations and his

69

silences, what he included and what he excluded. The strategy was to ease the mind of the uneasy by provisions securing rights, thereby winning them away from those who sought to change the constitutional structure and powers of the government. If any proposal from the state-ratifying conventions sought to make some right secure, Madison adopted it; if it combined security of a right with a restraint on a delegated power, Madison separated them and discarded half; and if it sought to strip away some power without reference to a right, Madison ignored it. What he left out was all-important to the leading spokesmen of the movement to call a second convention to rewrite the Constitution, but not to their followers. When Madison was through proposing his amendments, his opponents were left as leaders without followers, and the movement for a second convention was dead.

## Madison's Arguments in Favor of His Amendments

I will confine my observations on Madison's arguments to a few main points: his list of what is said in favor of bills of rights; Madison's own view of "the great object" of bills of rights; and a list of the objections to bills of rights, with Madison's responses to them.[23]

Madison began his commentary on the proposed amendments with some remarkably faint praise. Although he was aware that "a great number of the most respectable friends to the Government, and champions for republican liberty" have thought a bill of rights "unnecessary, . . . improper" and "even dangerous," still, Madison reminded the House, among the general public "a different opinion prevails in the United States," as evidenced by the prevalence of state bills of rights. But aside from the factor of public opinion, Madison said little in support of state bills of rights. He was "inclined to believe" that "although some of them are rather unimportant, yet, upon the whole, they will have a salutary tendency." With that not-quite-rousing tribute to state bills of rights out of the way, Madison turned to the question, What is a bill of rights intended to do?

Surveying the state bills of rights, he sees that they declare "the perfect equality of mankind," or they assert the rights of the people in establishing a government, or they list the rights retained by the people when others are surrendered to the legislature, or they specify positive rights under government, like trial by jury, or they lay down "dogmatic maxims," such as affirming the separation of powers. Madison does not say so at this point, but his own proposals do all of the above except for explicitly proclaiming equality. "The great object in

70

view" in any bill of rights, however, no matter what its form, is to "limit and qualify the powers of Government."

He then goes on to make a distinction between a bill of rights for a state and one for the United States. "In our Government," that is, the United States rather than the states, it is more important to restrain the legislature than the executive, and most important to restrain "the community."

> . . . in a Government modified like this of the United States, the great danger lies rather in the abuse of the community than in the legislative body. The prescriptions in favor of liberty ought to be levelled against that quarter where the greatest danger lies, namely, that which possesses the highest prerogative of power. But it is not found in either the executive or legislative departments of Government, but in the body of the people, operating by the majority against the minority.

This had long been a sticking point for Madison; how can any "paper barrier" restrain the power of the majority, the greatest danger because the greatest force in a popular government, when it is determined to "operate against the minority"? In short, where the majority rules, what power can control a bad majority? The answer Madison gave here, somewhat tentatively and not without reservations, is that public opinion may be strengthened in support of the rights proclaimed in a bill of rights, so that "the whole community" may be able to restrain the majority.

> As they [bills of rights] have a tendency to impress some degree of respect for them, to establish the public opinion in their favor, and rouse the attention of the whole community, it may be one means to control the majority from those acts to which they might be otherwise inclined.

This mild endorsement of state bills of rights, full of "tendencies," "some degrees," "may be's," and "might be's," is Madison's prelude to his taking up consideration of a list of objections to including a bill of rights in the Constitution of the United States: it is a paper barrier against the power of a majority; it is unnecessary in a republican government; it is unnecessary because the states have bills of rights; it endangers rights since it cannot enumerate every right and thus will disparage those not mentioned; and finally, bills of rights have not been successful in securing rights in the states.

Madison's responses to these objections to a bill of rights in the United States Constitution, briefly, are that abuses of power can exist even in a republican form of government, in the means used to carry

71

out constitutional powers, especially given the "necessary and proper" clause; that not all states have bills of rights, and some that do have inadequate and even "absolutely improper" ones; that the problem of the disparagement of unenumerated rights is addressed by one of his proposals (now the Ninth Amendment); and finally, granting that there have been "few particular States in which some of the most valuable articles have not, at one time or other, been violated; . . . it does not follow but they may have, to a certain degree, a salutary effect against the abuse of power," because the courts can use them to make themselves a bulwark against abuses of the executive and legislative branches.

It is fair to say that in all of Madison's responses to the objections—most of which objections he had expressed as his own in private correspondence over the years—Madison was very restrained in stating the case in favor of a bill of rights. In fact, he seemed to state the substantive objections to a bill of rights more forcefully and persuasively than the responses in favor of one. Right to the end of his comments on what are now the first ten amendments, the emphasis was on the public reaction. The most he would say on the substance of the proposals is that they were "proper," but he had much more to say about the consequences he hoped for:

> I conclude . . . that it will be proper in itself, and highly politic, for the tranquillity of the public mind, and the stability of the Government, that we should offer something, in the form I have proposed, to be incorporated in the system of Government, as a declaration of the rights of the people.

Again, in talking about what is now the Tenth Amendment, Madison did not urge the substance as a reason for action, but only the effect on part of the public. Several state-ratifying conventions were "particularly anxious that it should be declared in the constitution, that the powers not therein delegated should be reserved to the several states." That fact was the basis of his advocacy of an article that might, on its merits, be considered "superfluous" and "unnecessary."

> Perhaps words which may define this more precisely than the whole of the instrument now does, may be considered as superfluous. I admit they may be deemed unnecessary: but there can be no harm in making such a declaration, if gentlemen will allow that the fact is as stated.

Madison's effort throughout the speech was not to persuade by praising the excellence of the provisions, or to argue that the Constitution was defective without them, or that it would be improved in

any significant way by their addition. His emphasis was on their substantive harmlessness—they would make no meaningful change in
the Constitution. Almost all of the affirmative arguments on behalf of
the proposals concerned the beneficial political consequences. The
real change to be hoped for was greater public acceptance. That acceptance was the theme on which Madison concluded.

> I believe every gentleman will readily admit that nothing is
> in contemplation, so far as I have mentioned, that can en-
> danger the beauty of the Government in any one important
> feature, even in the eyes of its most sanguine admirers. I
> have proposed nothing that does not appear to me as proper
> in itself, or eligible as patronized by a respectable number of
> our fellow-citizens; and if we can make the constitution bet-
> ter in the opinion of those who are opposed to it, without
> weakening its frame, or abridging its usefulness, in the judg-
> ment of those who are attached to it, we act the part of wise
> and liberal men to make such alterations as shall produce
> that effect.

This self-appraisal does less than full justice to what Madison was
about to accomplish. Despite the setbacks he experienced in the debate as one or another of his proposals was voted down, consider his
successes. He succeeded in giving the nation a bill of rights quite different from any the world had seen before; he reassured the part of
the general public that had been uneasy about the new Constitution,
and thus brought to an abrupt halt the popular movement for a second constitutional convention; he saved the Constitution from every
contemplated radical amendment; and he gave an instructive display
of a new kind of statesmanship—democratic statesmanship on the
national scene—political wisdom artfully joined to popular consent.
This last, especially, deserves our attention.

Madison was acutely aware that there was a genuine constitutional problem to be addressed, but the problem was not in the document; it was in the public mistrust of the document and of the powers
of the new government it established. For a constitution establishing
popular government, based on consent of the people and majority
rule, with powers limited so as to secure the rights of the minority—
for such a constitution it is not enough to have majority support, even
a majority strong enough to carry every vote in the affirmative. Such
a constitution must have the allegiance of "the great mass of the
people," of "the whole community," or else the power of the majority
cannot be limited when it attempts to deny the rights of the minority
by the exercise of excessive or abusive power.

Despite his misgivings about bills of rights, Madison saw the necessity to act to gain the support of "the whole community" for the Constitution. But he was unwilling to attempt that by agreeing to popular but unwise provisions. As we have seen, his main objective was to keep the Constitution intact, to save it from radical amendments; he did so by proposing in their place his own nonamending amendments. In place of provisions put forth in the state-ratifying conventions and supported by popular demand, he proposed seemingly similar but quite different amendments, to which, as it turned out, the same public gladly gave its consent.

A familiar characteristic of democratic politicians is their tendency to satisfy public opinion by simply following the crowd, seeking out and doing whatever is calculated to be popular. A true democratic leader has the ability to discern the difference between what the public asks for and what it will accept. In presenting his amendments, Madison chose to do only what he considered "proper in itself," in a form that no one was asking for, and yet as it turned out something to which the people would gladly consent.

It is a commonplace to say that Madison changed his mind about bills of rights. I disagree. Madison's action in proposing his amendments was consistent with his long-standing opposition to reliance on a bill of rights. Since his amendments were intended to leave the Constitution unchanged, proposing them left unchanged his conviction that the greatest security for rights resides in the structure of the society and the government, that is, in the way the nation and the people constitute themselves.

Madison considered the Constitution itself to be a bill of rights. He would be distressed to know that American understanding of what truly secures rights has been so distorted that many today think the Bill of Rights is the Constitution.

# Appendix: Madison's Speech to the House of Representatives, June 8, 1789

Mr. Madison: I am sorry to be accessory to the loss of a single moment of time by the House. If I had been indulged in my motion, and we had gone into a Committee of the whole, I think we might have rose and resumed the consideration of other business before this time; that is, so far as it depended upon what I proposed to bring forward. As that mode seems not to give satisfaction, I will withdraw the motion, and move you, sir, that a select committee be appointed to consider and report such amendments as are proper for Congress to propose to the Legislatures of the several States, conformably to the fifth article of the constitution.

I will state my reasons why I think it proper to propose amendments, and state the amendments themselves, so far as I think they ought to be proposed. If I thought I could fulfil the duty which I owe to myself and my constituents, to let the subject pass over in silence, I most certainly should not trespass upon the indulgence of this House. But I cannot do this, and am therefore compelled to beg a patient hearing to what I have to lay before you. And I do most sincerely believe, that if Congress will devote but one day to this subject, so far as to satisfy the public that we do not disregard their wishes, it will have a salutary influence on the public councils, and prepare the way for a favorable reception of our future measures. It appears to me that this House is bound by every motive of prudence, not to let the first session pass over without proposing to the State Legislatures some things to be incorporated into the constitution, that will render it as acceptable to the whole people of the United States, as it has been found acceptable to a majority of them. I wish, among other reasons why something should be done, that those who have been friendly to the adoption of this constitution may have the opportunity of proving to those who were opposed to it that they were as sincerely devoted to liberty and a Republican Government, as those who charged them with wishing the adoption of this constitution in order to lay the foundation of an aristocracy or despotism. It will be a desirable thing to extinguish from the bosom of every member of the community, any apprehensions that there are those among his countrymen who wish to deprive them of the liberty for which they valiantly fought and honorably bled. And if there are amendments desired of such a nature as will not injure the constitution, and they can be ingrafted so as to give satisfaction to the doubting part of our fellow-citizens, the friends of the Federal Government will evince that spirit of deference and concession for which they have hitherto been distinguished.

It cannot be a secret to the gentlemen in this House, that, notwithstanding the ratification of this system of Government by eleven of the thirteen United States, in some cases unanimously, in others by large majorities; yet still there is a great number of our constituents who are dissatisfied with it; among whom are many respectable for their talents and patriotism, and respectable for the jealousy they have for their liberty, which, though mistaken in its object, is honorable in its motive. There is a great body of the people falling under this description, who at present feel much inclined to join their support to the cause of Federalism, if they were satisfied on this one point. We ought not to disregard their inclination, but, on principles of amity and moderation, conform to their wishes and expressly declare the great rights of mankind secured under this constitution. The acceptance which our fellow-citizens show under the Government, calls upon us for a like return of moderation. But perhaps there is a stronger motive than this for our going into a consideration of the subject. It is to provide those securities for liberty which are required by a part of the community: I allude in a particular manner to those two States that have not thought fit to throw themselves into the bosom of the Confederacy. It is a desirable thing, on our part as well as theirs, that a re-union should take place as soon as possible. I have no doubt, if we proceed to take those steps which would be prudent and requisite at this juncture, that in a short time we should see that disposition prevailing in those States which have not come in, that we have seen prevailing in those States which have embraced the constitution.

But I will candidly acknowledge, that, over and above all these considerations, I do conceive that the constitution may be amended; that is to say, if all power is subject to abuse, that then it is possible the abuse of the powers of the General Government may be guarded against in a more secure manner than is now done, while no one advantage arising from the exercise of that power shall be damaged or endangered by it. We have in this way something to gain, and, if we proceed with caution, nothing to lose. And in this case it is necessary to proceed with caution; for while we feel all these inducements to go into a revisal of the constitution, we must feel for the constitution itself, and make that revisal a moderate one. I should be unwilling to see a door opened for a reconsideration of the whole structure of the Government—for a re-consideration of the principles and the substance of the powers given; because I doubt, if such a door were opened, we should be very likely to stop at that point which would be safe to the Government itself. But I do wish to see a door opened to consider, so far as to incorporate those provisions for the security of rights, against which I believe no serious objection has been made by any class of our constituents: such as would be likely to meet with the concurrence of two-thirds of both Houses, and the approbation of three-fourths of the State Legislatures. I will not propose a single alteration which I do not wish to see take place, as intrinsically proper in itself, or proper because it is wished for by a respectable number of my fellow-citizens; and therefore I shall not propose a single alteration but is likely to meet the concurrence required by the constitution. There have been objections of various kinds made against the constitution. Some were levelled against its structure because the President was without a council; because the Senate, which is a legislative body, had judicial powers in trials on impeachments; and because the powers of that body were compounded in other respects, in a manner that did not correspond with a particular theory; because it grants more power than is supposed to be necessary for every good purpose, and controls the ordinary powers of the State Governments. I know some respectable characters who opposed this Government on these grounds; but I believe that the great mass of the people who opposed it, disliked it because it did not contain effectual provisions against encroachments on particular rights, and those safeguards which they have been long accustomed to have interposed between them and the magistrate who exercises the sovereign power; nor ought we to consider them safe, while a great number of our fellow-citizens think these securities necessary.

It is a fortunate thing that the objection to the Government has been made on the ground I stated, because it will be practicable, on that ground, to obviate the objection, so far as to satisfy the public mind that their liberties will be perpetual, and this without endangering any part of the constitution, which is considered as essential to the existence of the Government by those who promoted its adoption.

The amendments which have occurred to me, proper to be recommended by Congress to the State Legislatures, are these:

First, That there be prefixed to the constitution a declaration, that all power is originally rested in, and consequently derived from, the people.

That Government is instituted and ought to be exercised for the benefit of the people; which consists in the enjoyment of life and liberty, with the right of acquiring and using property, and generally of pursuing and obtaining happiness and safety.

That the people have an indubitable, unalienable, and indefeasible right to reform or change their Government, whenever it be found adverse or inadequate to the purposes of its institution.

Secondly, That in article 1st, section 2, clause 3, these words be struck out, to wit:

"The number of Representatives shall not exceed one for every thirty thousand, but each State shall have at least one Representative, and until such enumeration shall be made;" and that in place thereof be inserted these words, to wit: "After the first actual enumeration, there shall be one Representative for every thirty thousand, until the number amounts to——, after which the proportion shall be so regulated by Congress, that the number shall never be less than——, nor more than——, but each State shall, after the first enumeration, have at least two Representatives; and prior thereto."

Thirdly, That in article 1st, section 6, clause 1, there be added to the end of the first sentence, these words, to wit: "But no law varying the compensation last ascertained shall operate before the next ensuing election of Representatives."

Fourthly, That in article 1st, section 9, between clauses 3 and 4, be inserted these clauses, to wit: The civil rights of none shall be abridged on account of religious belief or worship, nor shall any national religion be established, nor shall the full and equal rights of conscience be in any manner, or on any pretext, infringed.

The people shall not be deprived or abridged of their right to speak, to write, or to publish their sentiments; and the freedom of the press, as one of the great bulwarks of liberty, shall be inviolable.

The people shall not be restrained from peaceably assembling and consulting for their common good; nor from applying to the Legislature by petitions, or remonstrances, for redress of their grievances.

The right of the people to keep and bear arms shall not be infringed; a well armed and well regulated militia being the best security of a free country; but no person religiously scrupulous of bearing arms shall be compelled to render military service in person.

No soldier shall in time of peace be quartered in any house without the consent of the owner; nor at any time, but in a manner warranted by law.

No person shall be subject, except in cases of impeachment, to more than one punishment or one trial for the same offence; nor shall be compelled to be a witness against himself; nor be deprived of life, liberty, or property, without due process of law; nor be obliged to relinquish his property, where it may be necessary for public use, without a just compensation.

Excessive bail shall not be required, nor excessive fines imposed, nor cruel and unusual punishments inflicted.

The rights of the people to be secured in their persons; their houses, their papers, and their other property, from all unreasonable searches and seizures, shall not be violated by warrants issued without probable cause, supported by oath or affirmation, or not particularly describing the places to be searched, or the persons or things to be seized.

In all criminal prosecutions, the accused shall enjoy the right to a speedy and public trial, to be informed of the cause and nature of the accusation, to be confronted with his accusers, and the witnesses against him; to have a compulsory process for obtaining witnesses in his favor; and to have the assistance of counsel for his defence.

The exceptions here or elsewhere in the constitution, made in favor of particular rights, shall not be so construed as to diminish the just importance of other rights retained by the people, or as to enlarge the powers delegated by the constitution; but either as actual limitations of such powers, or as inserted merely for greater caution.

Fifthly, That in article 1st, section 10, between clauses 1 and 2, be inserted this clause, to wit:

No State shall violate the equal rights of conscience, or the freedom of the press, or the trial by jury in criminal cases.

Sixthly, That, in article 3d, section 2, be annexed to the end of clause 2d, these words, to wit:

But no appeal to such court shall be allowed where the value in controversy shall not amount to——dollars: nor shall any fact triable by jury, according to the course of common law, be otherwise re-examinable than may consist with the principles of common law.

Seventhly, That in article 3d, section 2, the third clause be struck out, and in its place be inserted the clauses following, to wit:

The trial of all crimes (except in cases of impeachments, and cases arising in the land or naval forces, or the militia when on actual service, in time of war or public danger) shall be by an impartial jury of freeholders of the vicinage, with the requisite of unanimity for conviction, of the right of challenge, and other accustomed requisites; and in all crimes punishable with loss of life or member, presentment or indictment by a grand jury shall be an essential preliminary, provided that in cases of crimes committed within any county which may be in possession of an enemy, or in which a general insurrection may prevail, the trial may by law be authorized in some other county of the same State, as near as may be to the seat of the offence.

In cases of crimes committed not within any county, the trial may by law be in such county as the laws shall have prescribed. In suits at common law, between man and man, the trial by jury, as one of the best securities to the rights of the people, ought to remain inviolate.

Eighthly, That immediately after article 6th, be inserted, as article 7th, the clauses following, to wit:

The powers delegated by this constitution are appropriated to the departments to which they are respectively distributed: so that the legislative department shall never exercise the powers vested in the executive or judicial nor the executive exercise the powers vested in the legislative or judicial, nor the judicial exercise the powers vested in the legislative or executive departments.

The powers not delegated by this constitution, nor prohibited by it to the States, are reserved to the States respectively.

Ninthly, That article 7th be numbered as article 8th.

The first of these amendments relates to what may be called a bill of rights. I will own that I never considered this provision so essential to the federal constitution, as to make it improper to ratify it, until such an amendment was added; at the same time, I always conceived, that in a certain form, and to a certain extent, such a provision was neither improper nor altogether useless. I am aware, that a great number of the most respectable friends to the Government, and champions for republican liberty, have thought such a provision, not only unnecessary, but even improper; nay, I believe some have gone so far as to think it even dangerous. Some policy has been made use of, perhaps, by gentlemen on both sides of the question: I acknowledge the ingenuity of those arguments which were drawn against the constitution, by a comparison with the policy of Great Britain, in establishing a declaration of rights; but there is too great a difference in the case to warrant the comparison: therefore, the arguments drawn from that source were in a great measure inapplicable. In the declaration of rights which that country has established, the truth is, they have gone no farther than to raise a barrier against the power of the Crown; the power of the Legislature is left altogether indefinite. Although I know whenever the great rights, the trial by jury, freedom of the press, or liberty of conscience, come in question in that body, the invasion of them is resisted by able advocates, yet their Magna Charta does not contain any one provision for the security of those rights, respecting which the people of America are most alarmed. The freedom of the press and rights of conscience, those choicest privileges of the people, are unguarded in the British constitution.

But although the case may be widely different, and it may not be thought necessary to provide limits for the legislative power in that country, yet a different opinion prevails in the United States. The people of many States have thought it necessary to raise barriers against power in all forms and departments of Government, and I am inclined to believe, if once bills of rights are established in all the States as well as the federal constitution, we shall find that although some of them are rather unimportant, yet, upon the whole, they will have a salutary tendency.

It may be said, in some instances, they do no more than state the perfect equality of mankind. This, to be sure, is an absolute truth, yet it is not absolutely necessary to be inserted at the head of a constitution.

In some instances they assert those rights which are exercised by the people in forming and establishing a plan of Government. In other instances, they specify those rights which are retained when particular powers are given up to be exercised by the Legislature. In other instances, they specify positive rights, which may seem to result from the nature of the compact. Trial by jury cannot be considered as a natural right, but a right resulting from a social compact which regulates the action of the community, but is as essential to secure the liberty of the people as any one of the pre-existent rights of nature. In other instances, they lay down dogmatic maxims with respect to the construction of the Government; declaring that the legislative, executive, and judicial branches shall be kept separate and distinct. Perhaps the best way of securing this in practice is, to provide such checks as will prevent the encroachment of the one upon the other.

But whatever may be the form which the several States have adopted in making declarations in favor of particular rights, the great object in view is to limit and qualify the powers of Government, by excepting out of the grant of power those cases in which the Government ought not to act, or to act only in a particular mode. They point these exceptions sometimes against the abuse of the executive power, sometimes against the legislative, and, in some cases, against the community itself; or, in other words, against the majority in favor of the minority.

In our Government it is, perhaps, less necessary to guard against the abuse in the executive department than any other; because it is not the stronger branch of the system, but the weaker. It therefore must be levelled against the legislative, for it is the most powerful, and most likely to be abused, because it is under the least control. Hence, so far as a declaration of rights can tend to prevent the exercise of undue power, it cannot be doubted but such declaration is proper. But I confess that I do conceive, that in a Government modified like this of the United States, the great danger lies rather in the abuse of the community than in the legislative body. The prescriptions in favor of liberty ought to be levelled against that quarter where the greatest danger lies, namely, that which possesses the highest prerogative of power. But it is not found in either the executive or legislative departments of Government, but in the body of the people, operating by the majority against the minority.

It may be thought that all paper barriers against the power of the community are too weak to be worthy of attention. I am sensible they are not so strong as to satisfy gentlemen of every description who have seen and examined thoroughly the texture of such a defence; yet, as they have a tendency to impress some degree of respect for them, to establish the public opinion in their favor, and rouse the attention of the whole community, it may be one means to control the majority from those acts to which they might be otherwise inclined.

It has been said, by way of objection to a bill of rights, by many respectable gentlemen out of doors, and I find opposition on the same principles likely to be made by gentlemen on this floor, that they are unnecessary articles of a Republican Government, upon the presumption that the people have those rights in their own hands, and that is the proper place for them to rest. It would be a sufficient answer to say, that this objection lies against such provisions under the State Governments, as well as under the General Government: and there are, I believe, but few gentlemen who are inclined to push their theory so far as to say that a declaration of rights in those cases is either ineffectual or improper. It has been said, that in the Federal Government they are unnecessary, because the powers are enumerated, and it follows, that all that are not granted by the constitution are retained; that the constitution is a call of powers, the great residuum being the rights of the people; and, therefore, a bill of rights cannot be so necessary as if the residuum was thrown into the hands of the Government. I admit that these arguments are not entirely without foundation; but they are not conclusive to the extent which has been supposed. It is true, the powers of the General Government are circumscribed, they are directed to particular objects; but even if Government keeps within those limits, it has certain discretionary powers with respect to the means, which may admit of abuse to a certain extent, in the same manner as the powers of the State Governments under their constitutions may to an indefinite extent; because in the constitution of the United States, there is a clause granting to Congress the power to make all laws which shall be necessary and proper for carrying into execution all the powers vested in the Government of the United States, or in any department or officer thereof; this enables them to fulfil every purpose for which the Government was established. Now, may not laws be considered necessary and proper by Congress, for it is for them to judge of the necessity and propriety to accomplish those special purposes which they may have in contemplation, which laws in themselves are neither necessary nor proper; as well as improper laws could be enacted by the State Legislatures, for fulfilling the more extended objects of those Governments. I will state an instance, which I think in point, and proves that this might be the case. The General Government has a right to pass all laws which shall be necessary to collect its revenue; the means for enforcing the collection are within the direction of the Legislature: may not general warrants be considered necessary for this purpose, as well as for some purposes which it was supposed at the framing of their constitutions the State Governments had in view? If there was reason for restraining the State Governments from exercising this power, there is like reason for restraining the Federal Government.

It may be said, indeed it has been said, that a bill of rights is not necessary, because the establishment of this Government has not repealed those declarations of rights which are added to the several State constitutions; that those rights of the people, which had been established by the most solemn act, could not be annihilated by a subsequent act of that people, who meant, and declared at the head of the instrument, that they ordained and established a new system, for the express purpose of securing to themselves and posterity the liberties they had gained by an arduous conflict.

I admit the force of this observation, but I do not look upon it to be conclusive. In the first place, it is too uncertain ground to leave this provision upon, if a provision is at all necessary to secure rights so important as many of those I have mentioned are conceived to be, by the public in general, as well as those in particular who opposed the adoption of this constitution. Besides, some States have no bills of rights, there are others provided with very defective ones, and there are others whose bills of rights are not only defective, but absolutely improper; instead of securing some in the full extent which republican principles would require, they limit them too much to agree with the common ideas of liberty.

It has been objected also against a bill of rights, that, by enumerating particular exceptions to the grant of power, it would disparage those rights which were not placed in that enumeration; and it might follow, by implication, that those rights which were not singled out, were intended to be assigned into the hands of the General Government, and were consequently insecure. This is one of the most plausible arguments I have ever heard urged against the admission of a bill of rights into this system; but, I conceive, that it may be guarded against. I have attempted it, as gentlemen may see by turning to the last clause of the fourth resolution.

It has been said, that it is unnecessary to load the constitution with this provision, because it was not found effectual in the constitution of the particular States. It is true, there are a few particular States in which some of the most valuable articles have not, at one time or other, been violated; but it does not follow but they may have, to a certain degree, a salutary effect against the abuse of power. If they are incorporated into the constitution, independent tribunals of justice will consider themselves in a peculiar manner the guardians of those rights; they will be an impenetrable bulwark against every assumption of power in the legislative or executive; they will be naturally led to resist every encroachment upon rights expressly stipulated for in the constitution by the declaration of rights. Besides, this security, there is a great probability that such a declaration in the federal system would be enforced; because the State Legislatures will jealously and closely watch the operations of this Government, and be able to resist with more effect every assumption of power, than any other power on earth can do; and the greatest opponents to a Federal Government admit the State Legislatures to be sure guardians of the people's liberty. I conclude, from this view of the subject, that it will be proper in itself, and highly politic, for the tranquillity of the public mind, and the stability of the Government, that we should offer something, in the form I have proposed, to be incorporated in the system of Government, as a declaration of the rights of the people.

In the next place, I wish to see that part of the constitution revised which declares that the number of Representatives shall not exceed the proportion of one for every thirty thousand persons, and allows one Representative to every State which rates below that proportion. If we attend to the discussion of this subject, which has taken place in the State conventions, and even in the opinion of the friends to the constitution, an alteration here is proper. It is the sense of the people of America, that the number of Representatives ought to be increased, but particularly that it should not be left in the discretion of the Government to diminish them, below that proportion which certainly is in the power of the Legislature as the constitution now stands; and they may, as the population of the country increases, increase the House of Representatives to a very unwieldy degree. I confess I always thought this part of the constitution defective, though

83

not dangerous; and that it ought to be particularly attended to whenever Congress should go into the consideration of amendments.

There are several minor cases enumerated in my proposition, in which I wish also to see some alteration take place. That article which leaves it in the power of the Legislature to ascertain its own emolument, is one to which I allude. I do not believe this is a power which, in the ordinary course of Government, is likely to be abused. Perhaps of all the powers granted, it is least likely to abuse; but there is a seeming impropriety in leaving any set of men without control to put their hand into the public coffers, to take out money to put in their pockets; there is a seeming indecorum in such power, which leads me to propose a change. We have a guide to this alteration in several of the amendments which the different conventions have proposed. I have gone, therefore, so far as to fix it, that no law, varying the compensation shall operate until there is a change in the Legislature: in which case it cannot be for the particular benefit of those who are concerned in determining the value of the service.

I wish also, in revising the constitution, we may throw into that section, which interdict the abuse of certain powers in the State Legislatures, some other provisions of equal, if not greater importance than those already made. The words, "No State shall pass any bill of attainder, ex post facto law," &c. were wise and proper restrictions in the constitution. I think there is more danger of those powers being abused by the State Governments than by the Government of the United States. The same may be said of other powers which they possess, if not controlled by the general principle, that laws are unconstitutional which infringe the rights of the community. I should therefore wish to extend this interdiction, and add, as I have stated in the 5th resolution, that no State shall violate the equal right of conscience, freedom of the press, or trial by jury in criminal cases; because it is proper that every Government should be disarmed of powers which trench upon those particular rights. I know, in some of the State constitutions, the power of the Government is controlled by such a declaration; but others are not. I cannot see any reason against obtaining even a double security on those points; and nothing can give a more sincere proof of the attachment of those who opposed this constitution to these great and important rights, than to see them join in obtaining the security I have now proposed; because it must be admitted, on all hands, that the State Governments are as liable to attack the invaluable privileges as the General Government is, and therefore ought to be as cautiously guarded against.

I think it will be proper, with respect to the judiciary powers, to satisfy the public mind of those points which I have mentioned. Great inconvenience has been apprehended to suitors from the distance they would be dragged to obtain justice in the Supreme Court of the United States, upon an appeal on an action for a small debt. To remedy this, declare that no appeal shall be made unless the matter in controversy amounts to a particular sum; this, with the regulations respecting jury trials in criminal cases, and suits at common law, it is to be hoped, will quiet and reconcile the minds of the people to that part of the constitution.

I find, from looking into the amendments proposed by the State conventions, that several are particularly anxious that it should be declared in the constitution, that the powers not therein delegated should be reserved to the several States. Perhaps words which may define this more precisely than the whole of the instrument now does, may be considered as superfluous. I admit they may be deemed unnecessary: but there can be no harm in making such a declaration, if gentlemen will allow that the fact is as stated. I am sure I understand it so, and do therefore propose it.

These are the points on which I wish to see a revision of the constitution take place. How far they will accord with the sense of this body, I cannot take upon me absolutely to determine; but I believe every gentleman will readily admit that nothing is in contemplation, so far as I have mentioned, that can endanger the beauty of the Government in any one important feature, even in the eyes of its most sanguine admirers. I have proposed nothing that does not appear to me as proper in itself, or eligible as patronized by a respectable number of our fellow-citizens; and if we can make the constitution better in the opinion of those who are opposed to it, without weakening its frame, or abridging its usefulness, in the judgment of those who are attached to it, we act the part of wise and liberal men to make such alterations as shall produce that effect.

Having done what I conceived was my duty, in bringing before this House the subject of amendments, and also stated such as I wish for and approve, and offered the reasons which occurred to me in their support, I shall content myself, for the present, with moving "that a committee be appointed to consider of and report such amendments as ought to be proposed by Congress to the Legislatures of the States, to become, if ratified by three-fourths thereof, part of the constitution of the United States." By agreeing to this motion, the subject may be going on in the committee, while other important business is proceeding to a conclusion in the House. I should advocate greater despatch in the business of amendments, if I were not convinced of the absolute necessity there is of pursuing the organization of the Government; because I think we should obtain the confidence of our fellow-citizens, in proportion as we fortify the rights of the people against the encroachments of the Government.

NOTE: The text of Madison's speech is taken from Bernard Schwartz, *The Roots of the Bill of Rights*, five vols. (New York: Chelsea House Publishers, 1971), vol. 5, pp. 1023–34. The original source is *The Annals of Congress, 1789* (Washington, D.C.: Gales and Seaton, 1834).

# 5

# The Constitution and "Fundamental Rights"

*Lino A. Graglia*

Constitutional law is a potent force in American life, affecting the basic nature of our society and our ability to deal with social problems. Its potency, however, rests entirely on a misunderstanding, the mistaken belief of the American people that judicial declarations of unconstitutionality are in a meaningful sense based on the Constitution. Talk about "fundamental rights" in constitutional scholarship perpetuates this misunderstanding. "Such words as 'right,'" Justice Holmes warned, "are a constant solicitation to fallacy."[1] To add "fundamental" is only to make the solicitation more insistent. A legal right is simply a legally protected interest, not a difficult or mysterious concept. An asserted fundamental right, however, is typically not a right at all but a rhetorical suggestion that encourages judges to disallow as unconstitutional policy choices made in the ordinary political process, despite the absence of any apparent constitutional warrant for doing so. The nightmare of the American intellectual elite (broadly defined) is that control of public policy will fall into the hands of the American people. The function of judges, acting in the name of the Constitution, they believe, is to prevent that from happening. Fundamental rights are would-be improvements to a Constitution that is otherwise entirely inadequate to the task.

The Constitution, contrary to current popular belief, is not essentially about individual rights. It did not come into being because of a felt need to create new rights but to create a strengthened central government, primarily for reasons of commerce, finance, and defense, which was correctly seen as a new danger to individual rights. Alexander Hamilton and James Madison, the moving spirits for adoption of a new structure of government, argued against adopting a bill of rights—amendments limiting the national government's power in specific regards—on the ground that the Constitution was itself a bill of rights providing the two most effective (probably indispensable) protections for individual freedom and security. These protections are, first, a representative form of government, lawmaking by officials subject to regular elections; and second, a federalist form of government, a central government of limited powers, with local state autonomy retained over the bulk of social policy. Indeed, given these two constitutional rights, proponents of the Constitution argued, what need or justification can there be for any others? Why should a people enjoying decentralized self-government attempt to deprive themselves—or, worse, their successors—of rights of self-government? Constitutional restraints on self-government, which can easily become straitjackets as conditions change and amount to government of the living by the dead, require justification, and justifications are difficult to find. Constitutional rights are not costless benefits; to increase the protection of some interests is necessarily to lessen the protection of others. My right to solicit funds on the New York City subways, for example—a recent contribution to human welfare by a federal district judge, fortunately reversed by a higher court—lessens another's right to ride the subways without solicitation. Trade-offs are always involved, and the people of a given time have the most relevant experience and the best information to make them.

Although the Constitution does not use the term "fundamental rights," it can fairly be said that the two most fundamental rights it provides are to be governed by electorally accountable officials and to be governed primarily by local officials. Ironically, what proponents of fundamental rights are actually urging today is greater policy making by the courts and ultimately by the U.S. Supreme Court—a committee of nine lawyers, unelected and unremovable by elections, issuing decrees from Washington, D.C., for the governance of the nation as a whole. What they are urging, then, is not protection, but violation of our most fundamental constitutional rights.

## Individual Rights in the Constitution

The original, unamended Constitution says little of individual rights; that is, it places very few restrictions on the federal government's exercise of its limited authority and even fewer on the general residual authority of the states. Two sections of the original Constitution are specifically concerned with limitations on government power, Article I, section 9, applicable to the federal government, and Article I, section 10, applicable to the states. Although the two sections contain several limitations on power, most relate to federalism (section 9 begins, for example, with a provision prohibiting federal interference with the slave trade until the year 1808), and few today would be considered protections of individual rights.[2] Both the federal government and the states are prohibited from enacting bills of attainder (measures outlawing individuals) and *ex post facto* laws (laws retroactively creating crimes or increasing punishments), and the writ of habeas corpus (permitting judicial challenges to incarceration) is protected against federal action. By far the most important for constitutional litigation is the provision prohibiting the states from enacting laws "impairing the Obligation of Contracts," the specific purpose of which was to prohibit debtor-relief legislation.

In addition, under Article III the trial of federal crimes is to be by jury and in the state where committed, and the crime of treason is narrowly defined.[3] Finally, Article IV, section 2, restricts state discrimination against citizens of other states.[4] After searching the original Constitution in the light of its history for a specifically protected fundamental right, one could easily conclude that the most important of the few candidates is the right of moneylenders to collect their debts by force of law even against debtors in the direst circumstances. This is not one of the fundamental rights we are likely to hear about today, however, when supposed limitations on majority rule granted by the Constitution are being recited.

Additional personal rights were provided for by the adoption of the first ten amendments in 1791, the "Bill of Rights," two years after the ratification of the Constitution. Although today popularly seen as the point and essence of the constitutional enterprise, the Bill of Rights was adopted at the urging not of the proponents but of the opponents of the Constitution, such as Patrick Henry and other defenders of individual liberty and, its surrogate, local autonomy. They raised the popular cry of the need for additional restraints on the greatly strengthened national government in the hope of defeating ratification of the Constitution or at least bringing about a new convention in which much stricter limits on federal power could be formulated. They saw correctly that the national government's supposedly limited powers (specifically, the powers to tax and spend, regulate interstate commerce, and make war) would prove to be unlimited—would constitute full sovereignty leaving no matter exclusively for state control—unless those powers were much more narrowly defined.

Madison, Hamilton, and other principal proponents of the Constitution, who wanted as strong a national government as the states could be induced to accept, saw that the demand for a bill of rights could well defeat the Constitution; it was, in the event, only narrowly ratified by Virginia and New York, the two most important states. They therefore promised the state ratifying conventions that addition of a bill of rights would be the new government's first order of business. Madison, a member of the House of Representatives in the First Congress, drafted a number of amendments, which Congress combined and revised into a proposed twelve, all but the first two of which (having to do with numbers of representatives and with congressional salaries) were ratified by the requisite number of states. Thus, what was originally proposed as merely the Third Amendment became what is now the first.

The first and most important thing to note about the Bill of Rights is that it was intended to create rights only against the national government, not, as its origin makes clear, to limit the power of the states. The first word of the First Amendment is "Congress"; it is congressional, not state, legislative power that is restrained in regard to matters of religion and speech—a proposal by Madison to create similar rights against the states was rejected by Congress. As Chief Justice John Marshall stated for a unanimous court in *Barron v. Baltimore* in 1833, rejecting an attempt to find in the Bill of Rights a restraint on the power of the states, "These amendments demanded security against the apprehended encroachments of the general government—not against those of the local government."[5] He found it incredible that in proposing the amendments "Congress engaged in the extraordinary occupation of improving the constitutions of the several states by affording the people additional protection from the exercise of power by their own governments."[6]

Further, the Bill of Rights consists of what can be considered in modern terms a rather unimpressive list of guarantees, not at all comparable to the extensive and imposing lists of rights granted in, for example, the UN Declaration of Human Rights or the Soviet or Indian constitutions. The only substantive rights provided for are rights of freedom of religion and speech, in the First Amendment, a right to bear arms, in the Second Amendment—now more of an embarrassment than an asset to fundamental rights enthusiasts—and the right to compensation for private property taken for public use, in the Fifth Amendment. The Third Amendment, prohibiting the coerced quartering of soldiers in private homes during peacetime, has no apparent relation to modern conditions and is virtually never heard of. The remaining provisions of the Bill of Rights deal with procedure and, except for the Seventh Amendment, with procedure in criminal cases. The Seventh Amendment, also generally seen as an embarrassment, grants a right of jury trial in civil cases involving more than $20, a potential major obstacle to efficient judicial administration. It is hard to imagine that anyone would propose adoption of some of these amendments today as an original matter.

Many of the rights of the criminally accused created by the Bill of Rights are, to say the least, of dubious contemporary value. Is the Fifth Amendment privilege against self-incrimination, for example, anything other than an unnecessary impediment to the enforcement of the criminal law? This right may indeed be fundamental to the guilty but it is of little or no value to the innocent. No sensible system of law would exempt the accused from the duty imposed on all other citizens to assist in law enforcement by answering appropriate questions.[7] This and other rights of the criminally accused in the Bill of Rights were both applied to the states, without constitutional warrant, and expanded or distorted beyond recognition by the Supreme Court of the Warren era. The Court operated under the notion, then popular among advanced thinkers, that the criminally accused was the victim and society the criminal, so that the cause of justice was served when new ways were invented to permit criminals to escape punishment.

The privilege against self-incrimination, for instance—a bad idea to start with—was expanded by the *Miranda* decision[8] into a right of the accused to have the government provide him with a lawyer free of charge before he could be asked any questions, thereby guaranteeing his noncooperation with the police. Similarly, the Fourth Amendment protection against "unreasonable searches and seizures" was overlaid with the exclusionary rule[9] (prohibiting admission of improperly obtained evidence of crime), making it, like the privilege against self-incrimination, a right of value only to the guilty. The Sixth Amendment's right to the assistance of counsel, that is, to employ a lawyer, was converted to a right to have a lawyer provided at government expense.[10] The *Miranda* and exclusionary rule decisions created a virtually endless need for the services of lawyers, and the assistance-of-counsel decisions guarantee that demand for these services will not be subject to financial constraints.

The Court has, of course, worked similar wonders with the First Amendment's guarantee of freedom of speech and of the press, the primary purpose of which was to preclude federal imposition of "prior restraints" on speech, such as a requirement of a license before publication.[11] Freedom of speech turns out to protect, according to the justices of the Supreme Court, such things as nude dancing,[12] pornography,[13] the parading of vulgarity through a courthouse,[14] public burning of the American flag,[15] and, according to a lower federal court judge, the right to panhandle in New York City's subways.[16] The First Amendment's prohibition of federal interference in matters of religion has come to mean that the states may not provide for a moment of silence in their public schools (lest prayers be mumbled or mentally recited),[17] post a copy of the Ten Commandments in grade schools,[18] permit a crèche to appear in a county courthouse at Christmastime,[19] or deny unemployment compensation to persons claiming that the ordinary employment requirements conflict with their religious beliefs.[20]

The other substantive rights in the Bill of Rights have received a very different treatment. The Second Amendment guarantee of a right to bear arms has never engaged the solicitous attention of civil libertarians. History indicates that the framers and ratifiers considered this right to be extremely fundamental, the ultimate protection against tyranny, but it probably enjoys no more judicial protection today than it would if it were not mentioned in the Constitution.[21] The Fifth Amendment's prohibition of the government's taking of private property for public use does, unlike the Second Amendment, regularly receive Supreme Court attention and has been held applicable to the states by reason of "incorporation" in the Fourteenth Amendment. It has not, however, like the First Amendment and the criminal procedure provisions, received an expansive interpretation. The Court has held, for example, that a taking of private property may be considered to be for a public purpose even though the property is immediately transferred to other private owners.[22] Today the provision does not provide a significant impediment to most government confiscatory and redistributionist measures, despite Justice Antonin Scalia's apparent determination to give it a renewed vigor.[23]

The Civil War, of course, fundamentally changed the nature of the American constitutional scheme. Lincoln was determined to be president even though it meant the dissolution of the Union and waging war on the South to prevent or undo the dissolution. South Carolina, it was clear, was not to be accorded the rights currently being claimed by Lithuania. The Civil War established that the states were not members of the Union by choice. As a result, they could not leave or threaten to leave the Union to protect their freedom, greatly reducing their status.

The Thirteenth Amendment uncontroversially legitimated and extended Lincoln's Emancipation Proclamation. The Fourteenth Amendment was a very different matter, giving the federal government a role in the relationship between the individual state citizen and his state quite different from any contemplated before. The North made war on the South on the theory that the South could not leave the Union but, after successfully establishing by force of arms the correctness of this view, took the opposite position that the southern states had indeed left and could therefore be denied readmission unless and until they ratified the Fourteenth Amendment. Ratification of the Fourteenth Amendment was thus obtained only by coercion; indeed, it was never actually obtained at all, some states having rescinded their ratification before the process was complete.[24]

The purpose of the Fourteenth Amendment was, in any event, very limited. When reports from the South indicated that newly enacted "black codes" were denying blacks basic civil rights despite emancipation, the Radical Republicans, purporting to exercise legislative authority granted Congress by section 2 of the Thirteenth Amendment, enacted the 1866 Civil Rights Act. The act required that blacks be treated equally with whites in regard to such basic civil rights as owning property, making contracts, and bringing lawsuits. President Andrew Johnson vetoed the act on the ground, among others, that it exceeded Congress's authority under the Thirteenth Amendment because it went beyond enforcing the amendment's prohibition of slavery and involuntary servitude. Congress easily overrode the veto but had reason to fear that the Supreme Court would agree with Johnson. The Fourteenth Amendment was proposed and adopted to constitutionalize the 1866 act in two respects: remove all doubt as to Congress's authority to enact such a measure, which Congress then reenacted, and to raise the act's protections to the status of constitutional rights,[25] immune from repeal by ordinary legislation.

Later constitutional amendments extended the right to vote to blacks (the fifteenth), to women (the nineteenth), and to persons over the age of eighteen (the twenty-sixth), and the Twenty-fourth Amendment prohibits poll taxes in federal elections—gratuitously extended by the Court to include state elections.[26] In sum, the question of what individual rights, fundamental or otherwise, are protected by the Constitution is not a difficult one. The original Constitution granted very few personal rights, the one bearing most on actual litigation being the right of creditors to collect debts owed them under contracts that were legal when made. The Bill of Rights added important substantive rights relating to speech, religion, the possession of firearms, and compensation for government seizure of property, procedural rights of the criminally accused, and a right to a civil jury trial, but they restricted only the federal government. Other amendments prohibited slavery, granted basic civil rights to blacks, and extended the right to vote. All other alleged fundamental constitutional rights are the product of judicial policy making, almost always in the guise of interpreting the Fourteenth Amendment.

## The Supreme Court's Improvements on the Constitution

The states' loss of their power to withdraw from the Union as a result of the Civil War left them, as a matter of political reality, defenseless against whatever restrictions or controls national authorities sought to impose on them. This vulnerability was quickly and increasingly exploited by the justices of the Supreme Court. In the late nineteenth century and the first third of the twentieth century, the Court was dominated by libertarian-conservatives, strong believers in unfettered individualism, the sanctity of property rights, and free markets. The state governments and to a lesser degree the national government, in contrast, came increasingly under the control of proponents of extensive economic and social regulation in the interest of egalitarian and redistributionist ends.

The justices became keenly aware that the reduced status of the states meant that the Court, as an arm of the federal government, had the de facto power, if not the legitimate authority, to substitute the policy views of a majority of the justices for the views of elected state and local representatives. As always when the power to do so is clear, the temptation to impose one's views on others—to substitute "sound" for "unsound" views, as one sees them—proved irresistible. Socialist experimentation, the justices believed—as it happens, we now know a century later, correctly—was not only totally out of keeping with American tradition but also extremely unwise, inconsistent with freedom and prosperity.[27] The fundamental constitutional rights of the people to decentralized government and government by electorally accountable officials were not sufficient to persuade the justices to refrain from imposing their improvements on the results of the democratic political process.

Convention required the justices to assert, however implausibly, that they had a constitutional basis for frustrating the political process. Because the Constitution places very few restrictions on self-government—that is, creates very few individual rights—it does not lend itself at all well to such assertions. A Court that is supreme in fact as well as in name, however, subject to no review, is dependent on neither the logical correctness nor the factual accuracy of its assertions. The Court's decisions are not less binding and enforceable when they can be shown, as is often the case, to be logically and factually baseless.[28] As Justice Robert Jackson, unusually given to candor for a lawyer, once put it, "We are not final because we are infallible, but we are infallible only because we are final."[29] The justices have had to make use of whatever was available, and that as a practical matter meant the Fourteenth Amendment. The Bill of Rights, of course, did not even apply to the states, and the Thirteenth and Fifteenth Amendments were specifically limited to slavery and voting. The Fourteenth Amendment it had to be, and the Court therefore converted it from a guarantee of certain basic civil rights to blacks into a second Constitution that effectively granted the Court policy-making power of undefined scope. It has since served, as already noted, as the basis for virtually all the Court's assumptions of power over state policy making. This second Constitution has swallowed the first, substituting for the first's system of decentralized representative self-government a system of totally centralized decision making by officials not subject to elections.

The Fourteenth Amendment prohibits the states, as the Fifth Amendment had earlier prohibited the federal government, from depriving "any person of life, liberty, or property, without due process of law." On the basis both of plain language and of unambiguous history, the purpose of the clause is clear: it protects the individual from illegal punishment, punishment not imposed in accordance with the established legal procedures.[30] By the 1890s, however, the justices were citing the due process clause as if it authorized them to invalidate any legislation or other official act they considered "unreasonable," that is, not in accord with their view of good social policy.[31] The Court had invented the self-contradictory concept of "substantive due process," giving itself the veto power over state law that Madison in the Constitutional Convention had unsuccessfully sought to give to Congress. For half a century, until 1937,[32] the Court used this power to protect individual freedom and disallow Socialist experimentation by both the states and, particularly during the New Deal era, the federal government. Franklin Roosevelt's appointment of Justices Hugo Black and William O. Douglas, among others, to the Court, however, brought the Court's efforts on behalf of contract and property rights to a complete halt. The Constitution never gave either the New Deal or state economic regulation the least bit of trouble again.[33]

The post-1937 Court professed to swear off judicial policy making in general—no more would it act, as Black put it, as a "superlegisla-ture"—and "substantive due process" in particular.[34] The resolution, however, proved short-lived. Power and presumption—and Justices Douglas and William Brennan, for example, never lacked self-confidence—again had their predictable effect. Under a series of new rubrics—the "incorporation doctrine," "new equal protection" re-quiring "strict scrutiny," and "procedural due process"—the Court was soon back in the business of improving on democratic govern-ment. This Court, though, now pursued antitraditional and egalitar-ian goals that were the very opposite of those pursued by the old Court. Beginning with its 1954 decision in *Brown v. Board of Educa-tion*,[35] prohibiting state-imposed racial segregation, the Court be-came, for the first time in its history, not a brake on but an accelerator of social change.

New fundamental constitutional rights were now regularly dis-covered. The "incorporation" (and expansion) of the criminal proce-dure provisions of the Bill of Rights into the Fourteenth Amendment, for example, made the *Miranda* warnings and the exclusionary rule basic elements of state criminal justice systems; the "new equal pro-tection" disallowed virtually all discrimination on the basis of alien-age, illegitimacy, or sex;[36] and "procedural due process" produced rights to government benefits that could not be terminated except after notice and a hearing[37]—all of which operated greatly to increase the need for the services of lawyers. The *Brown* decision was no sooner made effective by the passage of the 1964 Civil Rights Act than the Court, looking for new worlds to conquer, stood it on its head. *Brown*, the Court told us, did not prohibit all racial discrimination by government, as everyone had thought, but on the contrary, required such discrimination where necessary to increase school racial integra-tion.[38] The fundamental right, it turned out, was not freedom from racial discrimination, but integration. Perhaps even more surprising and controversial was the new fundamental constitutional "right of privacy" discovered by Justice Douglas for the Court in 1965 in *Gris-wold v. Connecticut*.[39]

Connecticut had on its books an ancient law, unenforced and unenforceable, prohibiting all use of contraceptives, although contra-ceptives were in fact as fully and freely available in Connecticut as in, say, New York City, just down the road. The law was invoked, how-ever, to prevent the operation of a public birth control clinic, precisely the type of state social and business regulation, one might think, with which the Court had resolved not to interfere. The law, however, could be taken as a paradigm of the type of benighted social policy that can result from participation of the uninstructed masses in the governmental process. It nicely illustrated the clear need in a good society to impose on the unruly democratic process the guidance of an enlightened intellectual elite—which is precisely the function and justification of contemporary constitutional law.

The law clearly had to be invalidated, but how? The Court could not just announce that it was invalid because offensive to liberal sensibilities. Justice Douglas had by this time spent some decades vehemently denouncing "substantive due process" and insisting that the due process clause did *not* authorize the Court to substitute its view of good policy for that of legislatures. The true function of the due process clause of the Fourteenth Amendment, Douglas iterated in case after case, was, surprisingly enough, to make the "specifics" of the Bill of Rights applicable to the states. Although there is no basis for this "incorporation" doctrine (no reason to think that the states were any more willing to impose the restrictions of the Bill of Rights on themselves in 1868, when the Fourteenth Amendment was ratified, than they were in 1791), it served the purpose of seeming to give the Court more constitutional provisions to work with in state law cases, making it appear that the Constitution had something to do with the decisions reached.

Even a jurist of Justice Douglas's creativity, it seemed, would have difficulty finding a right to use contraceptives somewhere in the Bill of Rights, but he proved equal to the task. Explicitly continuing to eschew "substantive due process," Douglas announced that the Bill of Rights was not quite as specific as he had thought in previous cases. Indeed, it turned out that various provisions of the Bill of Rights have "emanations" and that these emanations form a "penumbra." In that penumbra Douglas was able to discern a "right of privacy." What privacy had to do with the operation of a public birth control clinic was no more clear than what a right of privacy might mean, but there could be no doubt that the statute was invalidated and that a new fundamental constitutional right had been born.

In the infamous *Roe v. Wade* decision,[40] eight years later, this constitutional right of privacy was found to include a near-absolute right to have an abortion, although the connection between privacy and obtaining an abortion was again not evident. Justice Harry Blackmun's majority opinion found its authority in *Griswold*, of course, but said nothing of emanations and penumbras—even a good joke does not necessarily bear repeating—choosing to rely offhandedly on substantive due process pure and simple. Thus did the Court come full circle to where it started in the 1880s. The conservative traditionalists of that era would surely have been surprised to see where their discovery of a fundamental right of "liberty of contract" in the due process clause had finally led—to a fundamental right to have an abortion.

This completes our catalog of major constitutional individual rights, both text based and judge made. In a word, the Constitution places very few restrictions on government, especially state government; the Court, the voice of America's intellectual elite in modern times, finding this unacceptably democratic, has created a great many more.

## "Fundamental Rights"—A Euphemism for Judicial Defeat of Majority Rule

The whole discussion of fundamental rights and where they might come from is, however, at best misleading; there can be no real doubt that the "fundamental rights" generally asserted—typically egalitarian or redistributionist requirements—are simply court-created restraints on popular government. If one wishes to approach constitutional law with at least a minimum of intellectual integrity, one must begin by recognizing two propositions necessary and sufficient to an understanding of the subject. First, contemporary constitutional law is in no sense derived from or dependent on the Constitution except that it is parasitical on the Constitution's good name. Second, the Supreme Court's controversial constitutional decisions of the past three and a half decades have uniformly served to substitute the policy preferences of the liberal-Left for the policy preferences of a majority of the American people. Constitutional law, that is, has become a means of removing control of government from the hands of the American people and permitting judicial enactment of a liberal political agenda.

That contemporary constitutional law has little or nothing to do with the Constitution can be easily seen by anyone willing to see. It is obvious, for example, in the fact that the vast bulk of constitutional decision making involves state, not federal, law and is almost entirely based on a single constitutional provision, the Fourteenth Amendment, and indeed, on four words, "due process" and "equal protection." If the Fourteenth Amendment were replaced with a provision of definite meaning—for example, a prohibition of all racial discrimination by government, which would follow and expand the Fourteenth Amendment's original purpose—constitutional law would be reduced to a subject of little general interest.

One does not need a high degree of jurisprudential sophistication to realize that the justices do not decide the vast array of difficult questions of social policy brought to them by studying four words.

No one can believe, for example, that the states lost the power to re-strict the availability of abortion in 1973 when *Roe v. Wade* was de-cided—that abortion on demand became a fundamental constitu-tional right and the laws of all fifty states on the subject therefore became invalid—because the justices noticed in the due process clause of the Fourteenth Amendment something that had previously escaped attention for 105 years. The Constitution obviously had noth-ing to do with the decision except to provide the phrase "due pro-cess" referred to by the Court in passing. The decision resulted solely from the belief of a majority of the justices that their views on abortion were superior to those of the people in each of the fifty states and from their willingness and power to impose their views on the coun-try in the name of the Constitution.

To take another example, the states did not lose the power to make provision for prayer and Bible reading in the public schools in 1962 and 1963[41] because of something a majority of the justices discov-ered in the First Amendment—supposedly applicable to the states by reason of "incorporation" in the fourteenth. The purpose of the reli-gion clauses of the First Amendment ("Congress shall make no law respecting an establishment of religion, or prohibiting the free exer-cise thereof") was not to authorize but to preclude precisely this type of federal intervention in matters of religion, matters to be left exclu-sively to the states. School prayer decisions can therefore be said to be an even more egregious abuse of judicial power than the abortion de-cisions in that they are not only not required or supported by any constitutional provision but are in fact directly contrary to a constitu-tional provision. Similarly, the Constitution's explicit contemplation of capital punishment in three provisions[42] in no way deterred Jus-tices Brennan and Thurgood Marshall from insisting on every occa-sion that capital punishment is nonetheless constitutionally prohib-ited. It cannot be insisted too strongly or too often that constitutional interpretation is almost never involved in Supreme Court rulings of unconstitutionality.

It should be clear, therefore, that Supreme Court rulings of unconstitutionality almost always represent the transference of decision-making power on issues of social policy from electorally ac-countable officials, usually on the state level, to a majority of the nine lifetime appointees on the Supreme Court. The result is a system of government by philosopher-kings similar to that recommended by Plato, except that the kings are not philosophers—persons presum-ably skilled in the art and science of government—but lawyers, per-sons skilled only in finding arguments for positions their interests require them to advance. The central question, the only serious question, presented by constitutional law is why the American people should prefer this form of government to the system of decentralized government with the consent of the governed contemplated by the Constitution.

The answer, of course, is that the American people do not prefer it, which is why its proponents cannot defend it openly and honestly. If government by judges could be openly defended, we would have no reason to confine our selection of judges to members of the legal profession; we would be able to seek real moral and political philosophers, social scientists, priests, and others presumably knowledgeable on the issues that our lawyer-judges now decide. We would not permit the occasion of the judges' policy pronouncements to be determined solely by the accidents of litigation. We would provide our judges with personnel and facilities suitable for the researches the issues require. Finally, we would not embarrass our judges with the convention that they present their decisions as interpretations of the Constitution.

Our system of government by judges in the guise of interpreting the Constitution exists because it is preferred, not by the American people, but by a liberal academic and intellectual elite. This elite sees it as not an ideal form of government—it is unfortunate, for example, that only lawyers are appointed Supreme Court justices—but as the only feasible means of removing control of major issues of social policy from the American people. The crucial fact about the Supreme Court's controversial constitutional decisions of the past three and a half decades is that they have not been random in their political impact. Although covering a myriad of issues—abortion, capital punishment, criminal procedure, prayer in the schools, government aid to religious schools, compulsory school racial integration through busing, pornography, libel law, street demonstrations, control of transients, Communist party members as public school teachers, discrimination on the basis of sex, alienage, or illegitimacy, and so on almost endlessly—these decisions have uniformly and invariably adopted and imposed the policy preferences of the liberal-Left.

The policies of the American Civil Liberties Union, anathema in the electoral process, have been the touchstone of enlightened progressivism and therefore of fundamental constitutional rights in the modern Supreme Court. It is not typically a matter of whether the Left will win or the Right will win on some substantive issue before the Court: either the Court intervenes in the political process to give the Left a victory it would otherwise be denied, or the Court does not intervene at all. For the Right—for example, opponents of unrestricted abortion—a "victory" in the Supreme Court is not to have the

Court impose the policy they prefer (protection of the fetus) as a matter of constitutional law but merely to be able to continue to fight for their position in the political process.

Because the American intellectual elite—academics in the social sciences and humanities, newspaper columnists, television commentators, mainline religious leaders, and other purveyors of the word—are predominantly well to the left of the American electorate, they see judicial activism—rulings of unconstitutionality not based on the Constitution—as the saving grace of the American political system. They therefore consider it part of their professional function to defend and justify what the Court has done. As more frequent judicial intervention in the political process makes the public aware of contemporary constitutional law, however, the intellectual elite finds judicial intervention more difficult to defend as a product of the Constitution in any meaningful or nonmystical sense. At the same time, policy making by unelected, life-tenured judges in accordance with the views of an intellectual elite and in defiance of the views of the electorate is also difficult to defend in the American context. Defenses of judicial activism are, however, invariably studded with warnings of the dangers of democracy and the need for restraints on majority rule. Astonishingly, as enthusiasm for democracy and decentralized government is growing in the rest of the world, it is waning among intellectuals in the land of its birth.

Defenders of judicial activism face the impossible task of convincing the public that while rulings of unconstitutionality may not be based on interpreting the Constitution in any ordinary sense, neither are they simply the result of the judges' political preferences. That the task is impossible means not that it is not attempted—the stakes, the very nature of our society, are too great for that—but that it has engaged some of the nation's very best legal minds. The judges, it is necessary to claim, are bound by something, even if not exactly by the Constitution, and the usual alternative is moral and political principle. Where these supposed principles are to be found is unclear, and how, if knowable, judges are to be confined to enforcing them is never explained.

The search, in any event, is futile. Problems of policy choice arise not because legislators fail to discern the resolving principle but because interests recognized as legitimate inevitably come into conflict. Value choices must be made, and representative self-government requires that they be made by officials subject to electoral control. To have them made by judges through the discovery of "fundamental rights" on the basis of moral and political philosophy is to have them made in accordance with the judges' rather than with the electorate's values. Moral and political philosophy is a pursuit, it is claimed, beyond the ken of the ordinary person, as is the extraordinary but happy coincidence that the fundamental rights that result from those pursuits dovetail precisely with the requirements of the liberal political agenda. "Fundamental rights" are mythical supports of a fraudulent structure built and maintained by America's intellectual elite on the conviction that government with the consent of the governed is undesirable in America.

# 6

# Republicanism and Rights

*Thomas L. Pangle*

What is the relationship between republicanism and rights? How is this relationship to be understood within the American constitutional tradition? Our initial response is likely to be that the relationship between republicanism and rights is surely very close. This response accurately characterizes the relationship within the *American* tradition, since 1787. But even superficial reflection on the history of ideas reminds us that the relationship between republicanism and rights is much more ambiguous than it first appears from the American constitutional perspective. *Republicanism* is a leading theme of Western political thought, from its first recorded beginnings in classical Greece. But the idea of rights—that is to say *human* rights, *natural* rights, rights of man, rights belonging to all human beings as individuals, and constituting the moral foundation of legitimate political authority—becomes a clear theme only in the mid-seventeenth century, in northern Europe and, especially, in England.

What is more, this relatively modern rise to preeminence of the idea of rights by no means necessarily entails a preference for republican government. The authors of *The Federalist Papers* found themselves compelled to argue for republicanism against the authority of "some celebrated authors, whose writings have had a great share in forming the modern standard of political opinions."[1] A fountainhead of this "modern standard of political opinions" was Thomas Hobbes, who might justly have claimed the honor of being the most powerful and influential theoretical originator of the focus on individual rights. Precisely because he believed that individual rights are fundamental, Hobbes was no friend of republicanism. Hobbes argued forcefully that to secure individual rights, the best form of government is monarchy; republicanism, with its endemic proclivity to factional strife, threatens individual rights. Hobbes aimed his attack on republicanism in the name of human rights not only against the moralistic ancient theorists like Aristotle, but even more directly against the very different and radically amoral republican principles of Machiavelli and his followers, who sought to revive admiration for the bloody republican imperialism of Rome: "What a beast of prey was the Roman people!"[2]

Later votaries of individual rights did not go nearly as far as Hobbes, but many—including most notably Montesquieu and Hume—did raise serious doubts as to whether republics were likely to secure rights or to curb their own tendencies to violate rights as effectively as well-designed monarchies like the English—that is, monarchies whose genuinely *mixed* constitutions included the checking and balancing advantages of a religious establishment, a hereditary and hence stable nobility, and a powerful but legally limited popular representative branch of the legislature. This kind of doubt was one important source of the opposition to ratification of the Constitution mounted by some thoughtful Anti-Federalists like Patrick Henry of Virginia and John Francis Mercer of Maryland.[3]

Nor were these or kindred thoughts alien to the Federalists, though they were less likely than the Anti-Federalists to express in public their doubts about republicanism. That Alexander Hamilton was deeply moved by such doubts is clear from his remarkable speech to the Constitutional Convention on June 18. Later, on June 26, Hamilton "acknowledged himself not to think favorably of Republican Government," despite or because he "professed himself to be as zealous an advocate for liberty as any man whatever, and trusted he should be as willing a martyr to it, though he differed as to the form in which it was most eligible."[4]

The doubts as to the harmony between republicanism and the securing of individual rights (or of liberty conceived in terms of such rights) are not obviously contradicted by the history of republicanism before the founding of the United States—as *The Federalist Papers* candidly concede.[5] Certainly, republican theory as well as practice prior to Hobbes—one might well argue, prior to the founding of the United States—can only with difficulty be associated with the idea of human rights or the rights of man. It is doubtful whether any text from the

Greco-Roman world or any biblical text ever mentions what can be translated as "human rights," "natural rights," or the "rights of man." Concern for fundamental rights of a kind does figure in classical republican political life and theory, but it is not the chief concern of the classical republic. Insofar as rights *are* of concern to the classical republics, the rights in question are mainly rights of *citizens* or specific groups of citizens, such as families, neighborhoods, and classes. The rights protected in classical republicanism are typically rights defined by and within a particular legal and political order—or they are the rights of the whole political society, vis-à-vis other societies but also vis-à-vis the citizens.

Republicanism, it would then appear, is a genus; the American republic, the first example in history of one relatively new species, is the republicanism that puts individual rights at the center of attention. What then *does* properly define republicanism per se? What new qualification on or supplement to republicanism—as it has been understood for most of its history—was required, and conversely, what change in the original theoretical understanding of a politics based on individual rights was needed in order to make possible the close link between republicanism and rights we find in the American tradition? Is the new, American synthesis of republicanism and individual rights altogether successful, or does there remain an important and troubling tension between the two elements of the new synthesis?

## Republicanism in the Constitution

Let us begin by considering the framers' conception of republicanism, as reflected in the Constitution itself. The framers were sufficiently confident as to the agreed meaning of "a republican form of government" that they included in the Constitution a guarantee of this form to every state, without further explanation (Article IV, section 4). What exactly was the meaning they thought would be understood?

Most of those who commented on this clause at the time of the framing conceived of the guarantee primarily as a bar against monarchy and hereditary aristocracy. More essentially, they defined the guaranteed republicanism by the criterion of *popular sovereignty,* or majority rule, expressed and channeled through elected, representative, legislative, and executive institutions, checked and balanced by the separation of powers, including an independent judiciary.[6] As Madison expressed it in a famous passage of *Federalist* 39, where he explicitly referred to the Constitution's guarantee of the republican form of government:

> If we resort for a criterion, to the different principles on which different forms of government are established, we may define a republic to be, or at least may bestow that name on, a government which derives all its powers directly or indirectly from the great body of the people; and is administered by persons holding their offices during pleasure, for a limited period, or during good behaviour. It is *essential* to such a government that it be derived from the great body of society, not from an inconsiderable proportion or a favored class of it. . . . It is *sufficient* for such a government that the persons administering it be appointed, either directly or indirectly, by the people; and that they hold their appointments by either of the tenures just specified.[7]

Madison prefaces this passage with an admission, however, that his criterion for republican government—popular rule—is controversial. He concedes, for example, that "Holland, in which no particle of the supreme authority is derived from the people, has passed almost universally under the denomination of a republic"; that the same is true of Venice; that Poland and England have frequently been designated republics, despite the fact that their governments do not rest, except partially at best, on popular sovereignty. Madison seems confident that his audience will agree on the "impropriety" of such undemocratic designations, which show, he claims, "the extreme inaccuracy with which the term has been used in political disquisitions." Indeed, throughout *The Federalist* Madison sees the more plausible and urgent challenge arising from those who would insist on a criterion for republican government even more democratic or popular than his own. Against those who, either out of misplaced enthusiasm for "pure democracy" or desire to discredit all democracy as unworkable, would insist on identifying democracy with what Madison calls a "pure republic," in which "the people meet and exercise the government in person," Madison defends a new sort of *representative* democratic republic. It would rest on "*the total exclusion of the people, in their collective capacity,* from any share in" government, thereby making possible the famous "extended" republic, whose basic principle and whose excellence as a cure for the fatal flaw of democracy—majoritarian faction and tyranny—Madison elaborates in *Federalist* 10.

Yet prominent writers on both sides of the debate over ratification continued to take note of the innovativeness, the break with republican tradition, that was implied in the new popular or democratic

American criterion for a republican government. Many Americans were familiar with, even if they did not accept, the republican theory of Montesquieu, generally acknowledged as the greatest political theorist of the age. And Montesquieu defines republican, in contrast to monarchic and despotic, government as

> that in which the body of the people, *or only a part of the people,* has the sovereign power. . . . When, in a republic, the people in a body holds the sovereign power, this is a *Democracy.* When the sovereign power is in the hands of a part of the people, this gives itself the name *Aristocracy.*[8] [Italics are mine.]

Montesquieu's silence here and throughout the *Spirit of the Laws* on the social contract, as well as his treatment of a strict aristocracy as a perfectly legitimate species of republican government, is an echo, though muted and altered, of the great tradition of classical republicanism rooted in the political theories of Thucydides, Socrates, Xenophon, Plato, and Aristotle, and in the practice of the cities of the Greco-Roman world. This classical republican tradition, as the American founders were to varying degrees aware, was fundamentally *aristocratic.* It did not define republicanism in terms of a social contract or popular sovereignty any more than it defined liberty in terms of universal individual rights.

The classical republicans knew of the *idea* that a presumed social contract among individuals ought to be the basis of legitimate civil authority; but Aristotle, in the preeminent classical republican discussion, rejected as wholly inadequate such a contractual grounding for civic justice and legitimacy.[9] Similarly, the classical republicans were of course familiar with democracy, or government based on popular sovereignty, as one form of republicanism; but they can hardly be said to have regarded such government as the sole legitimate form, let alone the best. In Aristotle's classification of regimes, one that remained authoritative for 2,000 years until the radical innovations of Machiavelli began to take hold, democracy (by which Aristotle does *not* mean mob rule, or radical democracy) was categorized as the least bad of the fundamentally unjust and hence defective kinds of polity.[10]

It begins to appear, then, that we were mistaken in our initial inclination to classify republicanism as a genus of which the new American form, with its stress on rights, is a species. The difference between the new republicanism chosen in the American founding and classical republicanism is a difference not of the species, but of the nature of the genus. The two types dispute the basic principles of republicanism; the classical understanding, which had reigned almost without challenge for the two thousand years prior to Machiavelli, did not conceive of republics in terms of the basic categories in which republics were redefined in the eighteenth century. What then were the defining principles of republicanism in the classical understanding, and just how do these principles contrast with and thus illuminate the principles underlying the new American republicanism?

## The Classical Conception of Republicanism

The massive concerns that preoccupy and distinguish republican government, in the classical view, are freedom and rule—conceived as inseparable. For freedom in the republican sense entails some meaningful degree of self-rule; freedom seems incompatible with being ruled by others. In this view, to be free is to be a citizen of a regime in which one has direct access to, or at the very least eligibility for participation in, sovereign office and the deliberations that authoritatively shape communal life.

This primary connotation of republicanism undergoes a considerable transfiguration, however, in the light of self-critical scrutiny. To begin with, of course, not everyone can rule all the time. Rule must be rotated. To be free is then to belong to a society in which one rules and is ruled in turn. To know how to rule as a republican one must know how to submit to being ruled. One must know how to obey—not as a slave, under compulsion, but as a free citizen, animated by an inner and voluntary obedience. On closer examination, then, freedom is not incompatible with being ruled, but rather presupposes being ruled and having the capacities of character that make one a good, that is truly obedient, follower. Citizens are and ought to be ranked—honored and dishonored—in accordance with their demonstrated capacity for such obedience. But if there are qualities of heart and mind that distinguish one individual from another in rank as citizen-followers, these qualities pale in comparison with the importance of the qualities that distinguish individuals as citizen-leaders or rulers. One must *deserve* to rule. Equal republican access to or eligibility for office is revealed on analysis to mean equal opportunity to earn the trust of one's fellow citizens on the basis of proven merit and potential.[11]

The qualities of character that ought to be considered in determining political merit are called the virtues, and are in the main well-known, in both their nature and their relative ranking, to all sensible citizens with any experience in public life. At the foundation of the list are the virtues reasonably demanded of all citizens, followers as well as leaders. These include a sense of shame or reverence, courage, moderation or self-control, truthfulness, justice, and piety. Then there are the rarer excellences that distinguish those few who deserve their fellow-citizens' trust and obedience: generosity, noble ambition, pride, justice as a quasi-paternal concern for the common good, and above all these moral qualities, a complementary intellectual insight, prudence, or practical judgment and wisdom that crowns what we all call "statesmanship" (*politikē*).

A sound republic will then be one where, as in Plato's *Republic*, the ruling offices are distributed as much as possible according to virtuous merit, and those who possess such merit are given the freest and fullest opportunity possible to exercise their capacities. But in actual fact, as Plato's *Laws* demonstrates, the rule of the wise and virtuous must be qualified by the principle of popular consent—that is, by the principle of majority rule. To speak constitutionally, aristocracy must be "mixed" with democracy. But with what right? What justifies the adulteration of the rule of the more public-spirited few by the power of the more selfish many, rich as well as poor?

The simplest, but for the ancients the most decisive answer was that the majority are by virtue of their numbers superior in *strength* to the minority. The nature of political life is such that in some measure might makes right—or, at any rate, might cannot be denied a decisive voice. Still, the might or strength in question is that of human beings, not animals: it is the might of those who are concerned not simply with sheer strength, but with the freedom and dignity that go with having some meaningful share in rule. The fact that some men are superior—sometimes vastly superior—in the moral and intellectual qualities that constitute the capacity to be a statesman, to care for the community as a whole, does not utterly eclipse the more modest talents, attainments, and hence deserts of the vast majority of ordinary folk. A decent republican society makes provision for education, as well as for at least minimal relief from blinding poverty and at least minimal restrictions on acquisitiveness.

This view of the claim of the majority only underlines, however, the degree to which consent or majority rule is a distinctly secondary and second-ranked principle of legitimacy. The principle that is first in rank and hence sovereignty is *virtue;* and consent must justify itself at least partly in terms of aspiration to and qualification for virtue. Strictly speaking, "popular sovereignty" is always an abridgment of civic justice, that is, of the sovereignty of the just.[12]

The preeminence of virtue over consent, as well as the redefinition of freedom and rule in terms of virtue, gains added weight when we observe that the virtues that qualify men for rule cannot be adequately comprehended as means to other ends. The virtues do indeed function as means to ends like collective security and prosperity; and the duties the virtues dictate do indeed compete with and compel the sacrifice of private interests and gratification; but the virtues also shine forth as themselves central to the fulfillment and perfection of human existence. Virtue does not guarantee and may not wholly constitute happiness; but it can be said to be the heart of happiness.[13]

Yet the contention that virtue is the heart or core of happiness is controversial. Many people doubt, if they do not reject, the centrality of virtue to human happiness—as regards both cities and individuals. These doubts compel serious attention because they are rooted in observation of troubling facts.[14]

In the first place, the security, prosperity, glory, and even beauty of the republic as a whole and of individuals sometimes seem compatible with and even dependent upon actions and men who are not virtuous. In the second place, virtue is not natural but dependent on early childhood habituation, which requires as a support the coercive, awe-inspiring, and frightening authority of the law. Indeed, this support from the law and legal sanctions seems required for all or almost all decent citizens throughout their lives. It is no accident that the greatest work of classical republicanism is called, simply, *Laws*. But nowhere is the dependence of moral virtue on coercive law, enforcing communal morals through punishment, more vividly highlighted than in the closing pages of Aristotle's *Nicomachean Ethics*, in a passage that includes a rather high praise of Sparta.[15]

That virtue is not natural in the sense of being spontaneous seems more than compensated by its being natural in the higher sense, of completing or actualizing the natural human potential. Yet if moral and civic virtue is "law-bred," or dependent on the external compulsion of law-enforced fear, shame, and honor, the question arises whether such virtue can be the true response to humanity's deepest natural needs.[16] John Adams was certainly correct to stress that republicanism has always been closely associated with the rule of law; but it is doubtful whether he grasped the problematic character of this assertion in the context of classical republican political theory.[17]

The fundamental problem is in a sense solved, but at the same time deepened, by the introduction of the divine law, or the natural law, conceived as the reasonable edict emanating from a divinely ordered cosmos. A classical republic has never existed, in history or in literature, that has not been grounded on an established civil religion. Whatever its other tenets, such a religion must include the belief that laws are sanctioned by and derivative from superhuman punitive authority.[18] The interweaving of human and divine law, lawgiving, and

109

prophecy surely lends to law and the virtues it sanctions awesome force. But the need to appeal to such support cannot help but raise, sooner or later, two very difficult questions. Why does civic and moral virtue need such massive external support? Who or what are the true gods, and how do we know?

These grave questions, in which culminate the whole gamut of difficulties I have just sketched, are the conundrums, arising directly out of serious reflection on the moral-political life, that open the door to philosophy in the classical republican, Socratic sense. The political philosopher in this sense is a man who intransigently raises, and having raised never ceases grappling with the question, "What is virtue?" What is the nature, the essence, of virtue, of true as opposed to apparent virtue, such as would explain its relation to happiness, to God, to our human nature, and to its needs?

This set of questions does not meet with a speedy or simple answer; it rather opens an alternative, more awakened, more fully rational, and hence more fully human and social way of life that lies above and beyond the life of even the lawgiver, not to mention the statesman or the citizen. The actual experience of this life, the classical republican philosophers insist, reveals that human nature is so constituted as to find its bliss in thinking or in the genuine self-knowledge that comes from thinking. The philosophic life therefore exemplifies a kind of virtue that is truly and radically nonutilitarian, as it seeks no end beyond the practice of the virtue or excellence itself.[19]

Yet there is a serious disharmony, as well as mutual need and benefit, in the relationship between philosopher and statesman. Philosophy, we have stressed, comes from a puzzled questioning of the meaning and purpose of law or lawfulness. This questioning of law, however reinforcing it may be in the final analysis, necessarily disturbs obedience to law nonetheless. For such obedience is only rarely and partially a matter of reason. As Aristotle says in a passage underlined by Thomas Aquinas in the latter's *Treatise on Law,* "The law has no strength to exact obedience other than habit, and this does not come into being except through lengthy passage of time."

The philosopher's activity poses the danger of undermining the traditions, bonds, and healthy limits on public speech that support the strongest lawful republican communities and the most lawfully dedicated republican leadership. Decent citizens can be deeply disoriented by philosophy, and the insights and questions of philosophy can sometimes be misused for evil ends by unscrupulous men. The wise philosopher must take responsibility for these dangers. He must philosophize in a manner, or communicate and publicize his philosophic speculation with a caution, that accords with the gravity of the threat his thought might otherwise pose to republican freedom and virtue.[20] The Socratic response is the "loving rhetoric" or "erotic rhetoric" Socrates teaches in Plato's *Phaedrus*.

But this most radical dimension of classical republican political philosophy casts an even longer shadow over our initial assumptions regarding the virtues that qualify men to rule in a republic. Those men who are most truly qualified to rule—because they are the most fully aware of the problematic character of human existence, and because they are so preoccupied with virtuous activity and friendship that they are immune to temptations to divert their lives from virtuous activity—practice a kind of virtue that leads them to wish not to have to assume the burdens of public office, and that leaves them unapt to attract the recognition or to assume the leadership of large numbers of unphilosophic citizens. As Plato's *Gorgias* and *Laws* and Aristotle's *Ethics* and *Politics* adumbrate, the most appropriate public role for such virtuous men is, in the best case, to give some crucial, general advice to decent, politically ambitious, and talented men engaged in framing laws or reforming republics under law.

Given, on the one hand, that full wisdom, the wisdom of self-knowledge and knowledge of ignorance, belongs to a rare few marginal philosophers like Socrates, who are neither easy to identify nor easy to draw into competition for rule, republican life is compelled in almost all actual situations to substitute some kind of approximation to wisdom or virtue. And on the other hand, since popular consent is necessarily consent of the less wise or less reflective, it is always consent colored by deception and self-deception. The complex task of constitution-making and of ruling, in the classical republican understanding, is then the weaving together of the impure simulacra of the twin roots of political authority—wisdom and consent.

## Liberal Government Centered on Rights

We can now appreciate more concretely the distinctively modern stress on individual rights, in contrast to the principles underlying classical republicanism.

The modern political theory of rights began with a radicalization of the problems concerning the naturalness of virtue, and of obligation grounded in the demands of virtue, that we have just traced in classical republican thought. The new liberal thinking rejects as unrealistic the classical republican attempts to contend with these difficulties. In particular, the classical attempt to subordinate naturally self-regarding passions to self-transcending habits or conventions,

111

supported by fear of divine as well as human punishment, is replaced by or drastically subordinated to a new alliance between reason and passion.

Reason ought to be viewed, the modern theory proposes, not as somehow constituting the end or purpose of human existence; instead, it is the marvelously effective servant of the passions. More precisely, reason is best understood as the servant of those strongest self-regarding passions that, when enlightened by their servant, point toward forms of competition and cooperation that bring about "the common benefit of each" (a striking phrase, coined by Machiavelli and then imitated by Locke).[21] Modern liberal thought certainly does not rule out concern for a kind of civic duty and virtue; but civic duty and virtue are reinterpreted as those limitations on behavior that can reasonably be shown to advance, in the long run and for most men, the satisfaction of their strongest passions.

The first step in constructing the new moral catechism is to bestow moral primacy on those passions that are by nature irresistible and therefore blameless. These are the passions by which all men are driven, and all men can therefore be said to be equally endowed with inalienable "natural rights" to seek the gratification of these passions. More specifically, all human beings may be said to have natural rights to pursue security, along with liberty—and especially the economic liberty to labor and acquire for themselves material wherewithal or property. Again, all human beings naturally pursue happiness, although the content of happiness is so diverse and so elusive that it is a mistake to suppose that anyone can or ought to dictate to another his or her goal in this respect: human beings may be said to have a right, inherent in their nature, to pursue happiness as they see fit, so long as they respect the same right in others.

The natural duties or laws are secondary to the natural rights or claims. Natural duties and laws are those imperatives that dictate the best means to the securing and promotion of these natural rights. The preeminent natural duty is to join, or join in constructing, government. Government is best understood as the rationally constructed artifice by which individuals contract with one another to create a collective police power that will limit everyone's pursuit of the objects of their passions so as to make such pursuit more secure for all. But how in practice is this police power to be organized and operated, and how in practice are the citizens' passions to be schooled in the new, enlightened self-interest guided by reason? The great series of debates over the answers to these questions animates the whole history of modern liberal political philosophy.

Hobbes stresses perhaps more than any subsequent thinker the need for education, of an intellectual or scientific rather than moral and habitual sort. The citizenry must be enlightened as to the true if somewhat frightening principles of human nature: the strength and the selfish or competitive character of the passions; the subordinate but decisive guidance given by reason; the artificiality, as well as the necessity, of law and politics as a cure for the sickness of man's natural condition.

This doctrine, as laid down in the philosophic treatises of Hobbes himself, is to be promulgated primarily in the universities and is to flow thence, through the pulpits and schools and public offices, to the great body of the people. The people will thus grasp the reasons for the onerous burdens and restraints imposed on their passions by law and government; they will understand why government must be authoritarian (in the best case, centralized monarchy), in order drastically to limit the natural drift of human selfishness and competitiveness toward civil war. The people will learn, in other words, that precisely their innate or natural equality requires, for their own protection, the drastic *inequality* of political power, artificially instituted by their presumed consent to the social compact.[22]

Mass enlightenment or education in this new scientific and philosophic sense remains a keynote of liberal thought. But it is supplemented and reformulated by Hobbes's successors, in the light of their insistence on the need for better fences against governmental oppression, as well as greater concessions to widespread human pride or ambition—both of which considerations dictate a much less restrictive distribution of political power. The considerable increase in the number of people having some share in political power can be made workable or safe, the later liberal thinkers argue, by a much more elaborate division and channelling of both governmental powers and economic pursuits, so as to constructively check and balance natural human competitiveness.

Locke and Montesquieu are the greatest theorists of this most characteristic central thread of liberal political thought. They propose a series of famous institutional schemes: representative government; separation of powers; "mixture," or regularized antagonism, of popular, hereditary-noble, and monarchic governmental bodies; and federalism, by which even imperfectly enlightened, selfish pursuits of power can be made to issue in constructive competition. They further argue that the competitive, commercial, or free-enterprise economic system, once liberated and protected, can wean even the most spirited men away from the thirst for militaristic vainglory, and toward the creation of vast new sources of collective welfare, security, and comfort.

Yet these proposals, Locke and Montesquieu concede, by no means obviate a considerable degree of economic as well as political inequality among the citizenry. Given the principled universal equality as well as liberty at the foundation of the modern liberal political teaching about rights, what is to ensure that the mass of men will not grow restive under the very unequal distribution that follows from the protection of the equal liberties embodied in the natural rights? This question intensifies if we keep in view—as Locke especially insists we ought—the power of the selfish, indeed dangerously selfish passions animating all men by nature.

The question becomes acute when we recognize in addition the threat posed by the human imagination, with its tendency to inflate and distort the original, simple passions through religious, heroic, and erotic fantasies, hopes, and fears.[23] Human beings, as individuals and in the mass, can be brought to their senses by grave threats or times of emergency; but what is to keep them in their senses as the more routine years pass, especially in a flourishing commercial and liberal society? Such a society, we must add, will tend to accumulate ever greater sources of administrative, economic, technological, and military power, whose irrational and destructive potential becomes greater as the years go by. The problem of mass education remains pressing, despite or even because of the efficacy of economic and institutional provisions.

In the case of Locke the problem is especially striking. Lockean liberalism depends not only on the persistence of respect for rights of unequally distributed property, as well as respect for never-ending hard labor and the burdens of familial responsibility; in addition, Locke stands at the opposite pole from Hobbes among the founders of the tradition of rights-based politics, by virtue of his doctrine of the popular right to revolution. This right places in the hands of the majority the right and the duty to rise in violent and dangerous rebellion in order to depose government that reveals itself to be aimed at the long-term enslavement and exploitation of the populace. But what will incline the people, or individuals among the people, to the heroism that the exercise of this right may well entail? And what will prevent the people from abusing the right, in fits of mass hysteria or under the delusions bred by soak-the-rich demagogues?

Two massive answers stand out in Locke's works. The first is a popular new religion: a Christianity reinterpreted and transformed so as to provide other-worldly sanctions for nothing more and nothing less than obedience to the laws of reason or nature dictated by Locke's liberal political philosophy. To the creation of such a radically liberalized Christianity, Locke devoted a large and very influential portion

114

of his published writings. The major difficulty is that the extraordinarily prosaic and almost transparently secular nature of the new "reasonable" religiosity renders rather questionable its capacity to bring authentic religious fervor to the support of the commands of Lockean reason.

The second Lockean answer is a new stress on moral education, outlined in Locke's famous treatise *Some Thoughts Concerning Education*. The character that is the goal of Locke's new system of character-formation is considerably less austere, self-transcending, or public-spirited than the character aimed at by the moral education envisaged in classical republicanism. Moreover, Locke views moral education as a private matter. Government is within its rights when it provides basic technical public education, but when government attempts to take on direct responsibility for the character-formation of its citizens it trenches on the sacred private sphere of basic individual rights to liberty and to the pursuit of happiness. Besides, Locke argues, parents—and tutors personally selected and hired by parents—are the appropriate directors of their own children's spiritual development. But this means that Locke's education is restricted to a small minority: to those few whose parents are financially able to afford the leisure and the tutors necessary for a fully elaborated education in the home.

It is not surprising, then, that Locke's greatest liberal successors, Montesquieu and Hume, look to less exclusive and more reliable sources for the popular education required if the new liberal institutions are to function well. Both Montesquieu and Hume place a new stress on the importance of subpolitical, climatic, and historical forces shaping a "general spirit of a nation"—a national character that welds human beings of all social strata into collectivities rooted in shared traditions, habits, customs, opinions, and beliefs. These national characters that are the result of generations of shared cultural and natural environments may be either well-disposed or ill-disposed to assimilate the new liberal principles and the modes of behavior those principles require.

Both Montesquieu and Hume bring out, in other words, the question of the degree to which the successful operation of enlightened self-interest requires preexisting habits and inner sources of discipline, trust, fellowship, or social solidarity that are not themselves necessarily or usually the product of enlightened self-interest. Accordingly, both thinkers are less sanguine than either Hobbes or Locke as to the degree to which liberal political systems and principles are likely to spread and take root throughout the world. And both thinkers are more troubled by the fragility of the institutional checks and balances and of the nascent economic freedoms that are

115

beginning to mark England, Holland, and even France in the eighteenth century.

As regards the protection of liberty and rights in England in particular, both Montesquieu and Hume, as we began by noting, stress the critical role played by the religious establishment, the hereditary nobility, and the monarchy within the mixed constitution of England. Montesquieu implicitly and Hume explicitly indicate grave reservations about the doctrines of the social contract, the right to revolution, and even human rights. Both philosophers worry that the incautious promulgation of such libertarian and egalitarian teachings might contribute to a breakdown of the traditional senses of reverence, deference, civility, responsibility, and allegiance, built up over generations and serving as the cement that prevents the disintegration and atomization of what these thinkers conceive to be essentially artifical civil societies.

## The American Synthesis

This sketch of the previous liberal tradition enables us to appreciate the daring and the problematic character of the American attempt to join republicanism and rights.

The framers' liberalism departs from the greatest previous forms of liberal or rights-oriented theory and practice in the degree to which it is married to a continuing dedication to popular self-government—seen partly as a means to securing rights, but partly as an additional end, as an essential additional manifestation of human dignity. But the American notion of self-government is decisively colored by the basic liberal principles of the social contract: the American notion of republicanism introduces the egalitarian and libertarian, or popular-sovereignty principles of the underlying social contract directly into the constitutional organization and administration of the government. The most prominent American founders—apart from John Adams, who in this key respect appears an anachronism—ignore or jettison the cautions that had been the great theme of Hume, Montesquieu, Blackstone, and other eighteenth-century liberals. The Americans insist on a government not only of and for, but to a considerable extent by the people.

To be sure, the Americans seek to construct, on a strictly popular basis, institutions that will play a role similar or at least akin to the role played by the nonpopular institutions of the English mixed Constitution. And of course the founders retain the great principle of representative as opposed to direct democracy. But they make the representative government much more directly responsible to, much more directly under the control of the people than had been the case in previous systems dedicated to the protection of individual rights. What is more, the system and the outlook they set in motion have in the two subsequent centuries developed far in an even more popular and individualistic direction than their original plan envisaged.

America's *republicanism* departs from previous forms of republicanism by taking as its chief goal the protection and fostering of individual or private rights and liberties. As a result, the Americans are at most only the distant heirs of the English republican tradition—the twofold tradition looking back to John Milton on the one hand and Algernon Sidney on the other. The American founders largely leave behind the austere blend of Isocratean classical republicanism and Calvinist political theology expressed so eloquently in Milton's *Areopagitica* and *Of Education*. They stand closer to Sidney's *Discourses on Government;* but they eschew even the softened militarism and imperialism of Sidney's much mitigated Machiavellian vision, while laying aside Sidney's still-classical reservations, voiced in the name of the claims of virtue against popular sovereignty. The American founders do not characteristically echo Sidney in speaking of the people's duty, under natural law, to elect their virtuous superiors as rulers or representatives.[24]

Yet, as republicans Americans do continue to express from afar a sense of kinship with the classical republican tradition. They give expression to a genuine admiration for the improbable self-overcoming exhibited by Plutarch's heroes and fostered by the cities those heroes inhabited and defended. Nor is this glance back to the classical republics merely perfunctory. The founders certainly restate, at important junctures, some of the principles of classical republican political teaching. They are concerned with recruiting men of virtue for public office under the new Constitution. They appeal to the proud, watchful, and fair-minded spirit of the people as the final bulwark against tyranny. They rely on the sturdy self-sufficiency and independence of the yeomanry to make up the moral backbone of the population.[25] But they integrate these classical or quasi-classical elements into a framework that makes very little provision for the inculcation, or fostering, or even preservation of these crucial excellences of character.

The question looming from the beginning, bulking ever larger as our constitutional system has evolved, especially in the past forty or fifty years, is whether and how the system provides for the moral and civic education of a people that becomes more fragmented in every sense, even as it is given more and more power and responsibility.

The form this question took in the founding period is instructive.

117

Those who did address the problem of preserving and fostering a reliable, popular, civic ethos tended to return again and again to two sources for guidance and inspiration: the classical republics and Protestant Christianity. They did so despite the fact that the founders tended themselves to be rather freethinking and were mostly opposed to any but the most minimal establishment of religion. They did so while exposing the classical republics to excoriating criticism: for their failure to protect individual rights, especially acquisitive property rights; for their anticommercial and stoical or moralistic austerity; and for the religious "superstition" that stained, in the Americans' eyes, their councils and public actions.

In other words, Americans during the founding period tried to imitate, if only in diluted versions, the classical virtues, while condemning or at any rate drastically subordinating the classical principles that sought to produce those virtues. The Americans celebrated the Revolution's spirit of brotherhood in arms, sacrifice of life, and martial manliness, while creating a society in which commerce was to reign supreme, explicitly displacing old-fashioned heroic republicanism. They tried to instill reverence for constitutional law and tradition, while insisting that the law could draw its only legitimacy from its service to the welfare of individuals. They assumed as pen names the names of Plutarchian heroes, while deploring and distancing themselves from the decisive aristocratic dimension of Plutarchian republicanism.

The rather slender threads that once linked the new rights-oriented republic to the ancient republican tradition have become increasingly frayed and tenuous. The check these threads provided on the more powerful mainsprings of the American republic have become weaker and weaker. For several generations we have been witnessing and experiencing the process by which the American republic, led by its "advanced" elites, has been radicalizing and making ever more unqualified both its liberal or libertarian and its democratic or egalitarian nature. The changes in our public and our private life that have resulted are troubling. The question is not the survival of the system and the republic, at least in the foreseeable future; at issue rather is the shrinking of the spirit, the shriveling of the heart, the banalization of existence that seems to loom as we look about us.

Certainly there are still glowing embers of a unique and strong national spirit warming American public life. The victory of the free world over communism is not merely a manifestation of the rottenness of Marxism; the victory is also a tribute, despite all the lapses and mistakes, to the resolve, the patience, the steadfastness, and the prudence of the American electorate and its cold war leadership over many years. The civil rights movement has eradicated or greatly diminished longstanding civic vices, through the victory of admirable civic virtues—of fraternity, fairness, courage, and compassion. Americans can take pride in the American economy, whose resilience testifies, in part at least, to the citizenry's hard work, discipline, commitment to education, and respect for talent and initiative. But these and other justifiable sources of pride are shadowed by a pervasive malaise that grips the vitals of the nation.

One need not look far for symptoms of the debility to which I refer: the political apathy and disenchantment of the American citizenry, borne out by steadily decreasing voting and steadily increasing disrespect for elected representatives; the powerful disinclination of those representatives to shoulder the responsibilities, to run the risks of truly governing the nation and facing the harsh choices such governing requires; the disintegration of the family, and the dissolution of relations between the sexes, manifested in rampant sexual promiscuity, staggering rates of divorce, child abuse, child abandonment (especially by divorced fathers), single-parent households and households in which marriage has been unknown for generations; the ever dwindling interest in serious literature, history, and the arts, which are increasingly replaced, (especially among the best-educated young people) by fascination with brutal, or sentimental, or escapist and mindless modes of entertainment; the appalling prevalence of drug consumption, now estimated at a level of $150 billion a year, and inducing in a growing number of civic leaders a call for surrender in the "drug war," for the legalization of all drugs.

Never has there been so much chatter about "community," "bonding," "empathy," "nurture," and "gentleness"; and never has there been so icy and thorough a disconnectedness between women and men, between generations, between fellow-citizens and workers and neighbors. With the erosion of the supports in tradition, religion, and reason for shared ties of reverence and meaning, "individualism"—the word coined by Tocqueville as the name of the peculiarly American pathology he so presciently diagnosed—becomes more and more the hallmark of American existence. Americans increasingly find themselves cast back upon nothing but themselves, in a floating anomie of lonely crowds denuded of trustworthy affective and intellectual sources of human fellowship.

In darker moments, one cannot help but wonder with trepidation whether the country might not be entering upon an irreversible trajectory. Is our debility not gathering a rather frightening momentum? Throwing themselves into essentially unpleasant or stultifying work with a view to the accumulation of greater material satisfactions and petty signs of prestige, to which they become ever more grimly enthralled; seeking escape in mindless entertainment, sports, travel, and short-lived, gripping diversions of all kinds; convulsed periodically with fantastic longings for revelatory erotic or religious experiences; may not future generations of Americans lead increasingly fragmented and purposeless existences, in a world of unprecedented materialism, desperate personal isolation, and inner psychological weakness verging on collapse?

Or will perhaps the inspiriting rebirth of enthusiasm in Eastern Europe, for *both* individual rights *and* republican self-government—for freedom not only in a negative but also in a more positive, civic, or virtuous sense, with all the rich challenges and stern but uplifting responsibilities this sense implies—infect us here in America with a renewed aspiration to recover the full meaning of both our dedication to rights and our dedication to republicanism? These questions seem to me to be among the most urgent of the coming century.

# 7

# The *Federalist* and the Institutions of Fundamental Rights

*Mark Tushnet*

In their defense of the institutions of the new Constitution they were recommending to their fellow citizens, the authors of *The Federalist* faced a dilemma. They needed to argue that these institutions of the new government would be sufficiently energetic to ensure the adoption of sound public policy yet not energetic enough to endanger the valued liberties of the citizenry. Yet their fundamental assumptions about human nature made it difficult to explain why these institutions satisfied this dual requirement. At crucial points the authors of *The Federalist* relaxed their assumptions about human nature, arguing that the occupants of particular positions in the new government— the president, members of Congress, and judges—would somehow be different from the majority of the citizenry. Because they understood that they could not adequately defend these relaxed assumptions, the authors created a rhetorical structure in which the confrontation between energy and the protection of liberty was repeatedly deferred: from the citizenry to Congress, then from Congress to the courts, then from the courts under the original Constitution to the courts under a Constitution amended to include a bill of specified rights, and finally to the courts under a Constitution with a relatively undefined protection of rights.[1] Here I examine the strategy of deferral. My primary aim is to develop a perspective on the theory of the Constitution somewhat different from those usually offered. My secondary goal is to point out how that theory came to undermine itself, both because of the strategy of deferral implicit in the original theory and because of the successes of the political and economic system that the Constitution underwrote.

The classic discussion in *Federalist* 10 states Publius's assumption about human nature: The fallibility of human reason gives rise to different opinions; the connection between reason and self-love amplifies the importance of those differences; and "the latent causes of faction are thus sown in the nature of man." Faction, in turn, entails either the invasion of the rights of other citizens or the failure to promote "the permanent and aggregate interests of the community," that is, the failure to adopt a sound public policy. As embodiments of majority rule, legislatures are bound to go awry under the influence of faction unless the institutions of government are carefully adjusted, for it is insufficient to rely on the good sense of "enlightened statesmen" to check the operation of faction. Although such statesmen may sometimes be in positions of power, they "will not always be at the helm."

## Institutional Design

The solution, according to *Federalist* 10, is to control the effects of faction by institutional design. Majority rule, "the republican principle which enables the majority to defeat [a minority faction's] sinister views by regular vote," is sufficient to control the threat of minority faction, but the problem of majority faction is more serious. *The Federalist* offers two solutions: to prevent the coexistence of the same passion or interest in a majority or to make it difficult for a majority that shares the same passion or interest to organize effectively to control the government. Both solutions are possible in a representative republic that extends over a large territory. Yet in the defense of the extended republic, the first strains in the scheme of *The Federalist* appear.

Representation, the authors argue, may "refine and enlarge the public views, by passing them through the medium of a chosen body of citizens, whose wisdom may best discern the true interest of their country." Given Publius's assumptions about human nature, however, why this should occur is unclear. Consider first the situation from the point of view of the citizenry. If the public's views are to be refined and enlarged, the citizenry must somehow choose representatives who, in the relevant sense, are better than the citizens themselves. Publius argues that they will do so because the size of the districts from which representatives will be selected can be adjusted to make it difficult for the electorate to select any one other than those with "the most diffusive and established characters." Although Publius offers a rather unpersuasive mathematical argument to this effect,[2] he presents a more substantial argument that the costs of corrupting a larger constituency through the practice of "the vicious arts by which elections are too often carried" will be too great. If the size of the constituencies is carefully determined, then, the only people well known enough to think it sensible to seek election will be, in the relevant sense, better than the majority of the electorate. Later, in the discussion of federalism, Publius argues that potential members of the national legislature would most likely come to prominence first through their service in state legislatures, where they will have the opportunity to demonstrate their characters to the electorate.[3]

Publius offers these arguments with some diffidence, and properly so. Madison's own experience in the election for the first House of Representatives is instructive here. Acting on Publius's assumptions, Madison failed to campaign for the office, believing that his service to the country was widely enough known to demonstrate his diffusive character to his constituents. James Monroe, who was more attuned to the operations of politics, campaigned vigorously for the position and nearly defeated Madison. Although Monroe did not behave badly in any sense, Madison's narrow victory points up difficulties in Publius's assumptions. Further, developments in the art of rhetoric—now called public relations—and in the technology of communication make it possible for people to become sufficiently widely known without having demonstrated their diffusive characters through prior service in public office. Radio broadcasters, stars of television situation comedies, and baseball and basketball players have successfully sought positions in the Senate and House of Representatives.

Even within the theoretical scheme Publius presents, he cannot eliminate the possibility that wealthy practitioners of "the vicious arts" will seek office. In the discussion of federalism Publius notes, for example, that "from the gift of [the states] . . . a greater number of officers and emoluments will flow." This suggests that successful state legislators might well be practitioners of the vicious arts rather than persons of the most diffusive character. Further, the close connection between state legislators and their constituents might lead constituents to select not the most diffusive characters, but the ones who have shown their ability to satisfy the factious desires of the electorate. Finally, as the argument develops, the ambition of representatives to hold and retain office plays a crucial role in keeping the national government from becoming oppressive. And ambition is defined as a form of that same self-interest that causes the problems of faction. Thus, representation alone is insufficient to guard against the dual dangers of unsound policy and incursions on liberty.

## Extending the Republic

To extend the sphere of the republic was another solution, which combined an attention to numbers with a concern for organization. This larger republic would encompass many more "distinct parties and interests" and would thereby make it less likely that the citizens in any single majority would share the same passions or interests. Even if citizens within the majority did share the same passions or interests, the larger territory would make it more difficult for them to communicate and to organize into a majority faction in the legislature. As Publius said, factions had to be united "by some common impulse of passion, or of interest." In modern terms, factions are single-interest groups.

Modern developments have revealed where the problems with this solution lie. Publius's discussion of organization indicates that he was aware of, but discounted, the possibility that logrolling and similar devices, used to assemble a majority coalition consisting of minority factions, could produce a majority faction. Once the possibility of a coalition is admitted, however, an extended territory and an increase in the numbers of "distinct parties and interests" will not offer a solution to the problem of majority faction. In this light, the development of a national party system, something about which many of the framers were quite ambivalent even as they assisted in constructing such a system, indicates the difficulty.[4] National parties coordinate the distinct interests that are otherwise geographically dispersed. And, again, modern technology substantially reduces the problem of communication in a large nation.

Perhaps, however, a majority faction consisting of the aggregation of minority factions is less troublesome than a majority faction united around a single common interest. First, a majority assembled in this way might have no permanent existence; it would form around a single, transitory array of issues, dissolve when the moment had passed, and then be replaced by some new aggregation. Yet, unless the new aggregation actually set aside what the prior one had done, the first faction's legislation would remain in place to thwart the broad permanent interests of the community. Second, however, the very processes of assembling a majority faction out of a group of minority factions might temper their desire to invade others' rights or defeat the public interest. Putting together such a coalition might set off bargaining and deal making that are fundamentally incompatible with the passions that motivated the factions constituting the coalition.

For all this, it remains unclear why a coalition coordinated through a national party might not *become* a majority faction of the troubling sort, even if not such a faction at the outset. In particular, those with the talent to put together a coalition seem likely to be ambitious people who could use the coalition to advance their interests. For one thing, they can take advantage of the perquisites of incumbency to entrench themselves further. For another, as proposals to "reform" campaign financing suggest, they can use their legislative power to reduce substantially the possibility of their replacement by people with fundamentally different notions about the public good.

Publius's emphasis on organization is more promising, though here too there are difficulties. The argument establishes that organizing a government encompassing an extended territory is more costly than organizing one over a smaller territory; the argument does not establish that it is more costly for majority factions than for a majority devoted to the public good and the recognition of the rights of citizens. Thus, the argument based on organization is in some tension with the fundamental effort to create an energetic government. To make that point, Publius argues that "where there is a consciousness of unjust or dishonorable purposes, communication is always checked by distrust in proportion to the number whose concurrence is necessary." Yet, Publius offers no reason to explain why the proponents of majority faction will be conscious of their unjust or dishonorable purposes. Indeed, the argument at the outset—that reason is connected to self-love—strongly suggests that people will become persuaded that they are acting in good faith to pursue the public good without infringing on anyone's rights, even though they are in fact either failing to pursue the public good or, in pursuing it, nonetheless infringing on rights.

Publius's conclusions in *Federalist* 10 are properly cast in terms of probability: a representative government over an extended territory is less likely to be oppressive and is more likely to pursue the public good than are the alternative forms of government such as direct democracy or small representative republics.[5] Later discussions of the separation of powers suggest, however, that Publius or the audience for *The Federalist* remained concerned that the new government might nonetheless be too powerful. If the extended republic is not sufficient to solve a problem, then the solution can be deferred to the operation of the institutions of that republic—the bicameral legislature, the presidency, and the courts.

The first step toward a solution that would create an energetic but limited government is to combine Publius's recognition that the legislature can be neither too small nor too large with his criticism of direct democracy on the ground that it provides the opportunity for a "common passion or interest . . . [to] be felt by a majority of the whole." Together, these observations imply that the representatives gathered in the legislature might themselves constitute a majority faction to the extent that they share a common passion or interest. And, Publius argues in *Federalist* 51, they *must* do so: for the system of separation of powers to work, "the *interest* of the man must be connected with the constitutional rights of the place." That is, in a well–designed system of separation of powers, all legislators share an interest in defending the rights of the legislature as such. There are a number of those rights, such as the constitutional protection afforded by the speech and debate clause, but it would seem that chief among them is the "right" to exercise the powers granted the legislature in the Constitution.[6]

This argument is, on the one hand, comforting, for it explains why Congress might be sufficiently energetic to enact important public policies. Yet, it is, on the other hand, threatening, for an energetic Congress bent on maximizing its power by exercising its constitutional right to legislate might intrude on rights or otherwise fail to advance the common good. If legislators were better than the electorate, the threat might be reduced. But, as we have seen, that solution cannot be guaranteed. The effects of the extended territory offer a different answer. In discussing the costs of organization, Publius stressed the difficulties of communicating from one state to another, using the metaphor of a "conflagration" that might arise in one state but fail to spread to another.[7] The cost of organization, however, can play a role even within the national legislature. Because of the great number and variety of factions, it will be difficult to assemble a majority coalition; the costs of organizing within Congress will be high because each legislator must figure out what package of positions will best satisfy the local electorate, thereby ensuring reelection. Yet, each legislator must be "ambitious" to ensure reelection, and that requires the exercise of congressional powers. Because the cost of organizing within Congress is high, if anything at all is to be enacted, it may well have to be legislation in the public interest; the factious desires of the various electorates may cancel each other out, leaving the members of

Congress with an incentive to do something but with nothing to do other than what is in the public good.

Again, however, the argument is incomplete. It is true that the costs of organizing within Congress, like the costs of organizing across state boundaries, may be high. The benefits of organization, though, must also be taken into account. Furthermore, Congress, having substantial powers, has the ability to confer large benefits on a factious majority, either a national faction willing to incur the cost of organization throughout the nation or a coalition of factions willing to incur the necessarily lower cost of organization within Congress. Fear of the factious exercise of Congress's substantial powers led opponents of the Constitution to propose that a bill of rights be added. From Congress's viewpoint, the addition would not bar enactment of legislation that advanced the public good and provided a further guarantee against the invasion of fundamental rights.

Publius resisted this effort, seeing it ambivalently as yet another effort to defer to another institution the problem of reconciling energy with the protection of liberty. Publius argued that no language inserted in the Constitution could provide the guarantees that the Constitution's opponents sought: "However accurately objects may be discriminated in themselves, . . . the definition of them may be rendered inaccurate by the inaccuracy of the terms in which it is delivered. And this unavoidable inaccuracy must be greater or less, according to the complexity and novelty of the objects defined."[8] Publius conceded that, over time, "a series of particular discussions and adjudications" might fix the meaning of constitutional terms more precisely. The general argument about the limitation of language, then, does not explain why a constitutional bill of rights would be pointless.

Indeed, the adoption of the Constitution might ensure that, in the short run—before fixing the meaning of terms in discussions and adjudications—the new government would not act in oppressive ways.[9] After the terms were fixed, when legislators were most public spirited, the Constitution would be clear enough to limit the national government.

The Supreme Court relied on a version of this argument in *Myers v. United States*, where it held unconstitutional a statute requiring congressional participation in presidential decisions to remove certain minor federal officials.[10] According to the Court's opinion by Chief Justice and former U.S. president Taft, the first Congress had expressly addressed this issue; in what came to be known in this area of law as "the Decision of 1789" Congress deliberately concluded that the president's power of removal could not be limited in this way. Yet, the erosion of the *Myers* decision in later years, evidenced by the independent counsel decision and the decision upholding the constitutionality of the U.S. Sentencing Commission, suggests that Publius's argument that a course of discussions can fix the meaning of constitutional terms needs careful qualification.[11]

Publius's argument that "a mere demarcation on parchment . . . is not a sufficient guard" against tyranny does not establish why the inclusion of a bill of rights in the Constitution would be pointless. For, as the later criticism of relying on "trust" in "parchment barriers" shows, the weight of the argument is carried by the word "mere." The opponents of the Constitution could readily concede that a "mere" set of parchment barriers could not in itself prevent tyranny. But, as Publius understood, one might design another institution to ensure that the parchment barriers were enforced; that is, one could create a system of judicial review to consider whether the barriers had been breached.

In *Federalist* 78 Publius's description of judicial review suggests that the courts could police the barriers. Yet, once again problems arose that required the solution's deferral from the original Constitution to a bill of rights. The difficulty lies in the basic structure of the separation of powers. To ensure that judges are not dependent upon the legislature, they are given tenure during good behavior and are given guarantees against salary reduction. Yet, these protections provide the judges with the opportunity to operate as their own faction. This type of faction, in which the judges cannot be removed by the operation of the republican principle of regular elections, is worse than a minority faction controlling the legislature.

Publius attempts to allay this concern in two ways. First and more prominently, he argues that "the judiciary, from the nature of its functions, will always be the least dangerous to the political rights of the Constitution."[12] The legislature "commands the purse [and] prescribes the rules by which the rights and duties of every citizen are to be regulated," while the executive "dispenses the honors [and] holds the sword of the community." These powers give those branches the ability to corrupt the citizenry or coerce it into relinquishing its rights. The judges, in contrast, have "neither *force* nor *will* but merely judgment." Lacking force, they cannot impose their views on a reluctant citizenry; lacking will, they cannot corrupt it. Their power resides in their ability to persuade their audience that their own views are correct. Publius's second argument against the possibility that the courts would become a faction of their own relies on the professionalism of

128

judges. Because few would combine the skills demanded with the integrity needed, judges would almost necessarily be "fit characters."

Neither argument is conclusive. First, on the question of professionalism, Publius establishes that only a few people possess the qualifications required for sound judging. The argument does not establish, nor does Publius establish elsewhere, that the processes for selecting judges will yield those, and only those, who possess the qualifications. Indeed, from the proposition that the pool of people qualified to be judges is likely to be small, one might conclude that there is a large chance that more than a few judges will in fact be *un*qualified. That chance would increase if the growth in the size of the judiciary outpaced the growth in the pool of lawyers qualified by learning and character to become judges. Second, their professionalism may increase the possibility that judges would come to constitute a faction. For, what is it that they are professionals in? As lawyers, judges will be skilled in the rhetorical arts by which people are persuaded that the advocate's asserted position is correct. Judges are therefore likely to be able to persuade their audience that the judges' views are correct; by exercising their rhetorical skills the judges may cloak their own will in the guise of judgment.

Third, in the general defense of the separation of powers, Publius noted the possibility that a majority faction could be avoided "by creating a will in the community independent of the majority."[13] The judges' guarantees of independence might make them such a will.[14] Yet, Publius argued, that sort of independent will provided "precarious security" in part because it might "espouse the unjust views" of the majority. The image here is of an alliance between the independent will and the majority. A similar alliance might be struck between the judges and the majority, thereby defeating the possibility that the judiciary would defend fundamental rights against the will of a majority.

This argument against judicial review might be strengthened by considering that Publius did not defend a strict separation of powers. He noted that

> in the constitution of the judiciary department in particular, it might be inexpedient to insist rigorously on the principle: first, because peculiar qualifications being essential in the members, the primary consideration ought to be to select that mode of choice which best secures these qualifications; second, because the permanent tenure by which the appointments are held in that department must soon destroy all sense of dependence on the authority conferring them.[15]

129

This argument seems to overlook two aspects of the dynamics of the operation of the system as a whole. First, and perhaps more important in the long run, if a political coalition sustains its power for long enough, it will repeatedly put in place judges who will—for the period it takes to dissipate the "sense of dependence"—act on behalf of that coalition. The occupants of judicial office, as a group, may thus be dependent on a majority faction in a troubling way. The possibility of this sort of dependence, however, weighs against another concern: that the judges, as an "independent will," would come to act as a faction on their own behalf.

Second, Publius offers no particular reason to believe that the "sense of dependence" will dissipate sooner rather than later, as he proposed. In our experience the Supreme Court justices, though with important individual exceptions, tend to adhere to the views that led the presidents to nominate them. This tendency may have resulted from a degeneration in the character of the legal profession or from the politicization of the judiciary over the past 200 years. Whatever the reason, though, Publius's confidence that the judges would not act as part of a faction seems to have been misplaced.

As the preceding difficulty suggests, the force of Publius's primary argument—that the judges exercise their judgment and not their will—turns almost entirely on the distinction between judgment and will. Yet, at least on the face of it, Publius's argument for separation of powers appears to turn on the exercise of will by the occupants of *each* branch, judges included. If, as the key argument states, "ambition must be made to counteract ambition," the judges too must be ambitious—selfishly alert to incursions by the other branches into the constitutional rights of the place the judges occupy: "The private interests of *every* individual may be a sentinel over the public rights." The ambitions of the judges could turn them into a self-interested faction. Although Publius makes no direct argument against this proposition, we might be able to develop one. Because they need not seek reelection, for example, judges must be alert only to incursions on their judicial function. That is, they need to act self-defensively but need not grab for greater power. I doubt whether the psychological proposition implicit in this counterargument, the proposition that people can act to maximize the achievement of their purposes in a limited domain without attempting to maximize elsewhere, is either sustainable or consistent with the fundamental scheme of *The Federalist*. Such a division seems to me unlikely and inconsistent with Publius's insistence that the Constitution can operate well, notwithstanding "the defect of better motives" in the society.

These considerations seem to justify Publius's ambivalence toward judicial review for the enforcement of fundamental rights. For, after establishing that judicial review would not be dangerous, Publius again asserted that a bill of rights was unnecessary. Publius cautioned that the inclusion of a bill of rights might cause people, including judges, to believe that the national government could do anything it wished so long as it did not invade the specified rights. This conclusion was inconsistent with the careful enumeration of powers conferred on the national government.[16] Perhaps more interesting was a point Publius made in a footnote. Opponents of the Constitution had argued that, by conferring the power to tax on the national government and in the absence of a bill of rights, the proposed Constitution authorized the government to infringe on the freedom of the press by setting taxes "so high as to amount to a prohibition." Publius responded that state governments, conceded by all to have general authority to impose taxes, could not be barred from imposing taxes on newspapers, even when provisions guaranteeing freedom of the press were written into their constitutions. Thus, "if duties of any kind may be laid without a violation of that liberty, it is evident that the extent must depend on legislative discretion, regulated by public opinion; so that, after all, general declarations respecting the liberty of the press will give it no greater security than it will have without them." Here Publius argued that a bill of rights would be inefficacious against authority exercised within the government's discretion. If a government's exercise of authority came within the terms of the power granted to that government, if a statute was a tax or a regulation of interstate commerce, it necessarily could not violate a right protected by a specification in a bill of rights. Only if a statute was not really a tax at all but was a naked effort to violate a right would it do so.

We have come to understand that a constitution need not operate on this model of the relation between powers and prohibitions. Indeed, our present understanding of that relation is precisely the opposite. We find it uninteresting whether a statute comes under the authority granted to the national government, for we believe that all our concerns can be addressed by conceding that the government has the power to enact the statute and by asking whether the exercise of that power infringes on a fundamental right.[17] Perhaps the opponents of the Constitution understood this as well. But perhaps not. The numbers of the advocates of a bill of rights, if not the force of their arguments, necessitated that supporters agree to adopt a bill of rights. Once again, at least from the active public's viewpoint, con-

cerns over the ability of the constitutional structure to ensure energetic but nontyrannous government were deferred to another part of
the constitutional system—to the Bill of Rights.

In this stage of deferral the solution presumably lay in the specificity with which rights were enumerated in the Bill of Rights. Specificity was advantageous in the operations of the political branches
and the courts. The existence of specified rights in the Constitution
would provide a benchmark for political discussion concerning the
political branches; rights would allow people to criticize legislators for
violating the Constitution and thus provide a political check against
oppression of the sort Publius alluded to in the footnote on the freedom of the press. If the enumeration was not specific, however, the
political check could not operate effectively; the criticized legislator
would create a legalistic fog of arguments designed to show how the
statute did not actually contravene the rights vaguely enumerated in
the Constitution.

Consider recent examples of both these phenomena. Opponents
of restrictions on the availability of firearms repeatedly invoke the language of the Second Amendment and attack legislators who propose
restrictions that the opponents believe would contravene the clear import of that amendment.[18] Here the Bill of Rights, because it is reasonably clear though subject to argument, serves as a political check on
legislative action. Where the Constitution is less clear, the political
check cannot operate effectively. Most notably, though outside the
context of the Bill of Rights, constitutional arguments cloud discussions of the proper allocation of authority in national security matters
between Congress and the President. The Constitution's general
principles certainly bear upon that allocation. But because the Constitution does not specify much about it, partisans on both sides deploy
arguments in ways that make it impossible for the public to evaluate
the constitutional propriety of either congressional regulation of executive authority or executive disregard of purported congressional
incursions on that authority.

## On Judicial Review

When we consider the judiciary, the advantage of a specific enumeration is almost the reverse. The courts are given the power of judicial
review to ensure that the political branches do not violate fundamental rights. Yet, unless that power is tightly confined, the courts themselves are in a position to violate those rights in the guise of enforcing
limitations on the political branches. Specificity keeps the courts
within bounds. With some exceptions, the provisions of the Bill of

Rights conform to this model. As Justice Black was fond of pointing out, the First Amendment says that Congress shall make no law abridging the freedom of speech, and no law means no law. Black's insistence on the clarity of the language comported with his understanding that the Bill of Rights looked in two directions: it limited Congress, of course, but in ways that substantially eliminated judicial discretion. Similarly, if we interpret the Fourth Amendment to give priority to the warrant clause rather than to the prohibition of unreasonable searches, as the Court has tended to do,[19] we can find specificity even in apparently open-ended provisions.[20]

Black's position seems unreasonable because its rigidity, an advantage from Black's point of view, nonetheless seems to bar Congress from enacting legislation that large majorities believe to be desirable. In the Pentagon Papers case, for example, Black refused to agree that a congressional ban on the publication of troop movements in wartime would be consistent with the First Amendment.[21] One might of course argue that if large majorities consistently believe that such legislation is desirable, the Constitution already provides the means for enacting it: amend the Constitution to revise the protection of free expression. Yet, somehow this seems unsatisfying because it seems unnecessary. Further, Black's position seems naive since, as sophisticated lawyers will explain, perhaps "no law" really does mean "no law." Even so, as we define "abridge" and the "freedom of speech," it is not nearly so clear that, for example, publication of troop movements falls within that "freedom of speech" in a way that a law prohibiting such publications abridges it.

Now, however, we may have returned to Publius's general argument against the ability of language to mark out with precision anything complex. For it would be difficult to imagine a constitutional provision that used *more* precise words than those in the First Amendment. The lack of specificity in the present context, however, is dramatic. When first offered, Publius's argument about the impossibility of precision supported his ambivalence toward the propriety of judicial review. Publius reluctantly embraced that institution, but only by sacrificing his views on language. The effects of that sacrifice are substantial once the institution of judicial review is in place. Give the courts power to interpret unclear constitutional terms, and, as Publius understood, you give them power restrained only by the judges' sense of professionalism. If, as I have argued, Publius's confidence in professionalism as a limit of judicial discretion was theoretically ungrounded and has proved to be erroneous, the dangers to the constitutional system are substantial. If judicial review is seen only as a power to negative legislation, it can nonetheless substantially interfere with legislative efforts that promote the common good without infringing on fundamental rights. If it takes on more affirmative forms, judicial review can itself interfere with fundamental rights by coercing action inconsistent with those rights.[22]

## The Enumeration of Rights

The drafters of the Bill of Rights could do little to avert these dangers. Publius had directed attention to another difficulty: the negative inferences drawn from an enumeration of specified rights that the national government was constrained only by these specified rights and not by other principles of sound government and that the Constitution protected no rights other than those enumerated. The Ninth and Tenth Amendments aimed at forestalling these negative inferences. The Tenth Amendment states that "the powers not delegated to the United States by the Constitution . . . are reserved to the States respectively, or to the people." Although the Supreme Court has said that this "states but a truism,"[23] the Tenth Amendment does a bit more than nothing. It drives home the point that the national government is one of enumerated powers and does not have, as state governments do,[24] general legislative authority. The Tenth Amendment insists that the national government's activities be tied to some enumerated power. The Supreme Court was correct, of course, in noting that the amendment cannot address the different question of whether national action really is connected to an enumerated power and, in situations where the national action in question has such a connection, the amendment certainly has no bearing whatever. In this sense the amendment states the truism that if a power has not been delegated, it has been retained by the states or the people.

For the purposes of this chapter, the Ninth Amendment is more interesting. Its terms directly address the problem of negative inferences: "The enumeration in the Constitution, of certain rights, shall not be construed to deny or disparage others retained by the people." The controversy over the interpretation of the Ninth Amendment arises from two connected issues. One is the *nature* of the unenumerated rights to which the amendment refers. The other is the *authority*—of the nation or the state—that might infringe on those unenumerated rights.[25] The unenumerated rights might arise from positive law outside the Constitution, or they might be natural rights existing independently of their recognition in positive law.[26] If the unenumerated rights arise from positive law, again there are two possibilities. The positive law might be a statutory law, or it might be a common law developed by the courts. At this point, however, the question of authority arises, for it is difficult to develop a theory of unenumerated rights as positive law rights derived from national positive law. The Bill of Rights is a limitation on national power, and it is hard to see how the enumeration of rights could possibly "be construed to deny or disparage" the existence of rights arising from positive national statutory law. If the relevant positive law is judicially developed, it would have to be a form of common law, and at the time of the framing many were hostile to the proposition that a federal common law should obtain in the field of crime, which was understood to be where the most sensitive questions of individual rights were implicated.[27] Even more, the distance between a judicially developed federal common law and judicial recognition of natural law rights preexisting their articulation in positive law seems too small to survive scrutiny; that is, the articulation of common law-like rights by the national judiciary would almost inevitably slide into the articulation of natural law rights.

If the Ninth Amendment refers to positive law rights, then the obvious source of those rights is state law. The enumeration of rights in the Constitution, that is, could not give rise to inferences that rights established by state statutory or common law were thereby eliminated. Here, too, complexities in interpretation arise. For it would be extraordinary, though not textually barred, were the Ninth Amendment to mean that Congress could not exercise one of its enumerated powers to abolish some rights established under positive law. That, after all, is the effect of national statutes that preempt state law.[28] Thus, if the Ninth Amendment refers to rights established by positive law, the most natural reading, and the one reflected in most of the commentary,[29] precludes the courts from invalidating state legislation and common law on the ground that state law recognizes more extensive rights than those recognized by the federal Constitution.[30]

The argument that the Ninth Amendment refers only to rights established by state law has no contemporary legal significance and was not compelled by either the language of the amendment or the theories of law prevalent in 1791. As Suzanna Sherry has shown,[31] a substantial body of law, reflected in Justice Chase's 1798 opinion in *Calder v. Bull,*[32] held that "there are certain vital principles in our free republican governments, which will determine and overrule an apparent and flagrant abuse of legislative power" even if the legislature's "authority should not be expressly restrained by the constitution, or fundamental law of the state." The principles to which Chase referred concern, in part, the necessary implications of a republican government for matters such as civic virtue. Further, they also include basic principles of individual rights that prevent a legislature from taking the property of A and giving it to B, an example that Chase used.

## Failure of the Deferral Strategy

I do not mean to suggest that a natural law interpretation of the Ninth Amendment is compelled by its language, but only that such an interpretation is not precluded by the terms of the amendment and its intellectual setting. The effects of such an interpretation are well known. It licenses the courts to develop constitutional limitations on the authority of legislatures by reference to notions of natural law. As John Hart Ely has argued, if, as many people now believe, there is no such thing as natural law, or, as I have argued, if too many people disagree about the content of a natural law that is universally thought to exist in some sense, the prospects for a stable constitutional law are rather slim.[33] For present purposes, however, I want to make a more limited point. The strategy of deferring difficulties in the theory of the Constitution seems to have reached its end point in the Ninth Amendment, and it is an end point that demonstrates the failure of that strategy. For recall that the strategy was designed to ensure that the risks of overreaching by legislators in the first instance and then by judges would be substantially reduced. At each point in the strategy a gap was noticed, and the decision was to defer the solution to some other institution. An enormous gap is created by the possibility of a natural law interpretation of the Ninth Amendment. And because the courts themselves will interpret that amendment and will have incentives to maximize their power, the courts are likely to adopt such an interpretation. According to this view, the modern development of a constitutional law of unenumerated rights could have been expected. It exploits a gap in the theory of the Constitution that the founding generation had no way to close without sacrificing other aspects of the constitutional system that they apparently valued more.

# 8

# Thomas Jefferson on Nature and Natural Rights

*Michael P. Zuckert*

No thread runs through the tangle of American politics more clearly than rights. When the Americans came to the most solemn moment of their founding activity, when they took the irrevocable step that they knew put at hazard their "lives, fortunes and sacred honor," they spoke the language of rights in order to justify themselves. The king's failure to "secure these rights" was precisely what imposed on them the right, even the duty, "to throw off [his] government."

Rights are not merely the oldest theme in our constitutional order, but the newest as well. The most important and far-reaching current constitutional controversy also centers on the question of rights: Do citizens have rights beyond those explicitly embodied in the Constitution and laws? If so, does the Supreme Court have a warrant to enforce them? The current agitation over the question of rights in constitutional circles is matched by parallel concerns in the sphere of international relations for human rights, and in the philosophic sphere for the development of a theory of rights. In all three arenas questions such as, What is a right? Where do rights come from? and What rights are there? press themselves upon thoughtful persons.

At the same time our national obsession with rights is paradoxical. Although the theme of rights obviously goes back to the founding era, those who are concerned with rights in the contemporary context hardly look to the founding on the question, while those who study the founding have largely abandoned the perspective of rights. Current discussions of "theories of rights" show remarkably little concern for the indigenous sources of the doctrine. While such a wide variety of rights-theories has been developed in the recent philosophic literature that it is difficult to characterize what they all share, it is easy to notice what they all omit: a consideration of rights in the perspective of the American founders. One is far more likely to find Kant cited as an authority than the Declaration of Independence; nay, one is nearly certain to find the one and not the other.

But students of the founding era have for the most part abandoned the perspective of rights in favor of a very different focus on republicanism, the latter understood in terms of a special tradition of "civic humanism," traced by its discoverers back to the Italian Renaissance and thence to Aristotle. In this new light the Americans are seen not as political innovators, but as the last flowering of an old tradition, itself antimodernist in character.

We lose something important on both sides of this paradox. By excluding the founders from our reflections on rights, we forsake some potentially valuable guidance as we attempt to "take rights seriously." We need not believe that we are bound to follow the doctrine of rights held by the framers in order to see the value of looking to their thought on the question. At the very least it can provide us a view with strong roots in our traditions, and with a real embodiment in the Constitution. Equally important, the original doctrine raises a strong claim to philosophical adequacy.

We lose something historically also when we attempt to grasp the founding without central reference to rights. The fact is, rights were the dominant and central political focus for the thinking and acting that produced the Constitution. As Forrest McDonald said in his recent effort to refocus attention on rights, "Almost to a man, patriots were agreed that the proper ends of government were to protect people in their lives, liberty, and property."[1] This belief was surely held by the authors of The Federalist, who were willing to consider jettisoning republican government if it could not be made compatible with rights-securing.[2] The reverse was not the case.

Central as rights have been to the American political experience, the facts suggest that they have been ill-understood. Current controversies over "fundamental rights" in constitutional law and "human rights" in international relations, as well as the shyness historians show toward the idea, suggest intellectual anarchy and confusion. Although we continue to speak the language of rights, it has to some

138

degree become what Latin became to Catholic lay people or Hebrew to most American Jews. We say the words but are not quite certain of what they mean.

Some of the reasons for this perplexity can be laid at the feet of the founding generation; some are due to shifts in intellectual fashions since the founding. The founders, in their most visible presentation of rights, declared them to be "self-evident truths"; most twentieth-century Americans find this claim not only difficult to accept but hardly intelligible. This difficulty is closely bound up with the idea of rights as natural rights. That nature is the source of political standards, of right or rights, has itself become a difficult idea for modern Americans.

## Nature

The Americans of the founding generation appear to have shared none of the perplexity about rights characteristic of the twentieth century. Although, as James Madison said, the Americans had no precedent for the revolution they made, they nonetheless spoke with great confidence in the document that purported to explain and justify that revolution.[3] They rested their actions on truths they "held to be self-evident," and trusted that "a candid world," to say nothing of "divine providence," would respect the reasons for their actions. The very language and rhythms of the Declaration of Independence reinforce the impression of confidence—stately yet simple, firm and even passionate, yet not shrill. The confidence of its tone and the seriousness of its content have conspired to make it, in the words of an editor of Jefferson's works, "probably the best known [paper] that ever came from the pen of an individual."[4]

The Americans spoke with such authority, it seems, because they found warrant for what they did in the "ultimate realities" of God or nature. The rights on behalf of which they acted were the gifts of "the Creator," and "the laws of nature and of nature's God" permitted them to take a "separate and equal station among the powers of the earth." God and nature—not the uncertainties, ambiguities, and groundlessness of human laws or human history.[5]

Although the concision of the Declaration's pronouncements on these "ultimate realities" contributes to the document's air of quiet confidence, it also hinders comprehension of how the Declaration understands those "ultimate realities," and of how they in turn ground the political principles they are invoked to support. Since the Declaration was a political document, it could only deploy, not discuss the philosophical and theological ideas it invoked. Yet its author was a philosophically minded man, as well as a politician, whose only book was largely an attempt to explore those same ultimate realities appealed to in the Declaration.

Thomas Jefferson's *Notes on the State of Virginia* seems at first to be anything but a philosophical book. Both in origin and in ultimate form it presents a series of answers to the set of quite specific questions about Virginia posed to Jefferson (and to leading figures in the other new states) by François de Marbois, the secretary of the French legation in America. The topics covered were those raised by Marbois's questions, and those questions were quite pedestrian—about the geography, climate, products, inhabitants, and so on, of Virginia. As Merrill Peterson puts it, "viewed in one aspect, the *Notes on Virginia* was simply a glorified guidebook, descriptive, crammed with facts, informative on a broad range of subjects from cascades and caverns to weights and measures."[6]

But as Peterson also notes, that aspect does not exhaust the riches of the book; it is also "touched with philosophy."[7] More than that, it is philosophical, if not philosophy through and through. The *Notes* may have been a response to Marbois' questions, but there is much evidence that Jefferson reframed them for his own purposes. Jefferson even changed the number of questions around which he organized his essays, and he thoroughly reordered the whole.

> Marbois' twenty-two queries came to Jefferson's hand in a jumble. Questions on colonial laws and charters and the Constitution preceded questions of a geographical nature, for instance, and some questions combined incongruous subjects. Jefferson sorted and arranged the whole under twenty-three heads, the order proceeding from the natural through the civil to the generally social and moral.[8]

Peterson very well captured the principle of Jefferson's reordering: "He thought it important to begin with nature." It is in any case the distinction between the natural and the nonnatural that governs Jefferson's presentation. Marbois' questions look to be a "jumble" compared with Jefferson's order, because the diplomat's purpose was merely information-gathering; Jefferson's imposition of a theoretically informed order implies a purpose altogether different from a "glorified guidebook."

Although the topics covered are nominally governed by Marbois' queries, in the *Notes* Jefferson obtrusively digresses or wanders off into issues not obviously necessary to answer the questions under discussion. One such digression relevant to our concern for the Declaration's appeal to the "ultimate realities" of God and nature occurs in query VI: in the midst of a catalog of the minerals of Virginia, Jefferson launches a substantial discussion of shells or shell-fossils found far from the seashore, and even in the Andes—far from Virginia as well. Jefferson considers the question, certainly foreign to the spirit of Marbois' inquiries, of how shells came to such unlikely places.

The chief point of his interest in this question is clearly, if cautiously, put: the fact that shells have been found on mountain tops "is considered by many, both of the learned and the unlearned, as a proof of a universal deluge."[9] Jefferson is thinking of those who accepted the biblical account of the flood in the book of *Genesis*.

> And the waters prevailed so mightily upon the earth that all the high mountains under the whole heaven were covered; the waters prevailed above the mountains, covering them fifteen cubits deep.[10]

While showing that a "universal deluge" could not account for the presence of shells on mountains, Jefferson shows by a very ingenious argument that there could not have been a universal flood at all. There is not enough water in the whole heavens to cover the earth. Although a "universal deluge" could not have occurred, Jefferson thinks it quite likely that there were "partial deluges" in the Mediterranean region, which were probably the basis for Hebrew and Greek "traditions" about a flood.[11]

Jefferson thus demotes the Bible to the level of a "tradition," one with a character and authority no different from other ancient traditions. Like those other traditions, it is of questionable authority. The biblical account was based (at best) on an undisciplined inference from a partial experience, generalized beyond the bounds warranted by the experience itself into a claim that went beyond the bounds of natural possibility. And, Jefferson insists, natural possibility is all there is: the universal deluge is rejected because it would be "out of the laws of nature."[12]

The "laws of nature" are thus identical to the laws of nature's God.[13] There is no mode of divine action other than nature, and there is no mode of knowing God other than through nature. Jefferson underlines his rejection of the truth-revealing character of the Bible by entertaining another hypothesis regarding the placement of the shells, a hypothesis that "supposes" events to have occurred "in times anterior to the records either of history or tradition."[14] According to this hypothesis, the earth is much older than the Bible says and has a history of which the Bible knows nothing. Jefferson does not accept that particular hypothesis, but he does not reject the idea of prebiblical times. In sum, he approaches the Bible just as he would later advise the young Peter Carr to do: "Read the Bible then, as you would have read Livy or Tacitus."[15]

In accord with his understanding of the nature of divine action, Jefferson could not understand the creation in anything like the biblical manner. In a subsequent discussion Jefferson interchangeably speaks of "nature" and of "creation"; at first he says nature was responsible for the characters of the mammoth and the elephant, then he says it was the creator, and then nature once again. Only if nature *is* the creator does his apparently wavering language make sense. This helps make intelligible another Jeffersonian practice: he frequently spoke of the creation, but scarcely ever of God as the Creator.[16]

Jefferson's use of the term "Creator" thus does not signify a relapse into biblical or quasi-biblical conceptions. When he says in the Declaration that men "are endowed by their Creator" with certain inalienable rights he means, we now see, that nature or nature's God is the source of rights.[17] The inalienable rights are indeed natural rights.[18] Nor does a later and very important passage in the *Notes* derogate from that conclusion: "And can the liberties of a nation be thought secure when we have removed their only firm basis, a conviction in the minds of the people that these liberties are the gift of God?"[19] This later passage speaks of the convictions necessary in the minds of the people; it does not speak of Jefferson's own view of the origins of rights, of liberty, or of the character of God. The passage helps, however, to account for Jefferson's employment of the potentially misleading term "Creator" in the Declaration. If it has produced a misunderstanding, it is a misunderstanding he would have welcomed.[20]

The ultimate reality to which the Declaration appeals is nature. But what do we know of nature? And how does nature ground the political truths announced in the Declaration? *Notes on Virginia* constitutes a sustained meditation on these questions. As we have already seen, the book begins with the natural and is organized around the distinction between the natural and the nonnatural. That theme appears from the very outset of the book in the first query, on the boundaries of Virginia. As a physical entity, Virginia is in some sense a natural object. The land is the "natural body," the base for everything else, natural and nonnatural, that it contains. And yet even as a merely physical entity, Virginia is hardly natural. Its boundaries are in part natural boundaries, such as the Atlantic Ocean, but more frequently humanly drawn lines, such as that "which was marked by Messrs. Mason and Dixon."[21] And, he points out, all the boundaries, including the "natural ones," derive their existence as boundaries of

Virginia from legal actions such as ancient charters, compacts between the colonies, and treaties. Virginia as a physical entity is thus a complex intermixture of nature and artifice: nature cannot so readily be extricated from nonnature.

The character of the intermingling of nature and human artifice becomes clearer in Jefferson's treatment of the rivers of Virginia in the second query. He presents them above all in terms of their navigability, that is, in terms of their fitness for human commerce, travel, and exchange. Human purpose or use dominates. But what of the rivers in themselves? Are there any such things? What about nature not viewed in terms of human purposes?

Mountains, the subject of the next query, do not seem to be so useful; at least Jefferson forbears from presenting them in terms of their usefulness. Mountains do not appear to be raw material for human use in the same way rivers are. Here nature is more natural, belongs more to itself, is not appropriated for human purposes.

The mountain is not something to use, but rather presents something to see: it is, he says, "one of the most stupendous scenes in nature." The perspective Jefferson takes on the mountains is far more theoretical, in the original sense of a viewing rather than a doing or making, than is the account of rivers. Furthermore, the mountain scene suggests to his mind a geological (that is, nonbiblical) account of the history of the earth, and reveals "the most powerful agents of nature," the creating or making forces, and their astonishing power.[22] When all use is stripped away, nature stands revealed as an awesome array of forces. "This scene," Jefferson wistfully concludes, "is worth a voyage across the Atlantic." Yet even people who live very near to the scene do not come "to survey these monuments of a war between rivers and mountains, which must have shaken the earth itself to its center."[23] When people cross the Atlantic, it seems, they do so for reasons of use. Nature, which appears to reveal itself only to a more theoretical attitude, thus goes largely unknown.

But if nature is revealed only in the attitude of putting aside all question of human use, then how can nature be the source of guidance for human life? How can nature be the ground of natural right? The discussion of mountains cannot exhaust the problem of nature. In the next query, Jefferson turns to the natural bridge, "the most sublime of nature's works." He concedes that this discussion too is a digression—it is "not comprehended under the present head"—but nonetheless it "must not be pretermitted."[24]

Like the mountain scene from the previous query, the natural bridge also shows the signs of "some great convulsion," which has "determined" its chief features. The bridge results from natural forces, and yet it is, or can be taken to be, a bridge, a product "made" by nature that resembles a product made by human beings for human use. The bridge stands between the natural and the human and connects them.[25]

The bridge is remarkable because it combines two very different views. One experiences the bridge from its top, looking over its edge; and one experiences it from the bottom looking up. Here is Jefferson's description of the view from the top:

> Though the sides of this bridge are provided in some parts with a parapet of fixed rocks, yet few men have resolution to walk to them, and look over the abyss. You involuntarily fall on your hands and feet, creep to the parapet and peep over it. Looking down from this height about a minute, gave me a violent headache.

But the view from beneath is entirely different:

> If the view from the top be painful and intolerable, that from below is delightful in an equal extreme. It is impossible for the emotions arising from the sublime to be felt beyond what they are here; so beautiful an arch, so elevated, so light, and springing as it were up to heaven! The rapture of the spectator is really indescribable![26]

One stands before this passage almost with the same sensation as Jefferson stood atop the bridge. Something dangerous and unexpected comes to light here; something complex and difficult as well. Nature reveals itself in two guises. From the top of the bridge she is "painful and intolerable," from below, "delightful." It takes great "resolution" to look nature in the face from the top; from beneath, the spectator is in "indescribable rapture." Can there be two such truths about nature?

Jefferson presents two perspectives on nature, one high, one low. Or better, one looking down and one looking up. The truly decisive difference between the two, however, lies in the different situation of the spectator. In the one case he is exposed, vulnerable. The danger is so great that Jefferson reacts in a most extreme manner—the involuntary falling onto hands and feet, the creeping to the edge, the violent headache. He experiences his—or humanity's—radical exposedness. Just as in the mountains, nature lies before him as a blind, cold, and cataclysmic force. But in the mountains he sees evidence of those forces at work in the distant past and far away. He does not feel the threat of nature. Here atop the bridge there is a more immediate vulnerability to great uncaring forces.

Jefferson becomes dizzy at the prospect of nature so understood.[27] He emphasizes the exposedness: he first speaks generally of "men," then of the more personal but still indefinite "you," but finally of "me." It is one of the very few moments in this very scientific book when Jefferson as unique individual allows himself to be caught sight of. In the experience of facing his exposed situation in nature, Jefferson is most emphatically an individual. That experience breaks through all disinterest, every merely aesthetic attitude. He reacts to the natural bridge as does Pascal's *libertin* to nature as conceived in the new science: "The eternal silence of these infinite spaces terrifies me."[28] For Pascal, as for Jefferson, it is the same "me." The bridge, unlike the mountain of the preceding query, once again juxtaposes nature with human concerns but not, like the rivers, as an object of use. The bridge reveals the limits of human domination and use of nature. From the perspective of human insecurity, the bridge shows the terrors of nature.

Beneath the bridge is security. From the perception of security achieved or promised, the bridge appears to soar toward heaven and testify to providence. This purely natural entity presents a form, an arch, that men produce in their own makings, and the intelligibility of which they discover in their mathematics. Beneath the bridge stands not the "I," but once again the impersonal "spectator," who can afford to indulge himself in an intensely aesthetic reaction, which converges with a moral and religious experience as well. Beneath the bridge, man, nature, and heaven are all joined in a beneficent harmony.

Jefferson's quest for nature gives him double vision. There is no "nature-in-itself," for the truth of nature varies with the perspective— secure or insecure—of the investigator. Nature must inevitably be juxtaposed with the human concern for security—all-knowing is, after all, human-knowing. Jefferson's perspectivism therefore is not Nietzschean. There are but two, rather than indefinitely many perspectives, and they are related to each other in a definite way. They do not throw nature into doubt, but rather rest on or ground it.

The human drive for security, that which orients the two human perspectives, is itself natural.[29] Human beings, too, are part of the natural kingdom. The natural bridge proves to be a bridge to nature not so much because it uncovers nature-in-itself, but because it uncovers the natural ground for what Jefferson saw as a necessary and a true, bifurcated grasp of nature. Security as the natural ground provides the rationale and ultimate justification for a utilitarian orientation toward nature.[30]

Beneath the bridge is the source of the rational theology that Jefferson from time to time propounded, very little in *Notes on Virginia*, but at greater length in some of his correspondence. Probably the best example is contained in an 1823 letter to John Adams.

> I hold (without appeal to revelation) that when we take a view of the universe, in its parts general or particular, it is impossible for the human mind not to perceive and feel a conviction of design, consummate skill and indefinite power in every atom of its composition. The movements of the heavenly bodies, so exactly held in their courses by the balance of centrifugal and centripetal forces . . . , it is impossible, I say, for the human mind not to believe that there is, in all this, design, cause and effect, up to an ultimate cause.[31]

This passage, I believe, expresses exactly what Jefferson means when he says of the arch of the rational bridge that it "springs as it were up to heaven." A natural theology of order and final causes, of intelligence and purpose, is the truth from beneath the bridge.

But that truth coexists with the other truth, the top-of-the-bridge view of nature. Jefferson does not present so detailed and explicit a statement of this alternative perspective, but he supplies many indications that the natural theological view from beneath the bridge is not the exclusive truth.[32] The natural theological "proof" he gives depends on the claim that "it is impossible for the human mind not to perceive and feel a conviction of design, consummate skill, and indefinite powers. . . . It is impossible . . . for the human mind not to believe that there is in all this, design, cause and effect, up to an ultimate cause."

But Jefferson knew very well of groups of thinkers whose minds found no such impossibilities. In an earlier letter to Adams he had spoken of "the school of Diderot, D'Alembert, D'Holbach," which accepted a "system of atheism." These atheists "agreed" with theists "in the order of the existing system," but drew different conclusions about the source of that order. These atheists "supposed" the order of nature "from eternity," rather than "having begun in time." They "descanted on the unceasing motion and circulation of matter thro' the animal vegetable and mineral kingdoms, never resting, never annihilated, always changing form, and under all forms gifted with the power of reproduction."[33]

It cannot, therefore, be an "impossibility," strictly speaking, for the human mind to fail to conceive of Jefferson's rational God and deistic system of nature. Perhaps it would be more accurate to say that the human mind can scarcely help but entertain such a hypothesis and that it cannot definitely disprove the hypothesis—or its atheistic counterthesis.[34] This paradox is but another way to state what Jefferson conveys in his parable of the natural bridge—that there exist two irreducible perspectives, and a thoughtful person stands undecided before them. A yet more thoughtful person, perhaps, affirms the deeper truth beneath the two: the point of reference for both is the human drive for security, and nature (or the universe) presents itself in these two guises as security is promised or threatened. Jefferson is not quite the Enlightenment rationalist he is most often taken to be.

## Human Nature

Human beings first come into view in the *Notes* not so much as part of nature but as knowers of nature; Jefferson shares the perspective of modern, or post-Cartesian philosophy, which is not a surprising conclusion, given his "trinity of the three greatest men that have ever lived, without any exceptions"—Bacon, Locke, and Newton.[35] But what comes into view about human beings as knowers is the determinative character of their security-seeking. All animals, perhaps all nature, seek their own survival; only human beings seek *security*, the reasonable confidence in the prospect for survival and the allaying of the anxieties arising from threats to existence. The truths uncovered in the discussion of the natural bridge necessitate a more particular discussion of human beings as a special species of natural being.

Jefferson begins that discussion in query VI, on natural productions: human beings too can be seen among nature's productions or creations. It is obviously a very important discussion for our purposes, because it contains the first mention in the *Notes* of two themes central to the Declaration of Independence—natural equality and rights.[36] Jefferson himself emphasizes the importance of the discussion when he suggests that it will vindicate "the honor of human nature."[37]

Human nature required vindication from the slur cast upon it by the French naturalist, Comte de Buffon. Buffon aroused Jefferson's indignation with his assertions about the unfriendliness of nature in America to "the production and development of large quadrupeds"; and of men as well.[38] Jefferson considered Buffon's theories an insult not merely to America; according to his own testimony, it would be the honor of human nature rather than of America that would chiefly benefit from his rebuttal of Buffon.[39]

The core of Buffon's position, as identified by Jefferson, is that "*heat* is friendly, and moisture adverse" to animal development.[40] The relative lack of heat and the surplus of humidity in America manifest themselves first and foremost in the deficient sexual powers of those human beings native to America. Buffon's chain of reasoning is tight and far reaching: adverse climate produces lowered sexual capacity, which produces lower sexual interest; since sexual drives appear to be the root of both individual energy and sociability, the Indian shows little of either individual or social development. As Jefferson quotes the great naturalist: "This indifference to the other sex is the fundamental defect which weakens their nature, prevents its development, and—destroying the very germs of life—uproots society at the same time."[41]

Buffon had insulted human nature, for he had made it a reflex of climate and sexual drive, two subhuman forces. Jefferson vindicates human nature by showing that Buffon's description of the Indians is quite mistaken factually and that his explanation for what he finds is quite misguided.[42] Jefferson observes that the Indians are affectionate, even indulgent toward their children, and that in general their affections operate just as do those of Europeans. The Indian "is neither more defective in ardor nor more impotent with his female, than the white reduced to the same diet and exercise."[43] The Indians have fewer children than whites not for Buffon's reasons, but because of "circumstances." Their way of life makes childbearing "inconvenient," planting "obstacles . . . of want and hazard." When these obstacles are removed, they produce as many children as the Europeans.

Jefferson thus rejects both of the chief links in Buffon's deterministic explanation. The sexual characteristics of the Indians do not derive from climate, but from "way of life." And their other qualities do not, in turn, derive from their lack of "sexual ardor," but either from nature or, again, from way of life, or circumstances. Jefferson vindicates the honor of human nature in large part by showing that nature is directly responsible for much less about human existence than Buffon had said. Nature operates on human beings not so mechanistically, but via human adaptation to circumstances.

Like Buffon, Jefferson was indeed an environmentalist, in the sense that he thought environment had a tremendous influence on mankind, but he saw it operating in a very different way.[44] For Buffon, nature in the form of climate acted directly, physiologically, and mechanistically on human beings, making them a part of nature and the chain of natural cause no different from other parts of nature. For Jefferson, nature or environment operates on humanity through human intelligence, via the more or less conscious adaptation of ways of life in rational response to circumstance. Human nature is for him much less fixed, much more flexible and variable, much more human and intelligent than Buffon had thought. Buffon, one might say, had a top-of-the-bridge view only.

Jefferson's discussion of the Indians provides the occasion for considering human nature, or more broadly, what nature supplies to human beings. The Indians were as close to nature or natural man as Jefferson thought he could get. Yet even here, the line between nature and "education" is very obscure. He found himself unable to distinguish between the roles of nature and education in the production of some important Indian practices.[45] Obscure and remote as pure nature remained, the Indians nonetheless seemed to provide insights into the natural truths about politics. According to Jefferson's account, they live in the condition the philosophers had called the state of nature. They have "never submitted themselves to any laws, any coercive power, any shadow of government."[46] This way of life corresponds precisely to the state of nature, as defined by John Locke, Jefferson's philosophic authority on "the general principles of liberty and the rights of man, in nature and in society."

> Those who are united into one body and have a common established law and judicature to appeal to, with authority to decide controversies between them and punish offenders, are in civil society one with another; but those who have no such common appeal, I mean on earth, are still in the state of nature.[47]

For Jefferson the state of nature is prepolitical but not necessarily presocial. In place of law, government, and coercion, the Indians live under control of "their manners, and that moral sense of right and wrong, which, like the sense of tasting and feeling, in every man makes a part of his nature."[48] Life in the state of nature is thus governed by a complex amalgam of nature and manners. Nature does not supply government, but she supplies a guide for human life, the moral sense. But even in the state of nature, nature does not serve as sole guide: manners or customs too play their part, and these are certainly not entirely natural. As Jefferson insists in his attack on Buffon's environmental determinism, human beings are rational and conscious creatures and their ways of life show the marks of these qualities. This conviction is perhaps why Jefferson believed he never could reach a state of pure nature, it being the nature of human beings always to add something to their strictly natural endowment, and why he tended to eschew the terminology of the state of nature.[49]

In crucial respects, however, the guidance supplied by nature is inadequate. That inadequacy appears most clearly in Jefferson's discussion of the "unjust drudgery" to which Indian women are subjected.

149

> This I believe is the case with every barbarous people. With
> such force is law. The stronger sex therefore imposes on the
> weaker.[50]

Nature may provide the moral sense, but that is insufficient to produce just or moral social relations. The rule among peoples most exclusively dependent on the moral sense (and on nature) is force.

Jefferson is led to draw a most paradoxical conclusion: "It is civilization alone which *replaces* women in the enjoyment of their natural
equality."[51] The state of the Indians obviously is not a pure state of
nature, for Jefferson measures their condition against a yet more pri-
mordial one in which, he insists, all human beings, emphatically including women (*pace* contemporary feminists), were truly equal. The
Indians lack government, but their life does not fully embody the
original natural equality. There can be subjection to forces other than
governments. Only further progress away from nature and into civilization can bring a return to natural equality. Civilization is thus in
one sense at least a restoration of a purer natural condition.

Civilization restores the natural situation because it "first teaches
us to subdue the selfish passions, and to respect those rights in others
which we value in ourselves."[52] The moral sense fails because the
"selfish passions" overpower it. Again, here is a bifocal view of nature's endowment for humanity: in accord with the view from beneath the bridge, the moral sense; from above, the selfish passions.
But the two aspects of nature are quite unequal here. The view from
the top is more powerful, even dominant.

The taming of the selfish passions occurs not through an unvar-
nished or even a strengthened moral sense, but through the discovery of rights. Rights appear to replace the moral sense as a more effective source of just social relations. As opposed to the moral sense,
which operates directly like any other sense, rights require some sophisticated figuring out. That is why rights operate in civilized and
not in barbarous conditions. Both the moral sense and the system of
rights counter the natural selfish passions, but the system of rights
makes peace with these passions in a way the moral sense does not.
Like the moral sense, the system of rights leads to consideration of
others; but it also allows people to consider themselves, and even
builds on that consideration. We come "to respect those rights in others which we value in ourselves."

The moral sense is deficient in at least two ways: practically, as a
motive to moral action, and epistemologically, as a source of moral
knowledge. Jefferson addresses the first insufficiency explicitly in the
*Notes on Virginia*. It is tempting to understand Jefferson's discussion in

terms of a hard and fast distinction between the practical and the epistemological: the moral sense is a faculty only for knowing or perceiving, not for doing. Thus it is easily overpowered by the selfish passions, which provide the motives for action. An analogy from the sphere of the senses may make the point clearer: the senses of taste and smell allow human beings to identify (within limits) some substances as food and others as not food, but the senses supply neither the ability to acquire the food so identified nor the practical motive to do so. One could imagine a being with the power to discriminate agreeable from disagreeable tastes or smells, but lacking hunger, with no particular impulsion to eat.[53] Jefferson's picture of the natural endowment for humanity is thus complex. On the one side, nature supplies the moral sense, which points to the moral course of action; on the other side, however, are the selfish passions, which point elsewhere, and are far the stronger. Despite the very un-Hobbesian moral sense, Jefferson could nonetheless conclude this world was a *"bellum omnium in omnia"*—a war of all against all.[54]

The moral sense fails to a degree in its epistemological function, also: the good varies from time to time and from place to place; the moral sense does not reveal the good action or the good social practice in itself. The moral sense sets up benevolence as the standard, a general "love of others, and a sense of duty to them."[55] But which specific actions embody benevolence, or genuinely benefit others, remains an open question. The moral sense allows for error: witness the Indians who reduce their women to drudgery, and claim this to be right. The moral sense is ineffective not only in producing moral action but also in articulating valid moral standards.[56]

The system of rights corrects or replaces the moral sense in both respects. With their intimate ties to the passions, rights are more effective than the moral sense; but rights also supply the specific standards of political action, of justice, as the moral sense does not. The moral sense does not entirely disappear from the scene, but it functions as a supplemental support to the system of rights.

Rights as Jefferson understood them make for sociability, for they contain within themselves an accommodation to the claims of others and a tempering of the selfish passions that set human beings against one another. Rights thus understood may be natural, but they derive from nature in a human rather than in a mechanistic manner. The system of rights does not involve a mechanism of causation like Buffon's, which ignores the source of human dignity, the capacity for rational and conscious action. The system of natural rights thus accords more fully with the honor of human nature than does even the vaunted moral sense.[57] Natural rights, as opposed to the moral sense, are compatible with both perspectives on nature that come to sight from the natural bridge. As claims justly raised by all, they are appropriately seen as an endowment from the Creator, and thus part of the perspective from beneath the bridge. As responses to and modifications of the selfish passions, they comport with the view from the top of the bridge.[58]

## Natural Rights

Jefferson's presentation of natural rights in the *Notes* is remarkably concise, and thus it imposes on the reader a formidable task of interpretation. The brevity of his statement does not imply that his understanding of the nature of rights was in any sense underdeveloped. Like much in the *Notes* it is understated; but on examination it bears the marks of having been very carefully thought through.

As we have already seen, nature, ironically, is not unequivocally the home of natural rights. Nature is home to "the selfish passions," and to "rights . . . we value in ourselves." At a later stage, a civilized stage, we learn to "respect those rights in others which we value in ourselves." Jefferson thus had in mind three entities: selfish passions, the initial rights, and the later rights. In order to keep these entities disentangled, I propose to refer to the first kind of rights as proto-rights and the second as rights-in-the-proper-sense. The reasons for this particular terminology should become clear as the discussion progresses.

In the first instance, rights are claims that each of us is inclined to raise on his own behalf, that is, claims based on the selfish passions that are nature's first legacy. The core of the selfish passions derives from the force Jefferson uncovered at the natural bridge: the natural drive to self-preservation in its human form, the natural drive to security. Driven by the desire for security rather than the desire for mere preservation, human beings are far more selfish and contentious than other animals.

> In truth I do not recollect in all the animal kingdom a single species but man which is eternally and systematically engaged in the destruction of its own species. . . . Lions and tigers are lambs compared with man as a destroyer.[59]

From this natural drive initially arise proto-rights. That these proto-rights are less than rights-in-the-proper-sense is apparent from their consistency with rule on the basis of force, or the rule of the selfish passions. This consistency falls far short of the situation Jefferson sought, rule based on "a right independent of force."[60] The selfish passions are scarcely distinguishable from the proto-rights, for proto-rights are also selfish in origin, rooted in the quest for individual security. Proto-rights are the selfish passions, decreed rightful. That those who are strong enough to indulge their selfish passions should so decree them is less intriguing than the fact that Jefferson at least partially endorses their doing so: in the *Notes* he says that they come to accept rights in others that they value in themselves. Thus, they claim and Jefferson accepts their claim to rights prior to the recognition of similar rights in others.

Proto-rights fall short of rights-in-the-proper-sense in two respects: no duty correlates to them, and they are not tailored to the security-seeking that is their actual and legitimate origin. Prior to the stage of mutual recognition of rights there can be only rights-assertions, with no reciprocal duties attached to the rights. The original proto-rights are thus more or less the same as Hobbes's right of nature—the right of every man to everything. Since each person has a right to everything, no person has an obligation to respect any right of another. It is a frequently contested question within political philosophy whether a right of this sort, a right with no correlative duty, is a right-in-the-proper-sense. We need not settle that question in order to proceed, however, for Jefferson clearly saw a difference between the situation where proto-rights are asserted and that where rights are mutually recognized. In the latter case, the rule of rights is both more universal and more secure.

Moreover, the selfish passions do not stop or perfectly align themselves with the means of security, but are, so to speak, imperialistic. That imperialistic tendency of the selfish passions is on the one hand checked by the moral sense, mainly a sense of compassion for others. But as we have seen, this check is decisively ineffectual. The selfish passions are, on the other hand, fostered and encouraged by human intellectual errors. Although they are part of a natural order, driven to seek their security, human beings nevertheless participate in that order via intelligence and choice. Prior to the emergence of "science," they are driven by a nature they do not understand. Their errors, coupled with the natural drives, produce distortions in the natural drives, for human beings posit a false but effective nature or God. Under the influence of such ideas, some people come to accept a right by nature to indulge their selfish passions; more remarkably, others come to accept "chains," or even come to see themselves as "born with saddles on their backs," and recognize "a favored few booted and spurred, ready to ride them legitimately, by the grace of God."[61]

These proto-rights, defective as they are, derive so far as they are rights at all from the law of nature, which impels human beings to their own security. Such a law is, in the first instance, an amoral law, expressing the necessity of nature. Rights, as Jefferson says elsewhere, are "founded in our natural wants."[62] When right-in-the-proper-sense arises it remains rooted in "natural wants," or in those claims that are made "for the relief of sensibilities made a part of . . . nature."[63]

Rights-in-the-proper-sense arise when human beings come to recognize a need for reciprocity in rights, when human beings recognize that to claim a right for oneself requires accepting the same right in others. That system of mutual recognition constitutes the system of natural duties correlative with natural rights. Human beings must recognize "the similar rights of other sensible beings."[64]

But why must they do so? The whole system of proto-rights serves security-seeking, but in fact it is very defective in that respect. It is obviously defective for those whose rights are not respected: that is, for those who are subjected to the rule of unrightful force. But it is unsuccessful even for those who rule. They deny the rights of some, of those they subject, and "monkish ignorance and superstition" may encourage some of the oppressed to accept or partly accept their oppression. Nonetheless, nature prompts the oppressed to seek their security also, to assert themselves in the face of their oppression. Their erroneous opinions can mask the rule of nature in them only so far. Thus the rule of the oppressors is always insecure.

Likewise the oppressors suffer from insecurity vis-à-vis each other. They raise claims to more than security—to domination. Their claims inevitably conflict not only with the oppressed, but with the claims of other oppressors as well. The rulers in such a system suffer insecurity not only from below, or vertically, but horizontally as well. Human history under the aegis of proto-rights is a history of rebellion and civil war. It is not a history of human security. Human security is promised when the drive for security and the rights derivative therefrom are recognized for all, when the oppressed are raised up and the oppressors scale back their claims.[65]

Thus the rights-in-the-proper-sense that replace proto-rights are greater than the latter in at least two ways. First, they are mutually recognized, and thus acquire a genuine moral quality. As recognized claims, they become rights with duties reciprocal to them. To recognize the other's claim as a right is to recognize in oneself, and others, a duty. No such reciprocity of right (or claim) and duty precedes that; only selfish claims. Nevertheless, rights do not derive from duties, as many contemporary scholars would have it; the duties derive from the rights, or better yet, they are co-constituted with rights in the process of mutual recognition.[66]

Moreover, not every claim that an individual might be inclined to raise on his or her own behalf can be eligible to become a right-in-the-proper-sense. Not every such claim can reasonably be expected to achieve mutual acceptance by all others. The kinds of "rights" to dominate others, for example, that barbarous peoples claim are not likely to win universal acceptance. One can then reverse the Jeffersonian formula: we value those rights in ourselves that we respect in others and expect them to respect in us.

Rights-in-the-proper-sense derive from a relatively complex process of mutual recognition and transformation. Can they really be considered natural rights? It would seem not. What derive from nature are the selfish passions, which in themselves produce only selfish claims, not yet full rights; what transforms the claims of the passions into rights is the "civilized" figuring out of the system of mutual respect for rights, a figuring out no doubt aided by the existence of civilized institutions like government and law, which lend practical effectiveness to the mutual recognition. One might be tempted to adopt the Kantian formula of "rational rights" rather than "natural rights."

Yet Jefferson himself in the Declaration of Independence traced these rights to the Creator—that is, nature. Recalling what Jefferson discovered at the heart of nature in his discussion of the natural bridge may help us to see how he understood rights to be natural. The core of nature is the human drive for security; the core of rights is the same. The recognition of rights, of mutual claims to security, is the system that both serves and ultimately (but not directly) derives from that same natural drive. A rational or civilized figuring out may intervene, but the natural drive for security guides and grounds that process at every stage. In this quite meaningful sense, the rights thus arrived at are indeed natural rights.

The process of mutual recognition is furthered to the degree that human beings become properly self-conscious about the basis for their rights claims. When they recognize that security-seeking is the basis of rights, they can not only become more rationally calculating with regard to the means for the achievement of security; they also pose to themselves the question of why other security-seeking, "sensible" beings do not possess the same rights. If security-seeking is the decisive title to rights, then they are driven by the mere force of reason to recognize that same title in others. Thus the mutual recognition of rights becomes something more than a mere matter of calculation; it becomes a rational principle that is "undeniable," and it becomes a matter of conscientious conviction. Certainly for a man like Jefferson himself the recognition of rights stood on this footing. At the same time, the evolution of the system of mutual recognition of rights gives greater play to the moral sense, or natural compassion and benevolence toward fellow human beings. So far as one's own security is part of a system of mutual security, the conflicts between self and others that allowed the selfish passions to overwhelm the other-regarding feelings are muted. Ironically, the moral sense can come most into its own once it has been supplemented by the system of rights and government.[67]

In *Notes on Virginia* Jefferson sketches only the nature of rights in general; he does not pause to derive or list specific natural rights. Of course, in the Declaration of Independence he has already specified rights to life, liberty, and pursuit of happiness. But that list is not complete, for the three rights listed are said to be "among" the rights with which men were endowed by their Creator. The treatment of rights in the Declaration is incomplete in yet another respect: it treats the claims about rights (and other propositions about the fundamentals of politics) as "self-evident truths," and it therefore contains no discussions of the basis for affirming these three rights as rights, or for understanding what other rights there may be.[68] But Jefferson presented a fuller discussion of the nature of specific rights in an important letter to his good friend Pierre Samuel Du Pont de Nemours in 1816, which remedies some of this incompleteness.

In that letter, Jefferson presents a slightly different list of rights from the one offered in the Declaration: he specifically mentions a right to property and he describes another right that appears to be equivalent to the Declaration's right to liberty. He does not specify either a right to life or a right to the pursuit of happiness.[69]

The difference between the two lists does not imply any inconsistency between them, however; neither claims to be exhaustive, and nothing said in either place explicitly or implicitly denies anything said in the other—unless we follow the line of argument taken by some scholars, that Jefferson's failure to include the right to property in the Declaration amounts to a rejection of that right. Jefferson's own testimony points to a very different answer: the two lists are to be added together. That approach would mean, in effect, that the right to property would be added as a fourth right to the list in the Declaration. No firm reason suggests that these four are an all-inclusive list of the natural rights, of course. But they provide a good beginning for understanding the nature of specific rights.

## The Right to Life

Both the natural-rights tradition and Jefferson's Declaration of Independence give pride of place to the right to life. The 1816 statement does not explicitly identify such a right, but it does so implicitly. The right to property, Jefferson says, "is founded in our natural wants."[70] Our natural wants, understood here in the eighteenth-century sense of a lack that is at once a need and a desire, ground the right to property, and, a fortiori, ground the right to life.

The right to life easily and readily flows from the general description of rights in *Notes*. The natural ground is precisely the drive for security, which is but an extended form of the desire for preservation; the right to life, a "selfish passion," a "right we value for ourselves"— this claim appears as a proto-right. It can also be easily redefined as a right-in-the-proper-sense. The right to life is the kind of claim that is restrained enough to be universally and unanimously adopted; it is the kind of claim, in other words, that can satisfy the requirements of mutual recognition. Each person can recognize the right to life of others, in return for recognition of his or her own right.

The right to life can be a right-in-the-proper-sense, however, only if it is what some would call a negative or liberty right, as opposed to a positive or claim right. The difference between the two types of rights is simple. The duty correlative to a negative right is merely negative—it is the duty to forbear from interfering with the exercise of the right. The duty correlative to a positive right is more active—it demands that the duty-bearer supply that to which the right's holder has a right. An example of each can help clarify the distinction. The right a person has to the funds in his or her bank account is a positive right, because the duty-bearer, the bank, has an obligation to supply those funds when they are properly applied for. The right to freedom of speech, however, is a negative right, for the duty-bearers in this case have no obligation to supply the right-holder with a speech to deliver, nor even to listen to a speech. Their obligation extends only to forbearing from interfering with valid exercises of the right.

Only a negative right to life can pass the test for becoming a right-in-the-proper-sense. Persons may raise a proto-right-claim to a positive right to life, or rather the means to life; there can never, strictly speaking, be a duty in another to supply life, as that is beyond human powers. But a positive right to life will not win mutual assent: it amounts to a blank-check demand on one's own life and liberty that a rational being would not accept. While human beings are not simply selfish or entirely indifferent to others, they nonetheless are moved most powerfully by self-love, and love of their own.[71] The system of rights counters the ill-effects of the selfish passions, but it is effective precisely because it builds on them. Moreover, no person who understands property the way Jefferson did would accept a positive right to life.

## The Right to Property

The first and to many the most striking feature of Jefferson's letter to Du Pont de Nemours is the fact that it asserts, clearly and distinctly, a right to property: "I believe that a right to property is founded in our natural wants, in the means with which we are endowed to satisfy these wants, and the right to what we acquire by those means."[72] Jefferson's affirmation of a right to property, not unique to this place, runs counter to a current scholarly consensus resting on his modification in the Declaration of the famous Lockean triad of "life, liberty, and property" to "life, liberty, and the pursuit of happiness."[73] As Richard Matthews puts it:

> Jefferson rejects the traditional Lockean triad of "life, liberty, and estate." The omission is significant. While Locke views property as a natural right and its accumulation as the fulfillment of human endeavors, Jefferson does not. Jefferson's vision of man and of man's telos is much grander.[74]

But Jefferson did not consider the substitution of the pursuit of happiness for the right to property in the Declaration to imply a rejection of the latter. Indeed, if we consult some of the parallel statements of the day, we see how implausible is the claim that the affirmation of the right to the pursuit of happiness in itself amounts to a rejection of the right to property. Prior to the Declaration, George Mason had written in the Virginia Bill of Rights of "certain inherent rights" human beings possess by nature, "Namely the enjoyment of life and liberty, with the means of acquiring and possessing property and pursuing and obtaining happiness and safety."[75] In the Massachusetts Bill of Rights, the "natural, essential, and inalienable rights" are said to include "the right of enjoying and defending their lives and liberties; that of acquiring, possessing, and protecting property; in fine, that of seeking and obtaining their safety and happiness."[76]

In the letter to Du Pont de Nemours, Jefferson stated quite precisely the origin of the right to property: it is in the service of our right to satisfy our natural wants or needs. The right to property is grounded in the right to life, but it marks an important and problematic extension of the latter. The right to life is a right to what is most clearly our own, but the right to property is a right to the external world. This right affirms, in effect, that the external world can become one's own (juridically), just as one's life is. The right to property is thus inherently paradoxical. Jefferson answered this concern along the same lines Locke did. Human beings cannot do without some sort of property in that they must appropriate, make entirely their own, parts of the external world in order to live. The basic metabolism of existence is the first ground of property.[77] Jefferson, concludes Charles Miller, "is surely close to Locke" in his theory of the origin of property.[78]

Yet only human beings have property and a right to property in the strict sense, although all living beings appropriate parts of the external world. Moreover, human beings turn other animals, and even other sensible beings, into property.[79] Humans do not merely share natural wants with other living beings, but are, says Jefferson, "endowed" with certain "means . . . to satisfy those wants." The human means are different and unique. It is equivalent to the difference between the drive for security that impels humans and the desire for preservation that impels other animals. Humans consciously understand their mortality and their vulnerability, and thus consciously shape their world so as to guarantee their survival. Humans project their insecurity into the future. The pervasive rather than intermittent sense of insecurity produces the more or less steady pursuit of security. Human beings thus labor for the sake of the security they seek. As they have a right to life, they have a right to this unique human means to secure that right, a right to the fruits of their labor, and a right to the wherewithal upon which to labor. Thus from the natural right to life arises a natural right to property. Jefferson no less strongly affirms this than did Locke himself.

Driven by their desire for security, human beings invest their labor in the external world. Labor is an investment of what is clearly one's own in that which is not. Labor is also painful; no one would invest it without promise of reward in the form of a right to its fruits, a "right to what we acquire by these means." The investment of labor is necessary not merely because human beings seek security, but because nature of her own accord does not produce enough to satisfy human wants. "A little land cultivated, and a little labor, will procure more provisions than the most successful hunt; and a woman will clothe more by spinning and weaving clothes than by hunting."[80]

Property is thus both instrumental to human life and expressive of the fundamental character of human being. The relation between life, property (the external world), and labor confirms the argument presented in the previous section regarding the right to life as a negative right. Human beings who understand the relationship as Jefferson did would only affirm a negative right to life, for life requires external goods, which in turn require labor—that is, painful interaction with the external world. A positive right to the means of life would not be accepted by all, for it would blur responsibility for labor and would threaten to put one's own labor and the fruits thereof at the service of others indiscriminately. Not merely would this be unacceptable in itself, but a rational person would discern that such a right would undermine the very incentive to labor and thereby discourage the activity that makes life more secure. Paradoxically, therefore, a positive right to life would make life generally less rather than more secure.[81]

## The Right to Liberty

Jefferson likewise affirmed a right to liberty: "No one has a right to obstruct another, exercising his faculties innocently for the relief of sensibilities made a part of his nature."[82] Again the source is nature. The natural right to liberty is both a broader right than the natural right to property and a narrower one. It is broader in that it arises not merely from "natural wants," but from "natural sensibilities." Sensibility is a difficult word in the Jefferson lexicon, but it surely is broad enough to encompass wants or needs, at the same time that it encompasses more. The right to liberty is a right to the means of satisfying needs as well as other "natural sensibilities"—"instincts of liking or aversion" (OED). An example might be tastes or likings, or other pursuits that are not, strictly speaking, pursuits of needs, such as the sensibility for beauty in art or for chocolate in ice cream. As long as those pursuits are innocent, that is, not infringing on rights of others, then there is a right to them, "without hindrance." The right to liberty is an all-things-equal guarantee of freedom of choice and action, without necessary reference to need.

The right to liberty is also narrower than the right to property in that it concerns the actions of the individual, "the exercise of his faculties," and not the appropriation of a part of the external world. To appropriate a part of the external world is to raise a claim to make something one's own, which is surely more problematic than the claim to exercise what is more clearly one's own—one's faculties.

The right to liberty as a right-in-the-proper-sense thus contains within it a tacit reference to the rights of others. As a natural right, a right responding to the promptings of nature, the right to liberty is, of course, an inalienable right. But the right only extends so far as it remains innocent. In a state of nature, where there is no known law or government to draw firm lines establishing where the rights of one end and the rights of another begin, there must be self-definition—self-limitation and self-defense of rights. Under such circumstances disagreement will arise over these boundary lines; and this disagreement alone would make a system of rights without government and law a very inconvenient thing. Some relatively neutral party is needed to judge which exercises of liberty are truly innocent and which not. The government and laws that do this do not restrict or infringe the inalienable right to liberty, but rather define what counts as innocent exercise of one's faculties, which is all the inalienable liberty-right-in-the-proper-sense amounts to anyway.

The Declaration implicitly retains a distinction between legitimate and illegitimate liberty, but the distinction rests solely on whether the parallel liberties and rights of others are invaded. The inherent value or quality of the exercise of liberty is not otherwise a factor in the judgment of whether we are in the presence of a genuine liberty-right or not. In this sense the Declaration clearly articulates a liberal conception of politics and morals.

The rights to life, liberty, and property thus complement each other and form a kind of system. The grounding right is the first, but it is productive of the other two because human beings are part of nature in a unique way, such that the right to life necessarily broadens out to a larger concern for security on the one hand and sensibility on the other. The latter leads to a right to liberty that is not strictly limited to the means to life, but is limited to the use of one's own faculties. The former broadens out to the use and appropriation of the external world. So there is a certain completeness to the triad of life, liberty, and property, which is no doubt responsible for its near pervasiveness in rights-thinking.

### The Right to the Pursuit of Happiness

But what then is the right to the pursuit of happiness? Forrest McDonald recently concluded that the introduction of the pursuit of happiness into the Declaration implied the superposition of an Aristotelian doctrine—happiness—on what was an otherwise Lockean "enthusiasm for natural law." He based this conclusion on the assertion that the source for the idea may have been Burlamaqui, who, "it seems evident," was "the first eighteenth-century philosopher to have developed the idea."[83]

The "pursuit of happiness," however, is a Lockean idea, and it was extensively developed in Locke's *Essay Concerning Human Understanding*, a work that even the most devoted anti-Lockeans, such as

161

Wills, concede was important to Jefferson. According to Locke, all animals seek pleasure and attempt to avoid pain, but human beings alone develop a notion of happiness as such that goes beyond the mere satisfaction of individual desires. The idea of happiness rather "consists in the idea of the enjoyment of pleasure without any considerable mixture of uneasiness."[84] The idea of happiness frees human beings from subjection to individual desires, but they remain emphatically subject to the desire for happiness itself. "Happiness . . . everyone constantly pursues and desires what makes any part of it."[85] Locke emphasized the pursuit rather than the achievement of happiness, for it is a goal that can never be achieved in this life. All happiness is temporary, every satisfaction soon followed by a new unease by which "we are set afresh on work in the pursuit of happiness."[86]

At the same time, Locke used his conception of the pursuit of happiness to give an account and justification "for the various and contrary ways men take, though all aim at being happy."[87] All pursue happiness, but the specific things they pursue necessarily and legitimately vary. Happiness, or its pursuit, stands as the comprehensive object of action within a human life; human beings are unalterably or necessarily directed to this pursuit by their nature.[88] Such is the nature of rights. Even though human beings are doomed to frustration in their pursuit of the ever elusive happiness, they are nevertheless unalterably committed to it. And because different people pursue different visions or objects of happiness, freedom or tolerance necessarily characterizes a society that attempts to live according to the guidance of nature as Locke described it in his doctrine of happiness.

The affirmation of a right to the pursuit of happiness in the Declaration seems to involve a commitment to this notion of a comprehensive yet individually variable object of universal human desire and action. It is an appropriate right to add to the list, for it serves as a kind of summation of all the aspirations and strivings that are expressed in the other rights.[89] Recall that John Adams concluded his list of the natural rights in the Massachusetts constitution as follows: "In fine, that of seeking and obtaining their safety and happiness." Ronald Hamowy captures very well the summative and variable quality of happiness in the Declaration:

> They may act as they choose in their search for ease, comfort, felicity, and grace, either by owning property or not, by accumulating wealth or distributing it, by opting for material success or asceticism, in a word, by determining the path of their own earthly and heavenly salvation as they alone see fit.[90]

The right to pursue happiness, like the rights to property and liberty, derives from the special way in which human beings fit into nature. The idea of happiness, originating in the unique capacity of the human mind to form general ideas, moves human beings to a place within the chain of natural causation altogether peculiar to them. It supplies them with freedom, or the nearest thing to free will that is attainable. It removes them from the chain of stimulus and response to which other animals are bound, and gives human beings the capacity to stand above the particular stimuli they encounter, and to form a life with some shape or other. The idea of happiness does not remove human beings from the natural chain of causation—they are as determined to that pursuit as other animals are to particular stimuli. Yet as a comprehensive, although variable, end of action, happiness stands at a remove from the passion for survival that grounds the right to life. The right to life is constituted by reference to a passion of antipathy, antipathy to death; in Hobbes's language it is a "from-ward" right. Happiness, on the other hand, is a "to-ward" right, a goal or end to be sought, not merely a fate to be fled. Between these two kinds of rights stands the right to liberty, which partakes to a degree of both impulses. As a right, it is constituted by its service as a means to the preservation of life. But it also betokens the human quest "to-ward," the human transcendence of mere survival as an end. Liberty is thus a most comprehensive right. As it often did for writers of the founding generation, it can stand as a shorthand expression for all the rights.

### Civil Rights and Political Imperatives— Some Implications of Natural Rights

It is easy to fall into confusion over the nature and number of rights, for the Americans spoke of a bewildering number of rights deriving from a great variety of sources. The recent efforts of John Phillip Reid to identify both the rights and their sources has been extremely helpful to all students of the revolutionary period, but his treatment suffers from failing sufficiently to distinguish natural from other rights, with the result that he underestimates the significance of natural rights for the Americans. "The revolutionary controversy," says Reid, "was concerned with positive constitutional right, not abstract natural rights."[91] This essay is not the place to survey the role of natural-rights thinking in the revolutionary controversies, but here I must attempt to lay out some conceptual matters that are indispensable for understanding the revolutionary era discussions of rights.

Natural rights are rights human beings possess prior to, that is, independent of, all government. Thus, not only is government not the source of the rights, but the rights do not concern government; they are rights that individuals hold in the first instance vis-à-vis other individuals.[92] When government is instituted, however, a new situation arises.

The institution of government creates a new kind of entity against which rights hold—namely, government itself. Government can threaten rights, indeed can be a particularly potent threat against rights, for it possesses the organized coercive power of the community. How to protect the people in their natural rights against government became one of the master questions of the political philosophy of rights and one of the major issues of contention during the founding era.

That question cannot be adequately approached, however, unless a yet more fundamental feature is recognized: with the institution of government a whole new class of rights emerges, not so much from nature itself as from the nature of the formation of government, from the universal consent or agreement that institutes government. The individuals, or citizens, have a new right—the civil right to protection in their natural rights. This right, although not natural, is in principle universal, once it is recognized what the purpose of government is.

In addition to not deriving directly from nature as the natural rights do, this fundamental civil right differs from the natural rights in several other important ways. The duty-bearer in this case is not another individual, but the new collectivity, the state, brought into existence or rationalized by the "social contract." Second, this right, unlike the natural rights, is a claim or positive right. The duty borne by the state is precisely to supply that to which the individuals possess a right—protection by the state. For reasons of justice and safety, protection is to take the primary form of protection by laws. Thus as a first consequence of the making or rationalizing of the state, individuals acquire a right to protection of the laws. Such a right is strictly reciprocal with a duty of allegiance in the citizens. John Adams captured this point exceedingly well in the debates culminating in the resolution to break with Britain.

> That, as to the king, we had been bound to him by Allegiance, but this bond was now dissolved by his assent to the last act of Parliament, by which he declares us out of his protection, and by his levying war on us, a fact which had long ago proved us out of his protection; it being a certain position in law, that allegiance and protection are reciprocal, the one ceasing when the other is withdrawn.[93]

164

The state's duty to supply protection of the laws is not satisfied by any mere act of forbearance, as the other duties correlative with the natural rights may be. This duty requires positive acts of supplying protection in order to be fulfilled.

Thus, with the institution of government, two new major rights or sets of rights arise: the right to protection by the state, and the right to protection from the state. These rights are the primary civil rights of citizens or persons under the jurisdiction of a government.[94] The two rights are more frequently expressed in a constitutional context as the right to protection of the laws and the right to due process of the law, respectively. Each of these large civil rights implies or is constituted by a cluster of more particular rights, which provide specific ways in which these rights are secured to the individual. These rights also are civil rights, but not generally so universal as their "parent" civil rights; the latter are so universal that they could (and sometimes were) said to be natural rights. The more particular rights may vary somewhat from one political society to another; trial by jury may be considered a necessary part of the right to due process of law in some places, but other means of impartial trial may be accepted elsewhere. As Reid makes clear, the early Americans for the most part clung to the specification of these rights as they had evolved within the English common law and the British constitution.[95]

The two chief civil rights of citizens point in two quite different directions, and thus render the task of governance both complex and difficult. In *Federalist* 51, James Madison gives the nonlegalistic formulation of the two political imperatives corresponding to the two fundamental civil rights:

> In framing a government which is to be administered by men over men, the great difficulty lies in this: you must first enable the government to control the governed; and in the next place oblige it to control itself.[96]

These political requirements correspond to the legalistic formulation of the right to protection of the laws and the right to due process of law, respectively. The legalistic formulations of the rights do not suffice, for the mere declaration of rights does not entail their security. The task of securing the basic civil rights transforms itself into a task of politically constructing a government that is strong and active enough to control the governed in the pursuit of supplying security of rights through protection of the laws, and that is also sufficiently controlled to secure rights without infringing upon them. Thus the founders' constitutional science is a form of political science far more than it is a form of constitutional law.[97] Nonetheless, that political science retains the most intimate links with the doctrine of rights, natural and civil: a doctrine whose importance goes beyond explicit reference to rights, for it shaped the very task of political construction.

# Appendix I: On Reading Jefferson

Almost the only proposition that most readers of Jefferson can agree to is that he was either very confused or very eclectic. I do not mean to deny either of these altogether, but systematic reflection on how Jefferson wrote, and therefore on how he should be read, helps to diminish the appearance of confusion a good deal. Jefferson seems to have followed a principle in his own writing that he discovered in one of his early intellectual heroes, Bolingbroke. Of the latter he once wrote:

> His political tracts are safe reading for the most timid religionist, his philosophical, for those who are not afraid to trust their reason with discussions of right and wrong.[98]

Jefferson firmly believed that certain things were properly said in some places and others not. That principle surely must be recalled when considering his most public, that is, his political writings; but it ought also to be kept in mind when considering the great variety of different things Jefferson said on moral and political topics in his voluminous correspondence. It made a difference to him whether his correspondent was a "timid religionist" or a "philosopher"—or one of the innumerable human types between those two poles.

Jefferson's writings fall into three main classes: public writings and sayings, undertaken by him in his political capacity and addressed to the community at large; private writings, mostly correspondence, addressed to a particular person; and his one book, *Notes on Virginia*, submitted like his political statements to the public at large, but submitted not in his public capacity.

The audiences differ and the modes of writing differ accordingly. Jefferson's public writings are most like the "political tracts" of Bolingbroke, which he praised as not offending even "the most timid religionist." It is well known that Jefferson frequently wrote in private correspondence to others of how much he hesitated to have his religious views become public.[99] His public presentations were certainly colored as well by his view that a healthy nation requires "the conviction in the minds of the people that [their] liberties are the gift of God."[100]

His private writings, upon which we are dependent for his views on so many subjects, present their own problems; for all were written to a specific person and very much tailored to that person. A particularly striking example is his correspondence with John Adams and with John Taylor, concerning the latter's attack in print on the former. With Adams, Jefferson commiserated: "I hope your quiet is not to be affected at this day by the rudeness of intemperance of scribblers."[101] To Taylor he wrote: "I found here the copy of your [book] for which I pray you to accept my thanks. . . . You have successfully and completely pulverized Mr. Adams' system of orders."[102]

167

In the private correspondence it is not only Jefferson's concern for sound public opinion at work, but rather tact and good taste, as well as a strong dislike for unnecessary personal conflict. One sees these qualities throughout Jefferson's life: he sought peace, harmony, and easy social relations whenever possible. When personal rifts occurred, as for example with Adams, he almost always made it a point to restore good feelings. Jefferson's great sense of tact is perhaps nowhere more visible than in his longstanding relationship with Madison. Few men have been such close friends over so long a time while disagreeing so much about the fundamentals of the pursuit, politics, to which both devoted their lives.

Throughout his private writings Jefferson displayed an astonishing tendency to be agreeable to his correspondent. Thomas Law, for example, sent him his book on the moral sense, and Jefferson replied that "it contained exactly my own creed on the foundation of morality in man." [103] William Short wrote him about Epicurus and Jefferson replied: "As you say of yourself, I too am an Epicurean." [104] Jefferson chose always to emphasize areas of agreement, and to say as much as he felt able of what his interlocutor wanted to hear. He himself expressed this policy in one of those pieces of advice he gave about life:

> In stating the prudential rules for our government in society, I must not omit the important one of never entering into dispute or argument with another. I never saw an instance of one of two disputants convincing the other by argument. [105]

These qualities of his private writings make for much of the confusion that scholars find in him. They also imply that the correspondence must be interpreted with great caution. It must and can be cited, but only with thoughtful analysis, including consideration of the recipient. For a striking case of Jefferson's accommodations, see his letter to John Adams of March 14, 1820. [106]

*Notes on Virginia* comes closest to the "philosophic tracts" of Bolingbroke, which Jefferson considered suited "for those who are not afraid to trust their reason with discussions of right and wrong." Since others also may pick up one of these tracts, they must be written with a bit of subtlety, as is *Notes on Virginia*. Nonetheless, by Jefferson's standard, *Notes* bears a specially privileged status among his writings; I have so approached this, his only book.

## Appendix II: Natural Rights and the Moral Sense

The account of the origin of rights presented here differs entirely from the well-known statement in Garry Wills's *Inventing America*. Wills traces Jefferson's position on rights back to the Scottish philosopher, Francis Hutcheson, who according to Wills derived rights directly from the moral sense. "Right was the exercise of the moral sense in some way that affected the lives of others for general good."[107] In so doing, however, Wills fails to bring into focus the distinction between right and rights. From the perspective of a moral-sense theory, it is true, "exercise of the moral sense in some way that affected the lives of others for general good" would be right, could indeed be the very definition of right. But the language of rights came about as a means of saying something different from mere rightness; as one contemporary legal theorist puts it: "Rights-talk is in part a way of talking about discretionary devices—about what one may or may not decline to do as distinct from what one ought or ought not to do.[108]

In addition to his insensitivity to the conceptual distinction between right and rights, Wills's discussion suffers from some fatal historical deficiencies. First, he discusses Hutcheson lengthily on rights, but he makes only the thinnest connection to Jefferson. Wills presents no evidence other than Jefferson's use of the term "inalienable" to establish his claim that Jefferson understood rights as he says Hutcheson did. The notion of inalienable rights is not sufficiently Hutchesonian for that purpose. Even Hobbes identified some rights as inalienable, and the entire thrust of Locke's liberal version of rights-theory rests on an acceptance of inalienability.[109]

More important, Wills entirely ignores the crucial discussion of rights in *Notes on Virginia*. There Jefferson, as we have seen, clearly presents rights as a kind of substitute for a more direct natural ordering to justice through the moral sense. And Jefferson is clear that reasoning, or figuring out, intervenes in the recognition of rights. Wills thus makes many claims about rights that run counter to Jefferson's discussion. Rights, Wills claims, build entirely on the nonselfish moral sense, and not at all on self-interest. To quote Wills, "The moral sense was directed to others—it was the principle of sociability, of benevolence, not selfishness. No politics built upon the moral sense could make self-interest the foundation of the social contract."[110]

But as we have seen, rights are indeed built up from the selfish passions, transformed into or restricted to the desire for security, and mutually recognized. The morality of rights is not a morality of self-love, but it is a morality that begins with and builds upon self-love. Rights supply a more effective means to achieve security, justice, and equality for all than the moral sense does, for the latter alone is swamped by the selfish passions, while the system of rights enlists those very passions. In this sense Jefferson's system of rights incorporates both the above- and below-the-bridge perspectives on nature.

# Notes

## Chapter 1: Introduction

1. "A Nauseous Project," *The Wilson Quarterly,* Winter 1991, p. 57.

## Chapter 2: Democratic Instrument or Democratic Obstacle?

1. Thomas Jefferson, cited in Richard K. Matthews, *The Radical Politics of Thomas Jefferson* (Lawrence, Kans.: University Press of Kansas, 1984), p. 78.

2. James Madison (1821), "Note to Speech on the Right to Suffrage," Saul K. Padover, *The Complete Madison* (New York: Harper, 1953), p. 40.

3. Jean Jacques Rousseau, *The Social Contract,* Book 2, chapter 2.

4. James Madison, *The Tree of Liberty: A Documentary History of Rebellion and Political Crime in America,* eds. N. N. Kittrie and E. D. Wedlock, Jr. (Baltimore, Md.: The Johns Hopkins University Press, 1986), p. 76.

5. E. Stanton, S. Anthony, and M. Gage, eds., "The Declaration of Sentiments and Resolutions of the First Women's Rights Conference," *History of Woman Suffrage* (New York: Fowler & Wells, 1881), pp. 170–73.

6. William Lloyd Garrison, in W. Garrison and F. Garrison, *William Lloyd Garrison: 1805–1879* (New York: Arno Press, 1969), p. 408.

7. L. Buchanan, *John Brown: The Making of a Revolutionary* (New York: Grosset & Dunlop, 1969), pp. 119–20.

8. 80 U.S. 19 (how.) 393. 400–54 (1857).

9. Madison, *Federalist* 54.

10. James Madison to Frances Wright, Sept. 1, 1825, *Letters and Other Writings,* vol. 3, p. 495.

11. See the unpublished working paper by Amitai Etzioni entitled "Too Many Rights, Too Few Responsibilities," Autumn, 1989, and Roger L. Conner, "Individual Rights Are Just Part of the Cocktail," *Wall Street Journal,* December 29, 1989, and the occasional publications of the American Alliance for Rights and Responsibilities.

12. Cited in the *New York Times,* April 20, 1990.

13. Proposition 111, passed by 52% of the vote in June, 1990, allows the state gasoline tax to double over the next five years to pay for repairing and expanding the highway system.

## CHAPTER 3: THE STRUCTURE OF THE GOVERNMENT

1. James Madison, *Federalist* 51, in *The Federalist Papers*, ed. Clinton Rossiter (New York: New American Library, 1961), p. 322, emphasis added.

2. Madison, *Federalist* 39, p. 241.

3. Madison, *Federalist* 10, p. 78.

4. Ibid., p. 84.

5. John Locke, *The Second Treatise of Government* (New York: Bobbs-Merrill, 1952), p. 75.

6. Alexis de Tocqueville, *Democracy in America*, vol. 1 (New York: Vintage Books, 1945), p. 168.

7. Hamilton, *Federalist* 31, p. 193.

8. Madison, *Federalist* 10, p. 79.

9. Ibid., p. 83.

10. Ibid., p. 78. Emphasis is added.

11. Martin Diamond, "The American Idea of Man: The View from the Founding," *The Americans 1976*, vol. 2, eds. Irving Kristol and Paul Weaver (Lexington, Mass.: Lexington Books, 1976), pp. 1–23.

12. Madison, *Federalist* 51, p. 324.

13. Ibid., emphasis added.

14. James Burnham, *Congress and the American Tradition* (Chicago, Ill.: Regnery, 1959), pp. 327–28.

15. Madison, *Federalist* 51, p. 325.

16. Diamond, "The American Idea of Man," pp. 1–23.

17. Madison, *Federalist* 51, p. 322.

18. Madison, *Federalist* 48, p. 309.

19. Judith A. Best, "The Item Veto: Would the Founders Approve?" *Presidential Studies Quarterly*, vol. XIV, no. 2 (Spring, 1984), pp. 183–88.

20. Hamilton, *Federalist* 73, p. 443.

21. James Madison, *Debates in the Federal Convention of 1787*, vol. 2, eds. Gaillard Hunt and James Brown Scott (Buffalo, N.Y.: Prometheus Books, 1987), pp. 405–07.

22. Madison, *Federalist* 51, p. 323.

23. Ibid.

24. Hamilton, *Federalist* 15, p. 106, emphasis added.

25. Ibid., p. 110.

26. Madison, *Debates*, vol. 1, p. 28.

27. Locke, *Second Treatise*, p. 4.

28. Ibid., p. 5.

29. Hamilton, *Federalist* 70, p. 423.

30. Clinton Rossiter, *American Presidency* (New York: New American Library, 1962), p. 13.

31. Madison, *Debates*, vol. 2, p. 282.

32. Locke, *Second Treatise*, p. 92.

33. Madison, *Debates*, vol. 2, p. 272.

34. Ibid., p. 282, statement of Morris.

35. John Philpot Curran, "Speech Upon the Right of Election of Lord Mayor of Dublin," July 10, 1790.

36. Madison, *Federalist* 55, p. 346.

## CHAPTER 4: Madison Proposes Amendments

1. Robert A. Rutland, "How the Constitution Protects Our Rights: A Look at the Seminal Years," in *How Does the Constitution Secure Rights?* ed. Robert A. Goldwin and William A. Schambra (Washington, D.C.: American Enterprise Institute, 1985), p. 3.

2. James Madison, Letter to Thomas Jefferson, October 17, 1788, *Writings of James Madison*, vol. 5 (New York: G.P. Putnam & Sons, 1904), pp. 269–275.

3. Except as noted, the citations in this section are taken from Schwartz, *The Roots*, vol. 5, pp. 1024–26.

4. Ralph A. Rossum, "*The Federalist*'s Understanding of the Constitution as a Bill of Rights," in *Saving the Revolution*, ed. Charles R. Kesler (New York: The Free Press, 1987), pp. 219–233.

5. For example, Madison's proposal dealing with excessive bail, now the Eighth Amendment, was unaltered as it passed through five stages of consideration: "Excessive bail shall not be required, nor excessive fines imposed, nor cruel and unusual punishments inflicted." An example of a Madisonian proposal that received slight modification is, "No soldier shall in time of peace be quartered in any house without the consent of the owner, nor at any time, but in a manner warranted by law." The final form, now the Third Amendment, was, "No soldier shall, in time of peace be quartered in any house, without the consent of the owner, nor in time of war, but in a manner to be prescribed by law." What is now the Ninth Amendment was proposed in these words: "The exceptions here or elsewhere in the constitution, made in favor of particular rights, shall not be construed as to diminish the just importance of other rights, retained by the people, or as to enlarge the powers delegated by the constitution; but either as actual limitations of such powers, or as inserted merely for greater caution." It was completely reworded as follows: "The enumeration in the Constitution, of certain rights, shall not be construed to deny or disparage others retained by the people."

6. Except as noted, all citations in this section are taken from Schwartz, *The Roots*, vol. 5, pp. 1026–28.

7. Herbert J. Storing, "The Constitution and the Bill of Rights," in *How Does the Constitution Secure Rights?* eds. Robert A. Goldwin and William A. Schambra (Washington, D.C.: American Enterprise Institute, 1985), p. 22.

8. This heading is almost always printed as if part of the Constitution, but there is a question whether it should be printed as such since it was not voted on and ratified by the states during the ratification process.

9. See Robert A. Goldwin, *Why Blacks, Women, and Jews Are Not Mentioned in the Constitution* (Washington, D.C.: AEI Press, 1990), pp. 4, 70–71, 89–90.

10. *Popular Sources of Political Authority: Documents of the Massachusetts Consti-*

*tution of 1780,* eds. Oscar and Mary Handlin (Cambridge, Mass.: Belknap Press of Harvard University, 1966), pp. 442–47.

11. "To promote their happiness and to secure the good order and preservation of their government, the people of this Commonwealth have a right to invest their legislature with power to authorize and require, and the legislature shall, from time to time, authorize and require, the several towns, parishes, precincts, and other bodies-politic, or religious societies, to make suitable provision, at their own expense, for the institution of the public worship of God, and for the support and maintenance of public protestant teachers of piety, religion and morality, in all cases where such provision shall not be made voluntarily."

"And every denomination of christians, demeaning themselves peaceably, and as good subjects of the Commonwealth, shall be equally under the protection of the law: And no subordination of any one sect or denomination to another shall ever be established by law." Ibid., pp. 442–3.

12. "That the people have a right to keep and bear arms: that a well regulated militia composed of the body of the people trained to arms, is the proper, natural and safe defence of a free state. That standing armies in time of peace are dangerous to liberty, and therefore ought to be avoided, as far as the circumstances and protection of the community will admit; and that in all cases, the military should be under strict subordination to and governed by the civil authority." Form of Ratification, which was read and agreed to by the Convention of Virginia, 17th Amendment. *The Ratification of the New Federal Constitution* (Richmond: Aug. Davis, 1788), p.20.

13. Schwartz, *The Roots,* vol. 4, p. 844.

14. Ibid., p. 843.

15. "Virginia Senators to the Governor of Virginia," September 28, 1789, ibid., vol.5, p. 1186.

16. "Virginia Senators to the Speaker of the House of Representatives in Virginia," September 28, 1789, ibid., p. 1187.

17. Hardin Burnley to Madison, November 28, 1789, ibid., p. 1188.

18. Ibid., p. 1105.

19. Ibid., pp. 1090–1103.

20. The motion to include "to instruct their representatives" was first raised by Thomas Tucker of South Carolina on August 15, 1789, during the debates of the Committee of the Whole. The Senate took up the question again on September 2, 1789.

21. On August 18th Thomas Tucker's motion to add the word "expressly" ("the powers not expressly delegated") to the reserved powers provision was defeated. On August 21, Elbridge Gerry's motion to amend the article in the same fashion was defeated. On September 7, in the Senate, the same motion was made and defeated.

22. Walter Berns, "The Meaning of the Tenth Amendment," in *A Nation of States,* ed. Robert A. Goldwin (Chicago: Rand McNally & Co., 1961), pp. 126–48.

23. All of the citations in this section are taken from Schwartz, *The Roots,* vol. 5, pp. 1026–33.

## CHAPTER 5: CONSTITUTION AND "FUNDAMENTAL RIGHTS"

1. Jackson v. Rosenbaum Co., 260 U.S. 22, 31 (1922).

2. Article I, section 9, provides:

> The Migration or Importation of such Persons as any of the States now existing shall think proper to admit, shall not be prohibited by the Congress prior to the Year one thousand eight hundred and eight, but a Tax or duty may be imposed on such Importation, not exceeding ten dollars for each Person.
>
> The Privilege of the Writ of Habeas Corpus shall not be suspended, unless when in Cases of Rebellion or Invasion the public Safety may require it.
>
> No Bill of Attainder or ex post facto law shall be passed.
>
> No Capitation, or other direct, Tax shall be laid, unless in Proportion to the Census or Enumeration herein before directed to be taken.
>
> No Tax or Duty shall be laid on Articles exported from any State.
>
> No Preference shall be given by any Regulation of Commerce or Revenue to the Ports of one State over those of another; nor shall Vessels bound to, or from, one State, be obligated to enter, clear or pay Duties in another.
>
> No Money shall be drawn from the Treasury, but in Consequence of Appropriations made by Law; and a regular Statement and Account of the Receipts and Expenditures of all public Money shall be published from time to time.
>
> No Title of Nobility shall be granted by the United States: And no Person holding any Office of Profit or Trust under them, shall, without the Consent of the Congress, accept of any present, Emolument, Office, or Title, of any kind whatever, from any King, Prince or foreign State.

Article I, section 10, provides:

> No State shall enter into any Treaty, Alliance, or Confederation; grant Letters of Marque and Reprisal; coin Money; emit Bills of Credit; make any Thing but gold and silver Coin a Tender in Payment of Debts; pass any Bill of Attainder, ex post facto Law, or Law impairing the Obligation of Contracts, or grant any Title of Nobility.
>
> No State shall, without the Consent of the Congress, lay any Imposts or Duties on Imports or Exports, except what may be absolutely necessary for executing its inspection Laws: and the net Produce of all Duties and Imposts, laid by any State on Imports or Exports, shall be for the Use of the Treasury of the United States; and all such Laws shall be subject to the Revision and Controul of the Congress.
>
> No State shall, without the Consent of Congress, lay any Duty of Tonnage, keep Troops, or Ships of War in time of Peace, enter into any Agreement or Compact with another State, or with a foreign Power, or engage in War, unless actually invaded, or in such imminent Danger as will not admit of delay.

3. Article III provides in part:

Section 2. . . . The Trial of all Crimes, except in Cases of Impeachment, shall be by Jury; and such Trial shall be held in the State where the said Crimes shall have been committed; but when not committed within any State, the Trial shall be at such Place or Places as the Congress may by Law have directed.

Section 3. Treason against the United States, shall consist only in levying War against them, or in adhering to their Enemies, giving them Aid and Comfort. No Person shall be convicted of Treason unless on the Testimony of two Witnesses to the same overt Act, or on Confession in open Court.

The Congress shall have Power to declare the Punishment of Treason, but no Attainder of Treason shall work Corruption of Blood, or Forfeiture except during the Life of the Person attainted.

4. Article IV, section 2, provides in part:

The Citizens of each State shall be entitled to all Privileges and Immunities of Citizens in the several States.

5. 7 Pet. (32 U.S.) 249 (1873).

6. Ibid.

7. See Robert M. Kaus, "Abolish the Fifth Amendment," *Washington Monthly*, Dec. 1980, pp. 12–19.

8. Miranda v. Arizona, 384 U.S. 436 (1966).

9. Mapp v. Ohio, 367 U.S. 643 (1961).

10. Gideon v. Wainright, 372 U.S. 335 (1963).

11. See Leonard Levy, *Legacy of Suppression* (Cambridge, Mass.: Belknap Press of Harvard University, 1960).

12. Schad v. Mt. Ephraim, 452 U.S. 61 (1981); but see Barnes v. Glen Theatre, Inc., 59 *Law Week* 4745 (June 21, 1991). Although deemed protected speech, totally nude dancing is subject to public indedency law.

13. Memoirs v. Massachusetts, 383 U.S. 413 (1966).

14. Cohen v. California, 403 U.S. 15 (1971).

15. United States v. Eichmann, 110 S. Ct. 2404 (1990).

16. Young v. New York City Transit Authority, 729 F.Supp. 341 (S.D. N.Y.), *rev'd in part, vacated in part*, 903 F. 2d 146 (2d Cir. 1990).

17. Wallace v. Jaffree, 472 U.S. 38 (1985).

18. State v. Graham, 449 U.S. 39 (1980).

19. County of Allegheny v. American Civil Liberties Union, 493 U.S.—, 109 S. Ct. 3086 (1989).

20. Sherbert v. Verner, 374 U.S. 398 (1963).

21. See Sanford Levinson, "The Embarrassing Second Amendment," *Yale Law Journal*, vol. 99 (1989), p. 637.

22. Hawaii Housing Authority v. Midkiff, 467 U.S. 229 (1984).

23. Nollan v. California Coastal Comm'n, 483 U.S. 825 (1987).

24. See Walter J. Suthon, Jr., "The Dubious Origin of the Fourteenth Amendment," *Tulane Law Review,* vol. 28 (1953), p. 22.

25. See Charles Fairman, *Reconstruction and Reunion 1864–88* (New York: Macmillan Co., 1971).

26. Harper v. Virginia Board of Elections, 383 U.S. 663 (1966).

27. See Lochner v. New York, 198 U.S. 45 (1905).

28. For an extended and detailed demonstration of this proposition, see Lino Graglia, *Disaster by Decree: The Supreme Court Decisions on Race and the Schools* (Ithaca, N.Y.: Cornell University Press, 1976).

29. Brown v. Allen, 344 U.S. 443, 540 (1953) (dissenting opinion).

30. See Frank Easterbrook, "Substance and Due Process," *1982 Sup. Ct. Rev.*, 85.

31. See Allgeyer v. Louisiana, 165 U.S. 578 (1897).

32. West Coast Hotel Co. v. Parrish, 300 U.S. 379 (1937).

33. A minor exception was Morey v. Doud, 354 U.S. 457 (1957), overruled in New Orleans v. Dukes, 427 U.S. 297 (1976).

34. Ferguson v. Skrupa, 372 U.S. 726 (1963).

35. 347 U.S. 483 (1954).

36. Graham v. Richardson, 403 U.S. 365 (1971) (alienage); Levy v. Louisiana, 391 U.S. 68 (1968) (legitimacy); Craig v. Boren, 429 U.S. 190 (1976) (sex).

37. Goldberg v. Kelly, 397 U.S. 254 (1970).

38. Green v. County School Board, 391 U.S. 430 (1958); Swann v. Charlotte-Mecklenburg Bd. of Educ., 402 U.S. 1 (1971).

39. 381 U.S. 479 (1965).

40. 410 U.S. 113 (1973).

41. Engel v. Vitale, 370 U.S. 421 (1962); Abington School District v. Schempp, 374 U.S. 203 (1963).

42. U.S. Constitution, Amendment V, Amendment XIV, section 1.

## Chapter 6: Republicanism and Rights

1. *Federalist* 14, in *The Federalist Papers*, ed. Clinton Rossiter (New York: New American Library, 1961), p. 100. The present discussion grows out of my treatment of the moral and political theory informing the founding in my *Spirit of Modern Republicanism* (Chicago: University of Chicago Press, 1988).

2. Thomas Hobbes, *Leviathan*, ed. Michael Oakeshott (Oxford: Basil Blackwell, 1960), chaps. 19, 29, 30, 46; pp. 122–25, 214, 216–18, 221–22, 447–48; *The Citizen*, ed. Bernard Gert (Gloucester, Mass.: Peter Smith, 1978), Epistle Dedicatory, p. 89.

3. *The Complete Anti-Federalist*, Herbert J. Storing, ed., seven vols. (Chicago, Ill.: University of Chicago Press, 1981), vol. 5, pp. 105–6, 233–34.

4. *The Records of the Federal Convention of 1787*, Max Farrand, ed., four vols. (New Haven, Conn.: Yale University Press, 1966), vol. 1, pp. 288–89, 424.

5. *Federalist* 9, pp. 71–73.

6. The account of the original meaning of the clause in W. Wiecek, *The Guarantee Clause of the U. S. Constitution* (Ithaca, N.Y.: Cornell University Press, 1972) wavers unsatisfactorily between the author's awareness of the considerable although by no means perfect precision and consensus of the founding generation's conception of republicanism, and his wish to clear the way for a judicial activism, based on the notion of "protean forms" in the Constitution and an "open-ended intent." Wiecek admits that "Federalists

and Antifederalists agreed on the desirability of republican government . . . and they agreed on its basic characteristics"; he quotes the passages in which Madison and others defined with some precision "republican government"; but he asserts, without citing any evidence, that "despite the authority" of Madison, these passages do not express "precisely the elements of republican government assured by the guarantee clause." On the contrary, Wiecek proclaims without evidence that it was the intention of the framers to give "an open-ended *command* to posterity that each succeeding generation define anew the character of republican government. . . . The ambiguity of the word 'guarantee' and the phrase 'republican form of government' was so great that they, like the clause itself, were *blank checks* to posterity" (pp. 5, 17–18, 24, 27, 72–73, 75, 242; my italics).

7. *Federalist* 39, p. 241.

8. Montesquieu, *Spirit of the Laws*, Book 2, chapter 1. My translation from the French.

9. Aristotle, *Politics*, 1280a7–1281a7.

10. Ibid., 1279a23–b10.

11. See ibid., 1276b18–1278b5.

12. *Laws*, 756e–758a; see also Aristotle, *Politics*, 1281a23–38; Isocrates, *Areopagiticus*, 21–22, 60–63, 69–70.

13. Plato, *Apology of Socrates*, 30b, and *Laws*, 631b–d; Aristotle, *Nicomachean Ethics*, Book 1.

14. The most profound and delightful introduction to the difficulties is Xenophon's *Education of Cyrus*. See also Plato, *Laws*, 627a–d, 638a–b, 706a, 707d, 770e, 936b.

15. Aristotle, *Nicomachean Ethics*, 1179b–end.

16. Plato, *Laws*, 631d–632c, 643e–645c, 653a–657b, and above all, 875a–d; Aristotle, *Nicomachean Ethics*, Book 2; Isocrates, *Areopagiticus*, 14, 40; Xenophon, *Education of Cyrus*, Book 1, chapter 2; Thucydides, Book 7, section 86 at the end.

17. "Defence of the Constitutions of Government of the United States of America," in *The Founders' Constitution*, eds. Philip B. Kurland and Ralph Lerner, five vols. (Chicago, Ill.: University of Chicago Press, 1987), vol. 1, p. 119.

18. Plato, *Laws*, 708b–724b; *Republic*, 427b–c; Xenophon, *Oeconomicus*, chapters 5–7, 11, 21; Aristotle, *Politics*, 1262a25–35, 1328b11–13, 1329a27–33.

19. Xenophon, *Oeconomicus*, chapters 6–7, 11–12; *Apology of Socrates to the Jury*, sections 5–9; Plato, *Republic*, Books 6–7; *Laws*, 803c–804b, 961a–969d; Aristotle, *Nicomachean Ethics*, 1152b1–3, 1177a12–1179a33; *Politics*, 1323a14–1325b31.

20. Plato, *Republic*, 487b–502c, 517d–521b, 549c–d; *Laws*, 803c–804b, 886c–894a, 967b–c; Xenophon, *Memorabilia*, Book 1, chapter 1 and Book 4, chapter 6; Aristotle, *Politics*, 1269a20–22; Thomas Aquinas, *Summa Theologica*, I–II, question 97, article 2.

21. Niccolò Machiavelli, *Discourses on the First Ten Books of Titus Livius*, Book 1, Introduction, beginning; John Locke, *Essays on the Law of Nature*, ed. W. von Leyden (Oxford: Clarendon Press, 1954), p. 206; this Lockean echo of Machiavelli was first pointed out by Leo Strauss: see "Locke's Doctrine of Natural

Law," in *What Is Political Philosophy?* (Glencoe, Ill.: The Free Press, 1959), p. 218.

22. See especially *Leviathan*, pp. 465–67.

23. See especially John Locke, *Two Treatises of Government*, Book 1, section 58; *Some Thoughts Concerning Education*, sections 103–105, 110, 119; *Essay Concerning Human Understanding*, Book 1, chapter 3, sections 3, 9, 13.

24. Algernon Sidney, *Discourses Concerning Government* (New York: Arno Press, 1979 reprint of 1698 ed.), chapter 1, sections 10, 13, 16, pp. 24, 29, 38–39.

25. See especially *Federalist* 1, 2, 14, 39, 52, 84; pp. 35, 38, 104, 240, 329, 353, 514.

## CHAPTER 7: *THE FEDERALIST* AND FUNDAMENTAL RIGHTS

1. The latter two stages occurred after the adoption of the Constitution, and strictly speaking the authors of *The Federalist*, considered as a corporate group, did not participate in these two stages. My discussion of the Bill of Rights and the Ninth Amendment works out what seems to me the logic of those provisions within the scheme developed in *The Federalist*.

2. See Mark Tushnet, "Constitutional Interpretation and Judicial Selection: A View from *The Federalist Papers*," *Southern California Law Review*, vol. 61 (1988), pp. 1669, 1674.

3. *Federalist* 46, in Clinton Rossiter, ed., *The Federalist* (New York: New American Library, 1961), pp. 296–97. All references to *The Federalist* are to this edition.

4. Richard Hofstadter, *The Idea of a Party System* (Berkeley, Calif.: University of California Press, 1969).

5. For a discussion of the points at which Publius offered certainty rather than probability, see Tushnet, "Constitutional Interpretation," pp. 1676–77.

6. I realize that it is possible to conceptualize the "constitutional rights of the place" as failing to include the right to exercise the powers granted. Such a conceptualization, however, seems to me difficult to defend (though I concede that further examination of the political theory of *The Federalist* might persuade me that Publius had such a conceptualization of the constitutional rights of the place).

7. *Federalist* 10, p. 84.

8. *Federalist* 37, p. 229.

9. I take this to be the standard explanation of the rhetorical effort embodied in *The Federalist*. The citizenry, aroused to consider the adoption of a new constitution, might momentarily set aside its more factious desires to show that it could establish "good government by reflection and choice" rather than by "accident and force." *Federalist* 1, p. 1.

10. 272 U.S. 52 (1926).

11. Morrison v. Olsen, 108 S.Ct. 2597 (1988); Mistretta v. United States, 109 S.Ct. 647 (1989).

12. *Federalist* 78, p. 465.

13. *Federalist* 51, p. 323.

14. This passes, for the moment, the proposition that judges exercise judgment and not will.

15. *Federalist* 51, p. 321.

16. *Federalist* 84, pp. 513–14.

17. One might consider, for example, the discussions of the propriety of amending the Constitution to deal with the Supreme Court's decisions invalidating statutes restricting flag burning. Almost no one paid attention to the question of where in the Constitution Congress finds its power to prohibit the burning of a national flag. The amendment that Congress rejected stated that Congress shall "have the power" to prohibit flag burning, but participants in the discussions assumed that this language did not confer new power on Congress but merely removed a bar to legislation that Congress already had the power to enact.

18. Sanford Levinson, "The Embarrassing Second Amendment," *Yale Law Journal*, vol. 99 (1989), pp. 637–59.

19. For an argument that the framers intended to give the reasonableness clause priority, see Telford Taylor, *Two Studies in Constitutional Interpretation* (Columbus: Ohio State University Press, 1969).

20. I doubt that anything similar could be done to transform the Eighth Amendment into a specific provision in the sense that I am using the term; "excessiveness" as to bail and fines, if not "cruel and unusual" as to punishments, seems to support a fair degree of judicial discretion in interpretation.

21. New York Times Co. v. United States, 403 U.S. 713, 715 (1971) (J. Black, concurring in the judgment). "In my view it is unfortunate that some of my Brethren are apparently willing to hold that the publication of news may sometimes be enjoined."

22. I should perhaps note here that, in my view, neither of these dangers has been substantially realized in the recent history of U.S. constitutionalism; I find unpersuasive recent conservative criticism of judicial activism. For me, the arguments in the text are more accurate as applied to earlier periods in U.S. history.

23. United States v. Darby, 312 U.S. 100 (1941).

24. This is true unless, as the Tenth Amendment also recognizes, their people choose to do otherwise.

25. This statement assumes that the amendment *can* be interpreted and is not, as Judge Bork suggested, like an inkblot on the document.

26. In the latter case one might have a theory of rights that implied that their recognition by courts—which seems to be implicit in the term "construed" in the Ninth Amendment—might convert them into positive law rights. In the literature on the Ninth Amendment, however, the term "positive law" usually refers to statutory or state common law.

27. See Levy, "Federal Common Law of Crimes," *Encyclopedia of the American Constitution*, vol. 2 (1983), pp. 962–63. See also Russell Caplan, "The History and Meaning of the Ninth Amendment," *Virginia Law Review*, vol. 69 (1983), pp. 223, 248–50.

28. I can imagine an interpretation of the Ninth Amendment that would

treat it as a limit on congressional power to preempt state law, but I cannot imagine why anyone would have supported the adoption of an amendment with that effect. Further, to the extent that such an amendment was desired, the Tenth Amendment would seem sufficient to accomplish the goal.

29. See, for example, Caplan, "History and Meaning."

30. This is not to say, of course, that the courts would be barred from invalidating state laws on the ground that they violated rights enumerated elsewhere in the Constitution, though at the time of the adoption of the Ninth Amendment the number of such rights was small. See U.S. Constitution, Article I, section 10. I will not deal here with the effect of the adoption of the Fourteenth Amendment on the implications of the Ninth Amendment except to note my agreement with Laurence Tribe. He wrote that the "shall not be construed to deny or disparage" phrase substantially undermines the Court's argument in Bowers v. Hardwick, 478 U.S. 186 (1986). It argued that considerations of legitimacy should incline it to be more reluctant to enforce unenumerated rights rather than enumerated rights. As Tribe points out, that argument is precisely a construction that denies or disparages the import of unenumerated rights. Laurence Tribe, "Contrasting Constitutional Visions: Of Real and Unreal Differences," *Harvard Civil Rights–Civil Liberties Law Review,* vol. 22 (1987), pp. 95, 101–8.

31. Suzanna Sherry, "The Founders' Unwritten Constitution," *University of Chicago Law Review,* vol. 54 (1987), pp. 1127–77.

32. 3 U.S. (3 Dall.) 386 (1798).

33. See John Hart Ely, *Democracy and Distrust* (Cambridge, Mass.: Harvard University Press, 1980), p. 50; Mark Tushnet, *Red, White, and Blue: A Critical Analysis of Constitutional Law* (Cambridge, Mass.: Harvard University Press, 1988), p. 108.

## Chapter 8: Thomas Jefferson on Natural Rights

This paper was partly prepared under a grant from the Woodrow Wilson International Center for Scholars, Washington, D.C. The statements and views expressed herein are those of the author and are not necessarily those of the Woodrow Wilson International Center for Scholars. I would especially like to thank a number of scholars who helped improve this essay by giving a previous draft their careful perusal and comments: Catherine Zuckert, William Galston, Adrian Piper, and Thomas Schrock.

1. Forrest McDonald, *Novus Ordo Seclorum* (Lawrence, Kan.: University of Kansas Press, 1985), p. 1.

2. *Federalist* 9, in *The Federalist Papers,* ed. Clinton Rossiter (New York: New American Library, 1961), p. 72.

3. *Federalist* 14, p. 104.

4. Moses Coit Tyler, "The Declaration of Independence in the Light of Modern Criticism," in *A Casebook on the Declaration of Independence,* ed. Robert Ginsberg (New York, 1966), p. 99.

5. Thomas Jefferson said almost fifty years after the Declaration of Inde-

pendence, but very much in its spirit, "our Revolution . . . presented us an album on which we were free to write what we pleased. We had no occasion to search into musty records, to hunt up royal parchments, or to investigate the laws and institutions of a semi-barbarous ancestry. We appealed to those of nature, and found them engraved on our hearts." Jefferson to Major John Cartwright, June 5, 1824, in *Jefferson*, ed. Merill Peterson (New York: Library of America, 1984), p. 1491.

6. Merrill D. Peterson, *Thomas Jefferson and the New Nation* (London, Oxford, and New York: Oxford University Press, 1970), p. 249.

7. Ibid.

8. Ibid., p. 250. See also the similar point in Charles A. Miller, *Jefferson and Nature* (Baltimore, Md.: Johns Hopkins University Press, 1988), pp. 18, 36–37; in Harvey Mansfield, Jr., "Jefferson," in *American Political Thought*, eds. Morton Frisch and Richard Stevens (Chicago, Ill.: E. E. Pencock Press, 1971), pp. 23–50; and in David Tucker, "The Political Thought of Thomas Jefferson: *Notes on the State of Virginia*," in Ralph Rossum and Gary McDowell, *The American Founding* (Port Washington, N.Y.: Kennikat, 1981), p. 108.

9. Thomas Jefferson, *Notes on the State of Virginia*, in Peterson, *Jefferson*, p. 154.

10. Genesis 7:17–24. See also Garry Wills, *Inventing America* (New York: Doubleday, 1978), p. 263.

11. Jefferson, *Notes*, p. 154.

12. Ibid.; see also p. 211. See also Harry V. Jaffa, "Humanizing Certitudes and Impoverishing Doubts," *Interpretation* (Fall 1988), pp. 116–17.

13. For a statement very much in the spirit of Jefferson's, and probably consciously echoing him, see John Adams's letter to Jefferson of September 14, 1813, in *The Adams-Jefferson Letters*, ed. Lester Cappon (Chapel Hill, N.C.: University of North Carolina Press, 1971), p. 373. See also Eva Brann, "Concerning the Declaration of Independence," *The College*, vol. 28 (1973); and Harry V. Jaffa, *How to Think About the American Revolution* (Durham, N.C.: Carolina Academic Press, 1978).

14. Jefferson, *Notes*, p. 155, and Miller, *Jefferson and Nature*, pp. 23, 26, 92, 94, 156 n. 4, 165. But see also pp. 32, 50 for Miller's confusions on this issue.

15. Jefferson to Peter Carr, August 10, 1787, in Peterson, *Jefferson*, p. 902. See also George Anastaplo, "The Declaration of Independence," *St. Louis University Law Journal*, vol. 9 (1965), p. 405.

16. Jefferson, *Notes*, p. 77, and also pp. 78, 86. For an exception on Creator, see Jefferson to Adams, April 11, 1823, in Peterson, *Jefferson*, p. 1466.

17. Here and elsewhere in his writings Jefferson is quite elusive as to his views on the ultimate relation of God and nature, and on the nature of God: he is clearest in rejecting the biblical notion of a God who acts independently of nature; he accepts neither miracles nor special revelation. Yet he distanced himself from the atheistic view that nature could be understood entirely self-sufficiently. Behind nature, he often affirmed, stands some sort of intelligence and purpose, but this intelligence and purpose operates solely through nature. This is the deism that has often been noted as central to his understanding of God and nature. On at least one occasion, however, Jefferson sug-

gested that the gap between his deism (or as he called it, theism) and atheism was not so great. See his letter to Adams of April 8, 1816, in Cappon, *Letters,* pp. 467–68, and the letter to Thomas Law, June 13, 1814, in Peterson, *Jefferson,* p. 1336.

18. See Jefferson to John Cartwright, June 5, 1829, in Peterson, *Jefferson,* pp. 1493–94.

19. Ibid., p. 289. See also Anastaplo, "Declaration," pp. 405–6.

20. For a similar understanding of "Creator," see Brann, "Concerning the Declaration," pp. 7, 9. See also Appendix I, "On Reading Jefferson."

21. Jefferson, *Notes,* p. 127.

22. See Miller, *Jefferson and Nature,* p. 26.

23. Jefferson, *Notes,* p. 143.

24. Ibid., p. 148.

25. Ibid.

26. Ibid.

27. See the alternate conventionalist reading, in Wills, *Inventing America,* pp. 259–72.

28. Blaise Pascal, *Pensées,* no. 68. Miller in *Jefferson and Nature* misses this dimension of the experience. See pp. 104–5.

29. See Jefferson, *Notes,* p. 174, on themes of fear and free government.

30. On Jefferson's own utilitarian attitudes toward science, see his letter to Adams, October 14, 1816, in Cappon, *Letters,* p. 491. Against this, see Miller, *Jefferson and Nature,* pp. 27, 101–4.

31. Jefferson to Adams, April 11, 1823, in Peterson, *Jefferson,* pp. 1466–67.

32. Jefferson's statement also needs to be considered in the light of the principles of reading described in Appendix I. It is true that Adams and Jefferson by 1823 were intimates, having corresponded regularly and more or less candidly since 1812. But there were definite limits to their candor (see Appendix I for an example). The letter begins with a typical Jeffersonian gesture of agreement with his correspondent: "The being described in [John Calvin's] five points is not *the God whom you and I acknowledge and adore . . .*" (emphasis supplied). This gesture responds to a longstanding expression by Adams of a need for a divinity in whose hands is divine consolation. For at least the previous six or seven years he had been writing to Jefferson of his hopes for another life, for a dualistic universe of spirit and matter, and for a God who could support that hope. For many years Jefferson had noticeably failed to join his voice in reassurance of Adams's hopes, but in 1823 he finally did so.

33. Jefferson to Adams, April 8, 1816, in Peterson, *Jefferson,* pp. 1382–83.

34. On Jefferson's argument from order, consider Locke, *Essay Concerning Human Understanding,* IVx, and Michael P. Zuckert, "An Introduction to Locke's *First Treatise,*" *Interpretation,* vol. VIII, 1978, pp. 70–74. Relevant also is Jefferson's materialism. See for example Jefferson to Adams, August 15, 1820, and his epicureanism. See for example Jefferson to William Smith, October 31, 1819.

35. Jefferson to John Trumbull, February 5, 1789, in Peterson, *Jefferson,* p. 939.

36. Jefferson, *Notes,* pp. 185–86.

37. Ibid., p. 183.

38. Ibid., pp. 169, 182.

39. Against this, see Miller, *Jefferson and Nature*, pp. 3, 63, 65.

40. Jefferson, *Notes*, p. 170. Emphasis in the original.

41. Quoted in Jefferson, *Notes*, p. 183.

42. See Miller, *Jefferson and Nature*, p. 64; Richard Matthews, *Radical Politics*, p. 54.

43. Jefferson, *Notes*, pp. 183–88.

44. Against this, see Miller, pp. 12–13, but see also pp. 56, 59, 61. See also Matthews, *Radical Politics*, pp. 34, 53, 56.

45. Jefferson, *Notes*, pp. 184–85. See also Miller, *Jefferson and Nature*, p. 64; Matthews, *Radical Politics*, p. 54.

46. Jefferson, *Notes*, p. 220. See also Jefferson to James Madison, January 30, 1787, in Peterson, *Jefferson*, p. 882: "[some] societies exist . . . without government, as among our Indians." Also see Jefferson to William Ludlow, September 6, 1924, in Peterson, *Jefferson*, p. 1496: the Indians "live under no law but that of nature."

47. John Locke, *Two Treatises of Government*, Essay II, 87; See also Miller, *Jefferson and Nature*, pp. 158–59; Jefferson to Thomas Mann Randolph, May 30, 1790, *Selected Writings*, eds. Koch and Peder, pp. 496–97.

48. Jefferson, *Notes*, p. 220; on Locke, see Thomas Pangle, *The Spirit of Modern Republicanism*, (Chicago, Ill.: University of Chicago Press, 1988), chapter 19.

49. But see "Summary View," Peterson, *Jefferson*, pp. 106–07.

50. Ibid, pp. 185–86.

51. Ibid. (Emphasis supplied.)

52. Ibid., p. 186. On the opposition between right and self-love, see Jefferson to Pierre S. Du Pont de Nemours, April 24, 1816, in Peterson, *Jefferson*, p. 1386.

53. The distinction between the moral sense as an epistemological and as a practical faculty can be overdrawn, however. According to Jefferson, the moral sense is not purely cognitive, for "every human mind feels pleasure in doing good to another," a feeling deriving from the moral sense, just as the other senses also include pleasure and pain; and pleasure and pain are motives to action. Jefferson to Adams, October 14, 1816, in Cappon, *Letters*, p. 492; Jefferson to Law, June 13, 1814, in Peterson, *Jefferson*, p. 1337.

54. Jefferson, *Notes*, p. 255; on the "war of all against all," see also Jefferson to Madison, January 1, 1797, in Peterson, *Jefferson*, p. 1039. But see Jefferson to Samuel Kercheval, July 12, 1816, in ibid., p. 1401. On Hobbes, see Jefferson to Adams, October 14, 1816, in Cappon, *Letters*, p. 492.

55. Jefferson to Law, June 13, 1814, in Peterson, *Jefferson*, p. 1338.

56. Jefferson, *Notes*, p. 186.

57. See the interesting but very different account of the origins of rights in nature in Larry Arnhart, "Charles Darwin and the Declaration of Independence," unpublished paper, American Political Science Association, 1982, pp. 3, 5, 17–19, 22, 29. Arnhart falls into a "biologism" more akin to Buffon than to Jefferson. The same might be said of Jacques Derrida's attempts to undermine natural standards of right in "Racism's Last Word," and of his *Otobiogra-*

*phies* (Paris: Galilée, 1984), pp. 13–32. See especially the extension of Derrida's argument to the Declaration in Catherine H. Zuckert's "Derrida and the Politics of Deconstruction," forthcoming in *Polity.*

58. For a clear indication of the degree to which rights supplant the moral sense as the basis for political society, see Jefferson's letter to John Norvell, June 11, 1807, in Peterson, *Jefferson,* p. 1176. For a fuller discussion, see Appendix II, this chapter.

59. Jefferson to Madison, January 1, 1797, in Peterson, *Jefferson,* p. 1039.

60. Jefferson to Du Pont de Nemours, April 24, 1816, in Peterson, *Jefferson,* p. 1387.

61. Jefferson to Roger Weightman, June 24, 1826, in Peterson, *Jefferson,* p. 1517.

62. Jefferson to Du Pont de Nemours, in Peterson, *Jefferson,* p. 1387.

63. Ibid.

64. Ibid.

65. For Jefferson's recognition that not all human beings are equally insecure in their rights, and for the role of the invention of gunpowder as the "great equalizer," see his letter to Adams, October 28, 1813, in Peterson, *Jefferson,* p. 1305.

66. See Morton White, *The Philosophy of the American Revolution* (New York: Oxford University Press, 1981), chapters 4–5.

67. See Jefferson to Peter Carr, August 10, 1787, in Peterson, *Jefferson,* p. 903.

68. On "self-evident truths" in the Declaration, see Michael P. Zuckert, "Self-Evident Truths and the Declaration of Independence," *Review of Politics,* vol. XLIX (1987), pp. 319–39.

69. The document Du Pont de Nemours had sent to Jefferson, to which the latter was replying, was titled, "Mémoire aux Républiques Equinoxiales." On its fate, see Ambrose Saricks, *Pierre Samuel Du Pont de Nemours* (Lawrence, Kan.: University of Kansas Press, 1965), p. 346. This instance is clearly another case of Jefferson's accommodating style in personal correspondence, as discussed in Appendix I. Nonetheless, Jefferson forcefully if gently made clear the areas where he disagreed with his friend's political project for the new republics of South America. The context may account for his inclusions and omissions, for he introduced the discussion of rights with the phrase, "I believe with you [Du Pont] that. . . ." He appears to have given explicit mention to themes that appeared in the discussion of politics that Du Pont had sent to him. We cannot specify with certainty the precise relationship between Jefferson's discussion and Du Pont's, however, for the latter's tract has been lost.

70. Jefferson to Du Pont de Nemours, April 24, 1816, in Peterson, *Jefferson,* p. 1387.

71. Jefferson, "Address to the Chiefs of the Cherokee Nation," January 10, 1810, in Peterson, *Jefferson,* p. 561.

72. Jefferson to Du Pont de Nemours, in Peterson, *Jefferson,* p. 1387.

73. See Wills, *Inventing America,* pp. 229–55; McDonald, *Novus Ordo,* pp. ix–x; White, *Philosophy,* pp. 213–28. For other places where Jefferson affirms a

right to property, see Jefferson to Adams, October 28, 1813, in Peterson, *Jefferson*, p. 1306; Jefferson to Kercheval, July 22, 1816, p. 1398; Jefferson to Brother Handsome Lake, November 1, 1802, p. 556; and his "Address to the Chiefs of the Cherokee Nation," January 10, 1806, p. 561.

74. Matthews, *Radical Politics*, p. 27.

75. George Mason, Virginia Bill of Rights, Article I.

76. Massachusetts Bill of Rights, Part I, Article I.

77. Locke, *Two Treatises*, Essay II, 26: "The fruit or venison, which nourishes the wild Indian . . . must be his, and so his, i.e., a part of him, that another can no longer have any right to it, before it can do him any good for the support of his life."

78. Miller, *Jefferson and Nature*, p. 200.

79. Jefferson nowhere indicates any doubts about the human practice of treating animals as property, but he does not accept the principle that other human beings can rightfully be treated as property. Except for the fact that much nonsense is frequently written on the subject it would be superfluous to mention Jefferson's denial of slavery's congruence with the principles of natural right. See his draft of the Declaration, Peterson, *Jefferson*, p. 22; Jefferson, *Notes*, pp. 270, 288–89.

80. "Message to the Brothers of the Choctaw Nation," December 17, 1803, in Peterson, *Jefferson*, p. 559; see also Locke, *Two Treatises*, Essay II, pp. 40–46.

81. I have presented here only the broad outlines of Jefferson's doctrine on the right to property. A fuller discussion would need to take account of the implications of inequality in property holdings and circumstances in which something like a right to welfare might emerge.

82. Jefferson to Du Pont de Nemours, in Peterson, *Jefferson*, p. 1387.

83. McDonald, *Novus Ordo*, ix–xi; see also Brann, "Considering," p. 12, for an Aristotelian reading.

84. Locke, *Essay* II, xxi 62.

85. Ibid., II, xxi 51.

86. Ibid., II, xxi 59.

87. Ibid., II, xxi 57.

88. See Locke, *Two Treatises*, Essay I, 86, II, 25.

89. Locke's doctrine of happiness and of the pursuit of happiness were not developed until he set out to revise his original treatment of free will and necessity for late editions of the *Essay*. The *Essay's* first edition, not containing the doctrine of happiness, was published in 1690. It is no surprise that the *Treatises on Government* did not contain it, for he had not worked it out by the time he published that book. Given the easy fit into his basic thinking on politics, however, I speculate that had he undertaken a substantive revision of the *Treatises*, as he did of the *Essay*, he might well have included it among the rights that receive special mention. In other words, Mason's and Jefferson's elevating pursuit of happiness into one of the basic rights may well accord with Locke's intent. See Strauss, *Natural Right*, pp. 226–27.

90. Ronald Hamowy, "Jefferson and the Scottish Enlightenment," in *William and Mary Quarterly*, vol. 36 (1979), p. 549.

91. John Phillip Reid, *Constitutional History of the American Revolution: The Authority of Rights* (Madison, Wisc.: University of Wisconsin Press, 1986), p. 90.

92. Against this, Miller, *Jefferson and Nature*, p. 40.

93. Jefferson, *Autobiography*, in Peterson, *Jefferson*, p. 5. See also his "First Inaugural Address," on "the equal rights" of minorities, which "equal law must protect." Ibid., p. 493.

94. Miller, *Jefferson and Nature*, p. 167, seems to be attempting to make this point.

95. Reid, *Constitutional History*, chapters 1–7.

96. *Federalist* 51, p. 322.

97. See Michael P. Zuckert, "What Next for Constitutional Studies?" *Constitutional Commentary*, vol. V (1988), pp. 35–38.

98. Jefferson to Francis Eppes, January 19, 1829, in Peterson, *Jefferson*, p. 1451.

99. See Jefferson to Adams, August 22, 1813, in Cappon, *Letters*, p. 369.

100. Jefferson, *Notes*, p. 155.

101. Jefferson to Adams, October 28, 1813, in Peterson, *Jefferson*, p. 1310.

102. Jefferson to Taylor, May 28, 1816, in Peterson, *Jefferson*, p. 1392.

103. Jefferson to Law, June 13, 1814, in Peterson, *Jefferson*, p. 1335.

104. Jefferson to Short, October 31, 1819, in Peterson, *Jefferson*, p. 1430.

105. Jefferson to Thomas Mann Randolph, November 24, 1808, in Peterson, *Jefferson*, p. 1995.

106. Cappon, *Letters*, p. 562.

107. Wills, *Inventing America*, pp. 215–16.

108. Michael J. Perry, *Morality, Politics, and Law* (New York: Oxford University Press, 1988), p. 185.

109. See Thomas Hobbes, *Leviathan*, chapter 14; *Two Treatises*, Essay II, 89.

110. Wills, *Inventing America*, p. 215.

# Index

Abolitionist movement, 31–32
ACLU. *See* American Civil Liberties
  Union
Adams, John, 32, 109, 116, 146, 167–
  68, 182–83n
  on rights, 162, 164–66
Adams, Sam, 26
Amendment process, 26, 50, 51
American Alliance for Rights and
  Responsibilities, 34
American Civil Liberties Union
  (ACLU), 34, 99
Anti-Federalists, 15, 24–25, 47, 103
  and Bill of Rights, 25, 60,
    67–70
Aquinas, Thomas, 110
*Areopagitica* (Milton), 117
Aristotle, 103, 106, 109, 110, 111,
  138, 161
Articles of Confederation, 47, 51

Bacon, Francis, 147
Barber, Benjamin R., 12–14
*Barron v. Baltimore*, 89
Berns, Walter, 69
Best, Judith A., 8–10, 12, 13, 14
Bicameralism, 48
Bill of Rights
  and Fourteenth Amendment,
    3–4, 92, 95, 96, 98, 181n
  and judicial review, 6, 128, 131;
    133–34
  as limit on central government,
    25, 61–62, 66–69, 88–90
  Madison's opposition to sepa-
    rate, 11–12, 27, 30–31, 36, 58–
    59, 62–64, 67, 74, 87

Madison's pre-Preamble proposal, 11–12, 62, 65–67
Madison's speech, 10–12, 57–
  85, 173n
negative and imperative character of, 63–64
omissions from, 66–67, 70, 90–
  91
specificity of, 7, 132–33, 134–35,
  180n
and state governments, 3–4, 89,
  93, 94, 96, 134–35, 180n
*See also* Rights; *specific amendments*
Black, Hugo, 94, 95, 133
Blackmun, Harry, 96
Blackstone, William, 18, 31, 116
Bolingbroke, Henry St. John, 167,
  168
*Bowers v. Hardwick*, 181n
Brennan, William, 95, 98
Brown, John, 31–32
*Brown v. Board of Education*, 35,
  95
Burke, Aedanus, 68
Burnham, James, 45

*Calder v. Bull*, 135
Central government, limits on, 24–
  25
  Bill of Rights, 25, 61–62, 66–69,
    88–90
  federalism, 50–51, 55, 56, 88
  separation of powers, 9, 47–50,
    55, 56, 125–26, 179n
  *See also* Anti-Federalists
Chase, Samuel, 135

Checks and balances. *See* Separation of powers
Citizenship, 28–29, 30
Civil Rights Act, 1866, 92
Civil Rights Act, 1964, 95
Civil War, 54, 91–92, 93
Civil War amendments. *See* Thirteenth Amendment; Fourteenth Amendment; Fifteenth Amendment
Congress, 12, 26, 45, 51, 55. *See also* Separation of powers
Consent, 8, 16, 30, 39–40, 55, 108, 109
Constitution
    amendment process, 26, 51
    Preamble, 31–32
    republicanism in, 15–16, 104–7, 177–78n
    rights implied in, 29, 56, 57, 75, 87, 88, 93–94, 174–76n
    *See also* Bill of Rights; Framers; *specific amendments; specific issues*
Courts. *See* Judicial review; Separation of powers
Curran, John Philpot, 56

de Buffon, Comte, 147–49
Declaration of Independence, 19, 31, 38, 64–65
    on natural rights, 19, 20, 21, 140–41, 142, 143, 156, 157–58, 162, 163–64
de Marbois, François, 140
Democracy
    vs. republican government, 13–14, 30, 68–70, 105–06, 174n
    and rights, 12–14, 27, 29
    *See also* Suffrage
Diamond, Martin, 44, 46
Dickinson, 49
Diderot, Denis, 146
*Discourses on Government* (Sidney), 117
Douglas, William O., 94, 95, 96
Dred Scott decision, 32
Due process, 4, 32, 94, 95, 96, 97–98, 165. *See also* Fifth Amendment; Fourteenth Amendment
Dupont de Nemours, Pierre Samuel, 21, 156, 158

Education, 17–18, 108, 113, 115, 117
Eighth Amendment, 173n, 180n. *See also* Bill of Rights
Electoral College, 45
Ely, John Hart, 136
Emancipation Proclamation, 92
Enumerated powers. *See* Ninth Amendment; Tenth Amendment
Equality, 13, 26, 28–30
*Essay Concerning Human Understanding* (Locke), 161, 183n
*Ethics* (Aristotle). *See Nicomacheian Ethics*
Etzioni, Amitai, 34
Exclusionary rule, 90
Executive. *See* Presidency

Factionalism, 25, 40, 43, 44–45, 105, 122. *See also* Human nature; Majorities
Federalism, 9, 44–47, 67–70, 113, 123
    as antidemocratic, 13, 26
    as limit on central government, 50–51, 55, 88
*Federalist, The*
    on human nature, 5, 121–22
    on judicial review, 6–7, 128–29, 131–34
    on majorities, 124–25
    No. 3, 41
    No. 10, 5, 122, 125
    No. 51, 126, 165
    No. 54, 32–33
    No. 78, 128
    on representation, 104–06, 122–25
    on separation of powers, 126, 129, 130
    *See also* Framers; Hamilton, Alexander; Madison, James
Federalists. *See Federalist, The;* Framers
Fifteenth Amendment, 13, 27, 32, 92, 94
Fifth Amendment, 90, 91, 94. *See also* Bill of Rights
First Amendment, 63, 69, 89, 91, 98, 133. *See also* Bill of Rights
Fourteenth Amendment, 13, 27, 32, 92
    Supreme Court use of, 3–4, 92, 94, 95, 96, 97–98

Fourth Amendment, 90, 133. *See also* Bill of Rights
Framers, 13, 14, 25, 28, 139
    on human nature, 5, 122–23
    *See also* Constitution; *Federalist, The; specific framers and issues*

Garrison, William Lloyd, 31
Gerry, Elbridge, 69, 174n
Goldwin, Robert A., 10–12, 13, 14
*Gorgias* (Plato), 111
Graglia, Lino A., 3–4, 5, 14
Green, T. H., 29
*Griswold v. Connecticut*, 95–96

Hamilton, Alexander, 25, 48, 49, 56, 87, 89
    on Articles of Confederation, 51
    on republican government, 15, 103
    on safety, 42
    *See also Federalist, The;* Framers
Hamowy, Ronald, 162
Happiness, pursuit of, 112, 158, 161–63, 186n
Harrington, James, 24
Hartz, Louis, 27
Henry, Patrick, 26, 67, 68, 88, 89, 103
Hobbes, Thomas, 17, 115, 151
    on forms of government, 15, 25, 103, 114
    on human nature, 46, 113
    on natural rights, 153, 163, 169
Holbach, Paul, Baron d', 146
Holmes, Oliver Wendell, 86
House of Representatives, 26, 45
Human nature
    framers' view of, 5, 122–23
    Jefferson on, 20, 147–52
    and natural rights, 115, 152–53
    and representation, 5–6, 114, 122
    *See also* Factionalism; Office-holder characteristics; Self-interest; Virtue
Hume, David, 15, 18, 103, 115–16
Hutcheson, Francis, 168
Hutson, James H., 2

Impeachment, 55
India, 89

Indians, 20, 148–49, 150
Individualism, 118, 119
*Inventing America* (Wills), 168

Jackson, Robert, 94
Jay, John, 32, 41
Jefferson, Thomas, 30, 35, 46, 50, 54, 181n
    as democratic, 25, 26
    on moral sense, 20, 150–51, 153, 183–84n
    on religion, 141–42, 146–47, 182n, 182–83n
    on slavery, 186n
    writings of, 167–68, 182–83n, 184–85n
    *See also* Declaration of Independence; *Notes on the State of Virginia*
Johnson, Andrew, 92
Judicial review
    as antidemocratic, 13, 14
    and Bill of Rights, 6, 129, 131, 132–34
    constitutional basis for, 9, 49–50
    as creator of individual rights, 35, 94–98, 99
    dangers of, 6–7, 50, 98–100, 128–30, 133–34, 180n

Kant, Immanuel, 155
Kennedy, Anthony, 35

Large republic, 8, 41, 44, 46–47
*Laws* (Plato), 108, 111
Law, Thomas, 168
Lee, Henry, 26
Legislature, checks on, 6, 48, 55, 71, 126. *See also* Separation of powers
Liberty, 160–61. *See also* Rights
Lincoln, Abraham, 54, 91, 92
Locke, John, 25, 42, 53–54, 147, 169
    on consent, 39, 55
    on property rights, 158, 159, 186n
    on pursuit of happiness, 161–62, 186n
    on safety, 8, 41
    on self-interest, 17, 18, 112, 113–115
    on state of nature, 42, 52

McDonald, Forrest, 138, 161
Machiavelli, Niccolò, 17, 24, 103, 107, 112
Madison, James, 38, 89, 123, 139, 165, 168
  on faction, 25, 43
  on federalism, 4, 94
  House of Representatives speech, June 8, 1789, 10–12, 57–85, 173n
  on majorities, 25, 43, 44–45, 71
  opposition to separate Bill of Rights, 11–12, 27, 30–31, 36, 58–59, 61–64, 66, 74, 87
  pre-Preamble proposal, 11–12, 61, 64–66
  on presidency, 48, 54
  on property, 43–44
  on representation, 5–6, 15, 104–05
  on separation of powers, 48
  on slavery, 32–33
  See also Federalist, The; Framers
Majorities, 9, 25, 44–47, 71, 108
  and judicial review, 6–7, 129–31
  large republic as limit on, 5–6, 8–9, 43–45, 122, 124–26
  separation of powers as limit on, 9, 44–45, 46–47, 126–28, 129
  See also Consent
Marshall, John, 89
Marshall, Thurgood, 98
Martin, Luther, 52
Mason, George, 32, 158, 186n
Massachusetts State Constitution, 11, 65, 158, 162, 173–74n
Matthews, Richard, 158
Mayflower Compact, 24
Mercer, John Francis, 49, 103
Michigan Department of State Police v. Sitz, 34
Militia, 66, 174n
Miller, Charles, 159
Milton, John, 117
Minority factions, 8, 9, 42, 44, 45, 122. See also Factionalism
Miranda v. Arizona, 90, 95, 96
Monroe, James, 123
Montesquieu, Charles-Louis de Secondat, 17, 24, 106, 113–15, 117
  on control of government, 15,

103
  on education, 17, 115
  on large republic, 8, 41
Moral sense, 20, 150–51, 154, 168–69, 184n
Morris, Gouverneur, 51–52, 54
Myers v. United States, 127–28

Natural law, 7, 112, 117, 136, 141. See also Natural rights
Natural rights, 20–21, 112, 139, 143, 152–63
  vs. civil rights, 21–22, 25, 42–43, 163–66
  and human nature, 115, 151
  and inequality, 17, 115, 154, 184n
  See also Natural law; Rights
Nature, 19–20, 141–47, 182
New Deal, 94
Newton, Isaac, 147
Nicomacheian Ethics (Aristotle), 109
Nineteenth Amendment, 92
Ninth Amendment, 7, 38, 72, 134–35, 136, 173n, 180n. See also Bill of Rights
Notes on the State of Virginia (Jefferson), 167–68
  on human nature, 19–20, 147–49, 151
  on natural rights, 19–21, 152–57, 169, 186n
  on nature, 19–20, 140–47

Of Education (Milton), 117
Officeholder characteristics, 121, 123–24, 129–30, 133. See also Human nature

Paine, Thomas, 26
Pangle, Thomas L., 14–19
Pascal, Blaise, 145
Pendleton, Edmund, 29
Pennsylvania Constitution, 26
Pentagon Papers case, 133
Peterson, Merrill, 19, 140
Phaedrus (Plato), 111
Pinkney, 49
Plato, 98, 106, 108, 111
Plutarch, 117, 118
Politics (Aristotle), 111

Presidency, 9, 47–48, 52–55
    indirect election to, 13, 26, 45
    *See also* Separation of powers
Property rights, 43–44, 114, 156–57,
    158–59. *See also* Natural rights;
    Rights
Proposition 13, 35–36
Proposition 111, 171n
Publius. *See Federalist, The*

Reason, 17, 56, 112, 122. *See also* Hu-
    man nature
Reid, John Phillip, 163, 165
Religion
    freedom of, 65, 91, 98, 174n
    and nature, 110, 141–42, 146–
        47, 182–83n
    and self-interest, 18, 114–15
    *See also* Rights
Representation, 5–6, 45, 87, 113,
    122–24. *See also* Republican gov-
    ernment
Republican government
    classical tradition, 16–17, 18–19,
        106–11, 117, 118
    and consent, 8, 16, 30, 39–40,
        55, 108
    in Constitution, 15–16, 104–07,
        177n
    vs. democracy, 13, 14, 30, 68–
        69, 105–06
    Lockean basis of, 39
    new American form of, 18–19,
        116–18
    as threat to individual rights,
        15, 102–04
    weaknesses of, 8, 25, 40–41, 43,
        102–04, 105–06
    *See also* Representation
*Republic* (Plato), 108
Rights
    absolutist view of, 14, 33–36
    American focus on, 1–2, 23–24,
        31, 137–38
    and citizenship, 30
    and democracy, 13, 14, 27, 29
    and equality, 13, 28–30
    government as danger to, 21,
        24–25, 38, 68, 164–65
    government as guardian of, 8,
        9–10, 24, 25, 37–39, 55–56
    implied in Constitution, 29, 57,

74, 87, 88, 92–93, 173–74
    and individualism, 117, 119–20
    judicial creation of, 3–4, 35, 86,
        90–91, 93–97, 98
    lack of constitutional basis for,
        86–88, 93–94, 97
    in liberal tradition, 111–16
    republican government as
        threat to, 15, 102–04
    and self-interest, 20, 150, 151,
        152, 153, 158–59, 169
    social character of, 13, 29, 30,
        33, 42–43
    suffrage as key to, 13–14, 27, 30
    traditional antidemocratic focus
        of, 24–26
    *See also* Bill of Rights; Natural
        rights; *specific amendments*
*Roe v. Wade*, 96, 98
Roosevelt, Franklin D., 94
Rossiter, Clinton, 52
Rousseau, Jean-Jacques, 29

Scalia, Antonin, 91
Second Amendment, 89, 91, 132. *See
    also* Bill of Rights
Self-interest, 5, 17–18, 111–16, 122,
    124
    and rights, 20, 150, 151, 152,
        153, 158–59, 169
    and separation of powers, 114,
        130
Senate, 13, 26, 45
Separation of powers, 13, 26, 53,
    54–55, 113, 130
    as limit on central government,
        9, 47–50, 56, 125–26
    as limit on majorities, 9, 44–45,
        46–47, 126–28, 129
Seventh Amendment, 90. *See also*
    Bill of Rights
Sherry, Suzanna, 135
Short, William, 168
Sidney, Algernon, 117
Sixth Amendment, 90. *See also* Bill of
    Rights
Slavery, 28, 31–33, 185n. *See also*
    Thirteenth Amendment
*Social Contract* (Rousseau), 29
Socrates, 16, 106, 110, 111
*Some Thoughts Concerning Education*
    (Locke), 115

Soviet Union, 30, 89
*Spirit of the Laws, The* (Montesquieu), 106
State governments, 91–92
    and Bill of Rights, 3–4, 89, 93, 94, 96, 134–35, 180n
    *See also* Federalism
Storing, Herbert, 61
Suffrage, 13–14, 27–28. *See also* Democracy
Supreme Court. *See* Judicial review; Separation of powers; *specific cases*

Taft, William H., 127
Taney, Roger, 32, 33
Taylor, John, 167
Tenth Amendment, 26, 69, 72, 134, 180n. *See also* Bill of Rights
Third Amendment, 90, 173n. *See also* Bill of Rights
Thirteenth Amendment, 13, 27, 32, 92, 94. *See also* Slavery
Three-fifths compromise, 28
Thucydides, 106
Tocqueville, Alexis de, 41, 50, 119

*Treatise on Law* (Aquinas), 110
*Treatises on Government* (Locke), 186n
Tribe, Laurence, 181n
Tucker, Thomas, 174n
Tushnet, Mark, 5–7, 8, 13
Twenty-fourth Amendment, 92
Twenty-sixth Amendment, 92

United Nations Declaration of Human Rights, 89

Virginia Constitution, 26, 158
Virtue, 16–17, 25, 56, 107–09, 110–11, 117
    vs. self-interest, 17, 112

Warren, Earl, 90
Wiecek, William M., 177n
Wills, Garry, 162, 168–69
Women's Rights Convention, Seneca Falls, 1846, 31

Xenophon, 106

Zuckert, Michael P., 19–22

A Note on the Book

*This book was edited by Cheryl Weissman*
*of the staff of the AEI Press.*
*The index was prepared by Do Mi Stauber.*
*The text was set in Palatino, a typeface designed by*
*the twentieth-century Swiss designer Hermann Zapf.*
*Graphic Composition, Inc. of Athens, Georgia,*
*set the type, and Edwards Brothers Incorporated,*
*of Ann Arbor, Michigan, printed and bound the book,*
*using permanent acid-free paper.*

The AEI Press is the publisher for the American Enterprise Institute for Public Policy Research, 1150 17th Street, N.W., Washington, D.C. 20036: *Christopher C. DeMuth*, publisher; *Edward Styles*, director; *Dana Lane*, assistant director; *Ann Petty*, editor; *Cheryl Weissman*, editor; *Susan Moran*, editorial assistant (rights and permissions). Books published by the AEI Press are distributed by arrangement with the University Press of America, 4720 Boston Way, Lanham, Md. 20706.